图书在版编目（CIP）数据

狂说会道：英语口语全攻略 / 刘冠奇编著.
北京：机械工业出版社，2024.7. —(冠奇英语秀).
ISBN 978-7-111-76229-4

Ⅰ. H319.9
中国国家版本馆CIP数据核字第20245XJ676号

机械工业出版社（北京市百万庄大街22号　邮政编码100037）
策划编辑：杨　娟　　责任编辑：杨　娟　张若男
责任校对：张晓娟　　责任印制：郜　敏
三河市宏达印刷有限公司印刷
2024年8月第1版第1次印刷
184mm×245mm・21.5印张・1插页・479千字
标准书号：ISBN 978-7-111-76229-4
定价：89.00元

电话服务　　　　　　　　网络服务
客服电话：010-88361066　　机　工　官　网：www.cmpbook.com
　　　　　010-88379833　　机　工　官　博：weibo.com/cmp1952
　　　　　010-68326294　　金　书　网：www.golden-book.com
封底无防伪标均为盗版　机工教育服务网：www.cmpedu.com

序 言

　　图书编辑催我好久了,"不务正业"的我今天终于坐了下来,安安静静地动笔写这本书的序言。并不是我生性懒惰或拖延,而是我一直在构思,想通过文字给你们展现除了阳光帅气、声音动听以外,我那些不一样的才华。希望你们能看到。

　　先简单自我介绍一下。我叫刘冠奇,男,1986年10月24日生人,身高183cm,体重不定。天蝎座,不记仇。出生于黑龙江省哈尔滨市呼兰县。在我之前这里最著名的人物是鲁迅的学生也是我国著名女作家萧红。对,我就是在她之后我们这儿"最"著名的作家、英语老师,兼抖音博主。

　　我2006年入行,开始从事英语教学,从新东方的助教做起,努力了8年之后,成为新东方"十大演讲师"之一。在新东方的职业生涯达到顶峰后,我辞了职。起因在于我离开前参与的最后一场新东方巡回讲座,讲座地点就在我的家乡哈尔滨。在那之前的几天哈尔滨举办了王菲的演唱会,接着就是我们新东方的励志公益巡讲"梦想之旅"。俞敏洪老师带着我们5位演讲师一起,为哈尔滨市各高校新入学的大学生的未来指点迷津。我当时作为当红"炸子鸡",给俞敏洪老师垫的场,其地位就相当于德云社的高峰,看到他,大家就知道郭德纲、于谦要出来了。这场讲座对我来说很有意义:第一,我爹当晚终于承认我不是"无业游民"了。第二,同事告诉我,当时现场有1万人,而在线还有20万人观看。我当时真的被震撼了,20万人在线是什么概念?周杰伦举办一场演唱会,线下观众也就是6万人。于是我当机立断决定裸辞,内心的声音告诉我,线上教育才是未来。

　　那时,中国在线教育大爆发,人人都想改变世界,人人都打着教育平等的概念去融资,招兵买马。有的人是真想做点儿事出来,而有的人则仅仅是想了或偷了一个概念,就拿着投资人的钱给自己开工资或做理财……但这些都不重要了,很快就全部销声匿迹了。

　　我在这个时候去了网易,正好网易有道词典积累了9亿用户,要做线上大班课程。这给我的概念就是,如果你站在用户的角度去思考,去做一个大家都需要且有效的课程,就算每人只收费1块钱,那9亿用户就是我做什么梦、拜什么神灵都不敢想的一个数字。但前提是要做出好的产品,这点是网易教我的。

　　我在网易做了三年,从刚开始讲别人让我讲的课,到做用户调研后讲用户需要的课;从在新东方课堂上讲励志讲精神,到现在要把自己"卖出去",要让用户知道他们的痛点是什么,我怎么帮助解决、为什么是我解决,我给用户什么样的产品,产品有多超值,现在有多实惠，知识无价，但……就别但了，3、2、1上链接……

自我销售是我当时不习惯且不接受的，但在这个不一样的时代，如果你自己都不知道自己哪儿厉害，不把你的优势和特长说出来，那么一些没什么实力、单纯糊弄人的老师既不能让学生学到知识又还挣了大钱，你生气不生气？我最早开始想售课，是因为我在一个平台上看到某个所谓的英语老师连拼音"n"和"l"都不分，导致"knife（小刀）"和"life（生活）"读的都是 life 的发音，还在问听讲的学生二者是不是有区别，而直播间的 1000 多人齐刷刷地刷屏"有区别"……我在新东方任教的时候，俞敏洪老师曾说过一句话，说每个人都为一件大事而来。虽然我不知道我的"大事"到底是什么，但起码我想告诉那些在直播间打"有区别"的人，这两个单词的读音是有区别，可那个老师读的没区别！

于是，带着心中的"大事"，我开始做用户调研，了解学生的需求，并做了"纠音大师"和"口语教练"两个产品。其中心思想是，英语发音想学好，只看课程是没有用的，你需要学、练、对比，然后有一个既懂你中文发音的问题又懂这些问题如何影响你的英文发音的中国老师来帮你纠正发音。注意，是中国老师，而不是外教！其实大部分外教并不懂音标，也不懂我们的各种方言。而想学好发音和口语，核心是脑子里要有正确的句型做支撑，再把单词放在这个框架下，需要什么你就背什么好了。知道怎么问、怎么答，还要练即时反应。一直练到像别人问你"How are you?"，你随口就能回答"I'm fine."一样熟练。记住，所有美好表象的呈现都要有所准备，你背下来，再演出来。人生如戏，在我以前每次找外国人聊天之前，你不知道我反复准备过多少个话题。连跟我聊天的外国人都觉得我很有原则，一看时间差不多了，就说自己马上要上课了，不能迟到，然后转身就走。而实际情况是，我把提前准备的话题聊完了，再不走我就露怯了……

我是一个做事很认真的人，如果你好好读读这本书，就能读懂我的心。口语表达中该注意的地方和我觉得你会忽略的地方都在这本书里有所体现。很多人觉得我很勤奋，但其实我觉得，只有懒惰的人才会想把一切都变得简单，就像在这本书里，我写的内容和方法都已经足够简单。内容可更改，方法永流传。

最后，我想用我非常喜爱的作家的书名作为结尾，那就是冯唐老师的《有本事》。请找到自己安身立命的本事。像老师教书、厨师做菜、司机开车……这都是本事，是别人偷不走的东西。无论我做过什么，成不成功，教书永远是我的本事。这一路走来，我经历过很多坎坷，但发生皆是好事，都是成长。在此感谢我爹妈给予我生命。感谢俞敏洪老师给那个 19 岁的孩子一个职业平台。感谢网易有道罗媛老师在人群中看到帅气的我，提升我的认知，帮助我成长。感谢我的学生在我经历人生起伏时的不离不弃。更感谢那个曾经在哈尔滨中央大街为了未来而拼命找老外聊天的刘冠奇。么么哒！

刘冠奇

2024 年 7 月

目 录

序 言

Chapter One　基础口语

Unit 1　自我介绍 Self-introduction　... 002
Lesson 1　打招呼 Greetings　... 002
Lesson 2　姓名、年龄和家乡 Name, Age and Hometown　... 004
Lesson 3　性格和爱好 Personality and Hobbies　... 007
Lesson 4　教育和职业 Education and Occupation　... 009
Lesson 5　告别 Goodbye　... 016

Unit 2　基本信息 Basic Information　... 018
Lesson 6　数字 Numbers　... 018
Lesson 7　星期与日期 Week and Date　... 023
Lesson 8　时间 Time　... 026
Lesson 9　天气和气温 Weather and Temperature　... 028
Lesson 10　建议、看法和重复 Suggestions, Opinions and Repetition　... 030

Unit 3　人际交往 Interpersonal Communication　... 033
Lesson 11　邀请 Invitations　... 033
Lesson 12　电话用语 Phone Calls　... 036
Lesson 13　帮助 Asking for and Offering Help　... 040
Lesson 14　感谢 Gratitude　... 044
Lesson 15　道歉 Apology　... 046

Unit 4　情绪态度 Emotions and Attitudes　... 048
Lesson 16　积极情绪 Positive Emotions　... 048
Lesson 17　消极情绪 Negative Emotions　... 050
Lesson 18　同意与反对 Agreement and Disagreement　... 052
Lesson 19　喜欢与讨厌 Likes and Dislikes　... 055
Lesson 20　支持、鼓励和祝贺，宽慰，信任与怀疑 Support, Encouragement and Congratulations, Comfort, Trust and Doubt　... 058

Chapter Two　场景对话

Unit 5　交通 Transportation　... 062
Lesson 21　办理登机、安检与登机 Check-in, Security and Boarding　... 062
Lesson 22　机舱服务 Plane Service　... 067
Lesson 23　过海关与领取行李 Customs and Reclaiming the Luggage　... 070
Lesson 24　乘坐地铁与公交车 Taking the Subway and Taking a Bus　... 072
Lesson 25　乘坐出租车与租车 Taking a Taxi and Renting a Car　... 075

v

Unit 6　酒店 Hotel … 079
- Lesson 26　预订酒店 Making Reservations … 079
- Lesson 27　办理入住 Check-in … 082
- Lesson 28　客房服务 Room Service … 084
- Lesson 29　投诉 Filing Complaints … 086
- Lesson 30　退房及后续服务 Check-out … 088

Unit 7　餐厅 Restaurant … 090
- Lesson 31　预订餐厅和到店 Making a Reservation and Arriving at the Restaurant … 090
- Lesson 32　点餐 Ordering Food … 093
- Lesson 33　用餐和投诉 During the Meal and Making Complaints … 096
- Lesson 34　打包和结账 Paying the Check … 099
- Lesson 35　快餐店 Fast-food Restaurants … 101

Unit 8　购物 Shopping … 104
- Lesson 36　选购 Shopping Around … 104
- Lesson 37　讨价还价和打折促销 Bargaining and Sales … 108
- Lesson 38　结账 Paying … 111
- Lesson 39　售后服务 After-Sales Service … 114
- Lesson 40　网上购物 Online Shopping … 116

Unit 9　娱乐 Entertainment … 119
- Lesson 41　游乐园 Going to the Amusement Park … 119
- Lesson 42　酒吧 Going to the Bar … 122
- Lesson 43　咖啡厅 Going to the Café … 125
- Lesson 44　健身房 At the Gym … 128
- Lesson 45　野营 Camping … 132

Unit 10　紧急事件 Emergency … 134
- Lesson 46　问路和指路 Asking for and Giving Directions … 134
- Lesson 47　突发疾病 Sudden Illnesses … 137
- Lesson 48　遭遇抢劫 Being Robbed … 142
- Lesson 49　护照遗失 Losing the Passport … 145
- Lesson 50　物品遗失 Lost Things … 147

Unit 11　情感 Relationship … 149
- Lesson 51　介绍 Introduction … 149
- Lesson 52　约会 Dating … 152
- Lesson 53　表白 Confessing Your Love … 154
- Lesson 54　分手 Breaking up … 156
- Lesson 55　婚姻 Marriage … 158

Unit 12　节日 Holidays … 160
- Lesson 56　圣诞节 Christmas … 160
- Lesson 57　感恩节 Thanksgiving Day … 162
- Lesson 58　万圣节 Halloween … 164
- Lesson 59　情人节 Valentine's Day … 166
- Lesson 60　其他节日 Other Holidays … 168

目 录

Chapter Three　基本问答

Unit 13　生活日常（一）Daily Life 1　　... 172
- Lesson 61　晨间日常 Morning Routine　　... 172
- Lesson 62　做家务 Doing Housework　　... 174
- Lesson 63　一日三餐 Meals　　... 177
- Lesson 64　学习 Studying　　... 179
- Lesson 65　工作 Working　　... 181

Unit 14　生活日常（二）Daily Life 2　　... 184
- Lesson 66　交通 Transportation　　... 184
- Lesson 67　购物 Shopping　　... 186
- Lesson 68　家庭成员 Family Members　　... 189
- Lesson 69　周末 Weekends　　... 191
- Lesson 70　社交 Socializing　　... 193

Unit 15　兴趣爱好（一）Hobbies 1　　... 195
- Lesson 71　养宠物 Having Pets　　... 195
- Lesson 72　看电影 Watching Movies　　... 198
- Lesson 73　玩游戏 Playing Video Games　　... 201
- Lesson 74　读书 Reading Books　　... 203
- Lesson 75　听音乐 Listening to Music　　... 206

Unit 16　兴趣爱好（二）Hobbies 2　　... 208
- Lesson 76　玩手机 Using Apps on Mobile Phones　　... 208
- Lesson 77　运动 Playing Sports　　... 210
- Lesson 78　拍照 Taking Photos　　... 213
- Lesson 79　旅游 Traveling　　... 215
- Lesson 80　看电视节目 Watching TV Shows　　... 217

Chapter Four　学会描述

Unit 17　描述人物 Describe a Person　　... 220
- Lesson 81　谁是你最好的朋友？Who is your best friend?　　... 220
- Lesson 82　你们是怎么认识的？How did you meet?　　... 223
- Lesson 83　她/他长什么样？What does she/he look like?　　... 226
- Lesson 84　她/他是什么样的人？What is she/he like?　　... 230
- Lesson 85　为什么她/他是你最好的朋友？Why is she/he your best friend?　　... 233

Unit 18　描述地点 Describe a Place　　... 236
- Lesson 86　你最近去过哪个城市？Which city have you been to recently?　　... 236
- Lesson 87　什么时候去的、和谁一起去的？When did you go there and who did you go with?　　... 240
- Lesson 88　你的第一印象是什么？What's your first impression?　　... 242
- Lesson 89　你在那里都做了什么？What did you do there?　　... 244
- Lesson 90　你喜欢去过的这个城市吗？Do you like this city you have visited?　　... 248

VII

Unit 19　描述事件 Describe an Event ... 252

- Lesson 91　什么事让你印象深刻？ What event made a lasting impression on you? ... 252
- Lesson 92　你和谁一起？ Who were you with? ... 254
- Lesson 93　过程中你的感受如何？ How did you feel during the event? ... 257
- Lesson 94　为什么这件事特别？ Why is this event special? ... 260
- Lesson 95　你从中学到了什么？ What did you learn from it? ... 263

Unit 20　描述物品 Describe an Object ... 267

- Lesson 96　你收到过的最好的礼物是什么？ What is the best gift you have ever received? ... 267
- Lesson 97　你什么时候收到这个礼物的？谁送给你的？ When did you receive the gift and who gave it to you? ... 271
- Lesson 98　你为什么收到这份礼物？ Why did you receive this gift? ... 273
- Lesson 99　你是如何使用它的？ How do you use it? ... 276
- Lesson 100　你为什么这么喜欢这份礼物？ Why do you like this gift so much? ... 279

Chapter Five　表达观点

Unit 21　社会话题 Social Issues ... 284

- Lesson 101　垃圾分类 Garbage Classification ... 284
- Lesson 102　网红 Internet Celebrities ... 287
- Lesson 103　叫车服务 Ride-hailing Services ... 290
- Lesson 104　共享单车 Bike Sharing ... 293
- Lesson 105　移动支付 Mobile Payments ... 295

Unit 22　生活话题 Daily Life ... 298

- Lesson 106　健身 Going to the Gym ... 298
- Lesson 107　外卖 Take-out Meals ... 300
- Lesson 108　相亲 Blind Dating ... 303
- Lesson 109　熬夜 Staying up Late ... 305
- Lesson 110　代购 Daigou ... 307

Unit 23　教育话题 Education ... 310

- Lesson 111　出国留学 Studying Abroad ... 310
- Lesson 112　在线学习 Online Learning ... 313
- Lesson 113　学习第二语言 Learning a Second Language ... 316
- Lesson 114　补习班 Cram Classes ... 318
- Lesson 115　课外活动 Extracurricular Activities ... 321

Unit 24　工作话题 Work ... 324

- Lesson 116　创业 Starting a Business ... 324
- Lesson 117　996 工作制 996 Working Hour System ... 326
- Lesson 118　居家办公 Working from Home ... 329
- Lesson 119　跳槽 Changing Jobs ... 332
- Lesson 120　斜杠青年 Slash Career ... 335

Chapter One

基础口语

导 语

本章"基础口语"涵盖了英语口语中最基础也是最日常的 20 个话题,共分成 4 个单元,每个单元聚焦于不同的基础口语技能,旨在全面提升你的英语交流能力。

- 第 1 单元:自我介绍——成功的交流始于良好的第一印象。在这个单元中,你将学习如何用英语进行自我介绍,包括打招呼,分享姓名、年龄、家乡、性格、爱好、教育背景和职业信息,以及如何礼貌地结束对话。

- 第 2 单元:基本信息——掌握日常生活中的基本信息是进行有效沟通的前提。本单元将教你如何用英语表达数字、日期、时间、天气,以及提出建议和看法。

- 第 3 单元:人际交往——日常交际技巧对于建立良好的人际关系至关重要。本单元覆盖了邀请、电话用语、提供帮助、表达感谢和进行道歉的地道英语表达。

- 第 4 单元:情绪态度——有效地表达情绪和态度是深化交流的关键。本单元将指导你如何用英语表达好心情、坏心情、同意和反对、喜欢和讨厌,以及提供支持与鼓励、安慰,表达信任或怀疑。

通过这 4 个单元、20 个话题的学习,你能掌握英语口语表达中最基础、最实用,同时也是最地道的表达,为进一步的口语学习打下坚实的基础。话不多说,让我们开始学习吧!

Unit 1　自我介绍 Self-introduction

Lesson 1　打招呼 Greetings

01 通用句型

提问

a. 正式

How are you? 你好吗?

b. 非正式

How are you doing? 你好吗?
How is it going? / How's it going? 近况如何?
How have you been? / How've you been? 最近过得怎么样?
How's life treating you? 过得如何?

回答

a. 特别好

Great. 很好。
Awesome. 特别好。
Pretty good. 非常好。
Couldn't be better. 不能更好了。

+ What about you? / You?
　那你呢? / 你呢?

词汇精讲　Word Study

awesome
英 /ˈɔːsəm/
美 /ˈɔːsəm/

a. 1. 很困难的；难得吓人的
　　It's an awesome task. 这是个艰巨的任务。
　2. 很好的，棒极了的
　　You look awesome today! 你今天看起来真美!

---

b. 一般好

Good. 挺好的。
Not bad. 还不错。
The same as usual. 老样子。

+ What about you? / You?
　那你呢? / 你呢?

c. 不好 / 忙

Not so great. 不太好。
Terrible. 很糟糕。
Couldn't be worse. 不能更糟了。
I've been a bit busy. 我最近有点忙。

+ What about you? / You?
　那你呢? / 你呢?

Unit 1　自我介绍 Self-introduction

🗨 场景对话 Conversation

A: Hey, Jack, how are you doing?
B: Not bad. What about you?
A: I'm good.

A：嘿，杰克，最近如何？
B：还不错。你呢？
A：我挺好的。

02 特殊句型

（1）What's up?

提问

What's up?
What up?
What's new?
最近怎么样？

}+man/buddy/bro/dude/mate!
兄弟！

回答

Not much, just chilling.
没什么，挺好的。
Not much, just watching TV.
没什么，就在看电视呢。

🗨 场景对话 Conversation

A: Hey, Jack, what's up?
B: Not much, man. I've been a bit busy. How are you doing?
A: Not bad.

A：嘿，杰克，最近怎么样？
B：没什么，就是有点忙。你过得怎么样？
A：还不错。

（2）好久不见

I haven't seen you for a long time.
I haven't seen you in ages.
It's been a while.
好久不见。

}+ How's it going?
最近过得如何？

Notes: 画横线部分可替换成上面提到的通用句型。

🗨 场景对话 Conversation

A: I haven't seen you for a long time. How's it going?
B: Yeah, it's been a while. I'm great. What about you?
A: The same as usual.

A：好久不见，近况如何？
B：是啊，好久不见。我很好，你呢？
A：还是老样子。

（3）正式场合

Ladies and gentlemen, thank you for giving me this opportunity. It's a great honor to be here.

女士们，先生们，感谢你们给我这次机会。很荣幸来到这里。

词汇精讲
Word Study

opportunity
英 /ˌɒpəˈtjuːnəti/
美 /ˌɑːpərˈtuːnəti/

n. 机会，良机
It's a great opportunity.
这是一个很好的机会。

Lesson 2 姓名、年龄和家乡
Name, Age and Hometown

Part 1 姓名 Name

01 关于姓名

提问

What's your name? 你叫什么名字？
May I have your name?
能告诉我你的名字吗？
Would you mind telling me your name?
你介意告诉我你的名字吗？
What do I call you? 我要如何称呼你？
How should I address you? 我该如何称呼你？

词汇补充 Word Supplement

nickname 英 /ˈnɪkneɪm/ 美 /ˈnɪkneɪm/ 昵称
family name/last name/surname 姓
given name/first name 名
full name 全名
Chinese name 中文名
English name 英文名

词汇精讲 Word Study

address
英 /əˈdres/
美 /əˈdres/

n. 1. 住址；地址；通信处
This is my home address. 这是我的住址。
2. （互联网等的）地址
What's your e-mail address? 你的电子邮箱地址是什么？
3. 演说；演讲
He delivered an address to the students. 他给同学们作了一场演讲。

v. 1. 演说；演讲
She will address the meeting tomorrow. 她明天要在会议上发言。
2. 称呼（某人）；冠以（某种称呼）
He addressed me as "Mrs. Zhang". 他称呼我为"张太太"。
3. 设法解决；处理；对付
I tried to address the issue. 我试图解决这个问题。

回答

My Chinese name is <u>Liu Guanqi</u>. 我的中文名字是刘冠奇。
My English name is <u>Jack</u>. 我的英文名字是杰克。
Just call me <u>Jack</u>. 叫我杰克就行。
I'm <u>Jack</u>, by the way. 随便说一下，我是杰克。
Feel free to call me <u>Jack</u>. 叫我杰克就行。

> **Notes:** 全书中画横线的部分均可根据自己的实际情况进行替换。

02 如何拼写

提问

How do you spell your name? 你的名字如何拼写呢？
Could you tell me how to spell your name? 你能告诉我如何拼写你的名字吗？

Unit 1　自我介绍 Self-introduction

回答

It's J-A-C-K, Jack. 是 J-A-C-K，Jack。

场景对话 Conversation

A: May I have your name?
B: My Chinese name is Liu Guanqi and my English name is Jack.
A: Could you tell me how to spell it?
B: It's J-A-C-K, Jack.
A: OK, I see. Nice to meet you, Jack.
B: Nice to meet you, too.

A: Hey, how are you doing?
B: Not bad, you?
A: Good. I'm Jack, by the way.
B: I'm Alex. Nice to meet you.

A：能告诉我你的名字吗？
B：我的中文名字是刘冠奇，我的英文名字是杰克。
A：你能告诉我如何拼写吗？
B：是 J-A-C-K，Jack。
A：好的，我知道了。很高兴认识你，杰克。
B：我也很高兴认识你。

A：嘿，你好吗？
B：还不错，你呢？
A：挺好的。顺便说一下，我叫杰克。
B：我是亚历克斯。很高兴认识你。

Part 2　年龄 Age

提问

How old are you? 你多大了?
When were you born? 你什么时候出生的?

回答

13/30. 13/30 岁。
I'm 13/30 years old. 我 13/30 岁。
I was born in 1986. 我 1986 年出生的。
I was born on October 24, 1986.
我 1986 年 10 月 24 号出生的。

语法点睛 Grammar Notes

- 年份前面使用介词 in
Beijing held the Summer Olympic Games in 2008.
北京于 2008 年举行了夏季奥运会。
- 具体日期前面使用介词 on
They arrived in Shanghai on May the first.
他们于五月一日到达上海。

场景对话 Conversation

A: Hey, how are you doing?
B: Not bad. What about you?
A: Good. How old are you?
B: 30. What about you?
A: I'm 24 years old.

A：嘿，你好吗？
B：还不错，你呢？
A：挺好的。你多大了？
B：30 岁。你呢？
A：我 24 岁。

Part 3　家乡 Hometown

01 简单问答

提问

Where are you from? =Where do you come from?
=Where is your hometown?
你来自哪里？

回答

I'm /come from <u>China</u>. 我来自中国。
I'm /come from <u>Harbin, Heilongjiang Province</u>. 我来自黑龙江省哈尔滨市。
I was born and raised in <u>China</u>. 我在中国出生和长大。
I was born and raised in <u>Harbin, Heilongjiang Province</u>.
我在黑龙江省哈尔滨市出生和长大。

02 进一步了解

提问

Could I know more about your hometown?
我能进一步了解你的家乡吗？
Can you say something about your hometown?
你能谈谈你的家乡吗？

回答

I was born and raised in <u>Harbin</u>, which is <u>a beautiful city and famous for Ice and Snow World</u>.
我在哈尔滨出生和长大，那是一个美丽的城市，以冰雪世界而闻名。

> **短语精讲** Phrase Study
>
> - be famous as 作为……而出名
>   He is famous as a singer.
>   他作为一名歌手而出名。
> - be famous for 因……而出名
>   He is famous for his novels.
>   他因他的小说而出名。

💬 场景对话 Conversation

A: Jack, where are you from?
B: I was born and raised in Harbin.
A: Could I know more about your hometown?
B: It is a beautiful city and famous for Ice and Snow World.

A：杰克，你来自哪里？
B：我在哈尔滨出生和长大。
A：我能进一步了解你的家乡吗？
B：哈尔滨是一个美丽的城市，以冰雪世界而闻名。

Lesson 3　性格和爱好
Personality and Hobbies

Part 1　性格 Personality

01 通用句型

I am a/an outgoing person/girl/guy. 我是一个外向的人 / 女孩 / 小伙子。

I'm (a little bit) shy. 我（有点）害羞。

I'm not very outgoing. 我不是很外向。

词汇补充 Word Supplement

词	英	美	中文
extroverted	/ˈekstrəvɜːtɪd/	/ˈekstrəvɜːrtɪd/	
=outgoing	/ˈaʊtɡəʊɪŋ/	/ˈaʊtɡoʊɪŋ/	外向的
introverted	/ˈɪntrəvɜːtɪd/	/ˈɪntrəvɜːrtɪd/	内向的
easygoing	/ˌiːziˈɡəʊɪŋ/	/ˌiːziˈɡoʊɪŋ/	随和的
shy	/ʃaɪ/	/ʃaɪ/	害羞的
honest	/ˈɒnɪst/	/ˈɑːnɪst/	诚实的
confident	/ˈkɒnfɪdənt/	/ˈkɑːnfɪdənt/	自信的
independent	/ˌɪndɪˈpendənt/	/ˌɪndɪˈpendənt/	独立的
creative	/kriˈeɪtɪv/	/kriˈeɪtɪv/	有创造力的
patient	/ˈpeɪʃ(ə)nt/	/ˈpeɪʃ(ə)nt/	有耐心的
open-minded	/ˌəʊpən ˈmaɪndɪd/	/ˌoʊpən ˈmaɪndɪd/	思想包容的
responsible	/rɪˈspɒnsəb(ə)l/	/rɪˈspɑːnsəb(ə)l/	有责任心的
optimistic	/ˌɒptɪˈmɪstɪk/	/ˌɑːptɪˈmɪstɪk/	乐观的
pessimistic	/ˌpesɪˈmɪstɪk/	/ˌpesɪˈmɪstɪk/	悲观的

02 补充细节

I am an outgoing and easygoing person. I'd like to make friends with everyone.
我是一个外向又随和的人。我想和大家交朋友。

I am very optimistic. I always look on the bright side of things.
我非常乐观，我总是看到事物好的一面。

I am not very extroverted. Sometimes I prefer staying alone.
我不是很外向，有时我更喜欢独处。

场景对话 Conversation

A: How would you describe yourself?

B: I am an outgoing and easygoing person. I'd like to make friends with everyone.

A：你会如何描述自己？

B：我是一个外向又随和的人。我想和大家结交朋友。

Part 2 爱好 Hobbies

提问

What's your hobby? /What are your hobbies? 你的爱好是什么?
What do you do in your spare/free time?=How do you spend your spare time?
你业余时间都喜欢干什么?

词汇精讲 Word Study

spare
英 /speə/
美 /sper/

a. 1. 备用的；闲置的
Do you have a spare key? 你有备用钥匙吗?
2. 空闲的；空余的
I like to paint in my spare time. 我喜欢在空余时间绘画。

v. 1. 抽出；拨出；留出；匀出
Can you spare me a moment? 你能给我一点时间吗?
2. 不吝惜（时间、金钱）
She spared no effort to help me. 她不遗余力地帮助我。

n. 备用品；备用轮胎
I've lost my key and I haven't got a spare. 我把钥匙弄丢了，还没有备用的。

回答

◇ I like/love to do/doing sth.
I like/love playing basketball.
I like/love to play basketball.
我喜欢/爱打篮球。

◇ I enjoy doing sth.
I enjoy listening to music.
我喜欢听音乐。

◇ I am crazy about sth.
I am crazy about football.
我非常喜欢足球。

◇ I am into (doing) sth.
I am into painting.
我喜欢画画。

词汇精讲 Word Study

crazy
英 /'kreɪzi/
美 /'kreɪzi/

a. 1. 不理智的；疯狂的
Are you crazy? 你疯了吗?
2. 非常气愤的
She is driving me crazy. 她快把我气疯了。
3. 热衷的；狂热的
He is crazy about basketball. 他非常喜欢篮球。

场景对话 Conversation

A: Jack, what's your hobby?
B: I like playing basketball. What about you?
A: I enjoy reading books.

A：杰克，你的爱好是什么?
B：我喜欢打篮球，你呢?
A：我喜欢读书。

Lesson 4　教育和职业
Education and Occupation

Part 1　教育 Education

01 关于年级

提问

What grade are you in?（美）
What year are you in?（英）
你上几年级？

回答

a. 小学生

　　I'm a sixth-grade student at Tsinghua University Affiliated Elementary School.
　　我是清华大学附属小学六年级的学生。

b. 初中生

　　I'm a middle school student at Beijing No.4 Middle School.
　　我是北京第四中学的一名中学生。

　　I'm an eighth-grade student at Beijing No.4 Middle School.
　　我是北京第四中学八年级的学生。

c. 高中生

　　I'm a high school student at Beijing No.4 High School.
　　我是北京第四中学的一名高中生。

　　I'm a tenth-grade student at Beijing No.4 High School.
　　我是北京第四中学高一的学生。

d. 大学生

　　I'm a freshman at Jilin University.
　　我是吉林大学大一的学生。

　　I'm a first-year student at Jilin University.
　　我是吉林大学大一的学生。

词汇补充 Word Supplement

1. 各阶段学校表达

   kindergarten [英] /ˈkɪndəgɑːt(ə)n/   [美] /ˈkɪndərgɑːrt(ə)n/   幼儿园
   primary school（英）/elementary school（美）小学
   （primary   [英] /ˈpraɪməri/   [美] /ˈpraɪməri/   初等教育的）
   （elementary [英] /ˌelɪˈmentri/   [美] /ˌelɪˈmentri/   初级的）
   secondary school（英）中学（包含初中和高中）
   （secondary   [英] /ˈsekənd(ə)ri/   [美] /ˈsekənderi/   中等教育的）
   middle school / junior high school（美）初中
   high school（美）高中
   college   [英] /ˈkɒlɪdʒ/   [美] /ˈkɑːlɪdʒ/   大学
   university   [英] /ˌjuːnɪˈvɜːsəti/   [美] /ˌjuːnɪˈvɜːrsəti/   大学
   vocational college 职业学院
   （vocational   [英] /vəʊˈkeɪʃ(ə)l/   [美] /voʊˈkeɪʃ(ə)l/   职业的）

2. 关于高中 / 大学不同年级的表达

   美国：
   freshman   [英] /ˈfreʃmən/   [美] /ˈfreʃmən/   一年级
   sophomore   [英] /ˈsɒfəmɔː(r)/   [美] /ˈsɑːfəmɔːr/   二年级
   junior   [英] /ˈdʒuːniə(r)/   [美] /ˈdʒuːniər/   三年级
   senior   [英] /ˈsiːniə(r)/   [美] /ˈsiːniər/   四年级
   英国：
   first/second/third/fourth year 一 / 二 / 三 / 四年级

02 关于学历

（1）在读学生

a. 关于学校

提问

Which school/university do you attend? 你在哪个学校 / 大学读书？

回答

I am studying at Jilin University. 我在吉林大学读书。

b. 关于学历

提问

Are you studying for a Bachelor's or Master's degree?
你正在攻读学士学位还是硕士学位？

Unit 1 自我介绍 Self-introduction

回答

I'm now in my first year of undergraduate/graduate study.
我现在正在本科/研究生学习的第一年。

词汇补充 Word Supplement

Bachelor's degree 学士
（bachelor　　英 /'bætʃələ(r)/　　美 /'bætʃələr/　　学士）
Master's degree 硕士
（master　　英 /'mɑːstə(r)/　　美 /'mæstər/　　硕士）
Doctor of Philosophy（Ph. D）博士
（philosophy　　英 /fə'lɒsəfi/　　美 /fə'lɑːsəfi/　　哲学）
undergraduate　　英 /ˌʌndə'grædʒuət/　　美 /ˌʌndər'grædʒuət/　　本科生
graduate　　英 /'grædʒuət/　　美 /'grædʒuət/　　研究生
post-graduate　　英 /ˌpəʊst 'grædʒuət/　　美 /ˌpoʊst 'grædʒuət/　　研究生

（2）已毕业

a. 关于学校

提问

Which school/university did you graduate from? 你是哪个学校/大学毕业的？

回答

I graduated from Jilin University. 我毕业于吉林大学。

b. 关于学位

提问

What kind of degree do you have? 你有什么学位？

回答

I have a Bachelor's degree in Literature. 我拥有文学学士学位。
I have a Master's degree in Law. 我拥有法律硕士学位。
I have a Ph. D in History. 我拥有历史学博士学位。

词汇补充 Word Supplement

主要的学科名称：
Economics　　英 /ˌiːkə'nɒmɪks/　　美 /ˌiːkə'nɑːmɪks/　　经济学
Law　　英 /lɔː/　　美 /lɔː/　　法学

011

Literature	英 /ˈlɪtrətʃə(r)/	美 /ˈlɪtrətʃər/	文学
History	英 /ˈhɪst(ə)ri/	美 /ˈhɪst(ə)ri/	历史学
Engineering	英 /ˌendʒɪˈnɪərɪŋ/	美 /ˌendʒɪˈnɪrɪŋ/	工学
Medicine	英 /ˈmedsn/	美 /ˈmedɪs(ə)n/	医学
Management	英 /ˈmænɪdʒmənt/	美 /ˈmænɪdʒmənt/	管理学
Art	英 /ɑːt/	美 /ɑːrt/	艺术学

03 关于专业

提问

What's your major? = What are you majoring in? 你的专业是什么?

回答

My major is English. = I'm majoring in English. 我的专业是英语。

词汇精讲 Word Study

major
英 /ˈmeɪdʒə(r)/
美 /ˈmeɪdʒər/

n. 1. 少校
He used to be a major in the army. 他曾经是一名陆军少校。
2. 专业（学生）
My major is English. 我的专业是英语。
a. 主要的；重大的
She played a major role in it. 她在这件事中发挥了重要作用。
v. 主修，专攻
I'm majoring in English. 我的专业是英语。

04 综合介绍

I'm a freshman at Jilin University, and I'm majoring in English.
我是吉林大学的大一新生，主修英语。

I'm an English major student at Jilin University. I'm a sophomore.
我是吉林大学英语专业的大二学生。

场景对话 Conversation

A: Are you studying for Bachelor's or Master's degree?　　A: 你正在攻读学士学位还是硕士学位?
B: I'm now in my third year of undergraduate study.　　B: 我现在是本科三年级。
A: What's your major?　　A: 你的专业是什么?
B: Economics. What about you?　　B: 经济学。你呢?
A: I am majoring in English.　　A: 我主修英语。

Unit 1　自我介绍 Self-introduction

Part 2　职业 Occupation

01 有工作

（1）简单问答

提问

What's your job? 你的工作是什么？
What do you do (for a living)？你以什么为生？

回答

I'm a teacher. 我是一名教师。
I work as a teacher. 我的工作是教师。
I've been working as a teacher for ten years. 我已经当了10年教师。

词汇补充 Word Supplement

常见职业：

单词	英	美	中文
teacher	/'tiːtʃə(r)/	/'tiːtʃər/	教师
doctor	/'dɒktə(r)/	/'dɑːktər/	医生
nurse	/nɜːs/	/nɜːrs/	护士
coder	/'kəʊdə(r)/	/'koʊdər/	程序员
=programmer	/'prəʊgræmə(r)/	/'proʊgræmər/	
chef	/ʃef/	/ʃef/	主厨
cook	/kʊk/	/kʊk/	厨师
accountant	/ə'kaʊntənt/	/ə'kaʊntənt/	会计
journalist	/'dʒɜːnəlɪst/	/'dʒɜːrnəlɪst/	记者
policeman	/pə'liːsmən/	/pə'liːsmən/	（男）警察
policewoman	/pə'liːswʊmən/	/pə'liːswʊmən/	（女）警察
cashier	/kæ'ʃɪə(r)/	/kæ'ʃɪr/	收银员
freelancer	/'friːlɑːnsə(r)/	/'friːlænsər/	自由职业者

taxi driver 出租车司机　　　product manager 产品经理

（2）进一步了解

提问

What do you have to do in your job? 你在工作中需要做什么？

回答

I've been working as a teacher for ten years. I'm responsible for/I'm in charge of course design and online teaching.

我已经当了 10 年教师。我负责课程设计和在线教学。

> **短语精讲** Phrase Study
>
> - **be responsible for 为……负责**
>   Each should be responsible for their own life decision.
>   每个人都要为自己的人生决定负责。
>   The storm is responsible for the building damage. 这场暴风雨造成建筑受损。
> - **be in charge of /take charge of 掌管……**
>   She is in charge of organizing the meeting. 她负责组织会议。
>   The new manager has taken charge of the project. 新任经理已掌管该项目。

02 找工作

I'm looking for work now. 我现在正在找工作。

I'm trying to find a job in online education. 我正在尝试在在线教育行业找工作。

03 失业

通用表达：

I'm out of work. 我失业了。

被炒鱿鱼：

I got fired (from my job). 我被解雇了。

主动辞职：

I have resigned from my job. 我辞职了。

I quit my job. 我辞职了。

> **词汇精讲** Word Study
>
> **quit**
> 英 /kwɪt/
> 美 /kwɪt/
>
> v. 1. 停止，放弃
>   I quit smoking. 我戒烟了。
> 2. 离开，辞（职）
>   I quit my job. 我辞职了。

04 创业

I'm trying to start up my own business now. The good thing is that I have already got a few investors who are willing to finance my project.

我现在正在努力创办自己的公司。好消息是我已经有了一些愿意为我的项目提供资金的投资者。

I'm trying to start up my own business now. But I'm still looking for some investors.
我现在正在努力创办自己的公司。但我还在寻找投资人。

05 退休

I have been retired for almost five years. 我已经退休快五年了。

I used to be a dancer. 我之前是一名舞者。

I worked as a teacher for almost 30 years. 我曾担任教师近 30 年。

I was a teacher at NetEase for ten years. Now I'm retired.
我曾在网易任教 10 年。现在我退休了。

词汇精讲 Word Study		
retire 英 /rɪˈtaɪə(r)/ 美 /rɪˈtaɪər/	v. 1.	退休，退役 He has been retired for ten years. 他已经退休 10 年了。
	2.	退下，退出，撤退 He had to retire from the competition because of injury. 他因伤不得不退出了比赛。

 场景对话 Conversation

A: Jack, what do you do for a living?
B: Well, I'm an English teacher and I've been teaching English for ten years.

A：杰克，你以什么为生？
B：我是一名英语教师，我已经教英语 10 年了。

015

Lesson 5　告别
Goodbye

01　日常生活

（1）前奏

It's a bit late. 有点晚了。
Well, it's getting late. 哦，时间不早了。

> **词汇精讲** Word Study
>
> **late**
> 英 /leɪt/
> 美 /leɪt/
>
> a. 1. 接近末期的；在晚年的
> She married in her late twenties. 她快 30 岁时结的婚。
> 2. 迟到的；迟发生的；迟做的
> I'm sorry I'm late. 对不起，我迟到了。
> 3. 近日暮的；近深夜的
> It's getting late. 时间不早了。

（2）不情愿走

I hate to say goodbye, but I have to. 我不想说再见，但是我不得不说。

（3）我得走了

I gotta go. 我得走了。
I must be going. 我必须得走了。

（4）和你聊天很愉快

It was nice talking with you. 和你聊天很愉快。

（5）让我们保持联系

Let's keep in touch. May I have your number/WeChat/E-mail?
让我们保持联系。能给我你的号码 / 微信 / 邮箱吗？

（6）再见

See you/ya. 再见。
See you soon. 一会儿见。
See you later. 回头见。
See you then. 到时候见。
See you around. 有缘再见。
Goodbye/Bye. 再见。
Take care. 保重。

> **短语精讲** Phrase Study
>
> ● keep in touch（with sb.）保持联系
> Let's keep in touch.
> 咱们保持联系。
> ● get in touch（with sb.）取得联系
> I'm trying to get in touch with her.
> 我在设法与她取得联系。
> ● lose touch（with sb.）失去联系
> I have lost touch with him.
> 我已经和他失去了联系。

Unit 1　自我介绍 Self-introduction

🗨 场景对话 Conversation

A: Jack, I gotta go. See you later.
B: OK, see ya. Take care.

A：杰克，我得走了，回头见。
B：好的，再见。保重。

02 正式场合

Thank you for your attention! 感谢您的关注！

词汇精讲 Word Study

attention
英 /əˈtenʃ(ə)n/
美 /əˈtenʃ(ə)n/

n. 1. 注意；专心；留心；注意力
May I have your attention, please? 请注意听我讲话好吗？
2. 兴趣；关注
The problem has drawn great attention. 这个问题引起了极大的关注。
3. 特别照料（或行动、处理）
The patient needs medical attention. 这个病人需要医疗护理。

自我介绍通用版：

Ladies and gentlemen, thank you for giving me this opportunity. It's a great honor to be here.

My Chinese name is Liu Guanqi and my English name is Jack. I'm from Harbin, which is a beautiful city and famous for Ice and Snow World. I'm actually 36 years old and I like playing basketball. I am an outgoing and easygoing guy. So that's it. Thank you for your attention.

女士们，先生们，感谢你们给我这次机会。很荣幸来到这里。
我的中文名字叫刘冠奇，英文名字叫杰克。我来自哈尔滨，那是一个美丽的城市，以冰雪大世界而闻名。我今年36岁，我喜欢打篮球。我是一个外向、随和的人。就这些了，谢谢你们的关注。

Unit 2 基本信息 Basic Information

Lesson 6 数字 Numbers

Part 1 基数词 Cardinal Numbers

01 基数词的读法

（1）个位数

0	zero	英 /ˈzɪərəʊ/	美 /ˈzɪroʊ/	零
1	one	英 /wʌn/	美 /wʌn/	一
2	two	英 /tuː/	美 /tuː/	二
3	three	英 /θriː/	美 /θriː/	三
4	four	英 /fɔː(r)/	美 /fɔːr/	四
5	five	英 /faɪv/	美 /faɪv/	五
6	six	英 /sɪks/	美 /sɪks/	六
7	seven	英 /ˈsev(ə)n/	美 /ˈsev(ə)n/	七
8	eight	英 /eɪt/	美 /eɪt/	八
9	nine	英 /naɪn/	美 /naɪn/	九
10	ten	英 /ten/	美 /ten/	十

（2）十几

11	eleven	英 /ɪˈlev(ə)n/	美 /ɪˈlev(ə)n/	十一
12	twelve	英 /twelv/	美 /twelv/	十二
13	thirteen	英 /ˌθɜːˈtiːn/	美 /ˌθɜːrˈtiːn/	十三
14	fourteen	英 /ˌfɔːˈtiːn/	美 /ˌfɔːrˈtiːn/	十四
15	fifteen	英 /ˌfɪfˈtiːn/	美 /ˌfɪfˈtiːn/	十五
16	sixteen	英 /ˌsɪksˈtiːn/	美 /ˌsɪksˈtiːn/	十六
17	seventeen	英 /ˌsev(ə)nˈtiːn/	美 /ˌsev(ə)nˈtiːn/	十七
18	eighteen	英 /ˌeɪˈtiːn/	美 /ˌeɪˈtiːn/	十八
19	nineteen	英 /ˌnaɪnˈtiːn/	美 /ˌnaɪnˈtiːn/	十九

Notes:
1. 11 eleven 和 12 twelve 需要单独记忆。
2. 剩下的 13~19 都以 -teen 结尾。
3. 其中，14 fourteen，16 sixteen，17 seventeen，19 nineteen 这四个数字都是在 4 four，6 six，7 seven，9 nine 后面直接加上 -teen 组成。
4. 18 eighteen 是 8 eight 去掉 t 之后再加上 -teen。
5. 13 thirteen 和 15 fifteen 中的 thir- 和 fif- 是由 3 three 和 5 five 转化而来。

（3）几十

20	twenty	英 /ˈtwenti/	美 /ˈtwenti/	二十
30	thirty	英 /ˈθɜːti/	美 /ˈθɜːrti/	三十
40	forty	英 /ˈfɔːti/	美 /ˈfɔːrti/	四十

50	fifty	英 /ˈfɪfti/	美 /ˈfɪfti/	五十
60	sixty	英 /ˈsɪksti/	美 /ˈsɪksti/	六十
70	seventy	英 /ˈsev(ə)nti/	美 /ˈsev(ə)nti/	七十
80	eighty	英 /ˈeɪti/	美 /ˈeɪti/	八十
90	ninety	英 /ˈnaɪnti/	美 /ˈnaɪnti/	九十

（4）几十几（几十 + 个位数）

21	twenty-one	二十一
32	thirty-two	三十二
43	forty-three	四十三
54	fifty-four	五十四
65	sixty-five	六十五
76	seventy-six	七十六
87	eighty-seven	八十七
98	ninety-eight	九十八
29	twenty-nine	二十九

Notes:
1. 整十数字都以 -ty 结尾，其中 twenty 需要单独记忆。
2. 60 sixty, 70 seventy 和 90 ninety 都是在 6 six, 7 seven, 9 nine 后面直接加上 -ty 组成。
3. 80 eighty 是 8 eight 去掉 t 之后再加上 -ty。
4. 30 thirty 和 50 fifty 与上面提到的 13 thirteen 和 15 fifteen 类似，其中的 thir- 和 fif- 是由 3 three 和 5 five 转化而来。
5. 40 forty 中的 for- 比 4 four 少一个 u。

Notes: 以上这些都是由整十数字加上个位数字构成，注意中间需要加上连字符。

（5）万，十万，百万，千万，亿

100	one hundred	百
1,000	one thousand	千
10,000	ten thousand	万
100,000	one hundred thousand	十万
1,000,000	one million	百万
10,000,000	ten million	千万
100,000,000	one hundred million	亿
1,000,000,000	one billion	十亿
10,000,000,000	ten billion	百亿
105	one hundred and five	
123	one hundred and twenty-three	
1,005	one thousand and five	
1,023	one thousand and twenty-three	
1,234	one thousand, two hundred and thirty-four	

Notes:
1. 1000 及以上的数字，从后往前数，每三位加一个逗号；读数时看逗号，一个逗号 thousand，两个逗号 million，三个逗号 billion。
2. 英文中的"万"用"十个千 ten thousand"表示，"十万"则是"百个千 hundred thousand"，"千万"用"十个百万 ten million"表示，"亿"用"百个百万 hundred million"表示，"百亿"用"十个十亿 ten billion"表示。
3. 注意十亿/百万/千/百位和十/个位之间需要加上 and。

10,005　　ten thousand and five
12,234　　twelve thousand, two hundred and thirty-four
123,456　　one hundred and twenty-three thousand, four hundred and fifty-six

02 基数词的应用场景：询问基本信息

提问

What's your ID number?
你的身份证号是多少？

May/Can/Could I have your phone number?
你能告诉我你的手机号码吗？

Do you have WeChat?
你用微信吗？

词汇补充 Word Supplement

ID number	身份证号
passport number	护照号
phone number	电话号码
student card number	学生卡号
post code	邮政编码
e-mail address	邮箱地址
WeChat	微信
Twitter	推特
Facebook	脸书

回答

My phone number is 123 4567 8910.
我的手机号是 12345678910。

My ID number is 65830932.
我的身份证号是 65830932。

It's 87249512.
是 87249512。

知识拓展 More to Know

电话号码的读法：

一般情况（一个一个数字地说）：
139 1234 5678　　one three nine, one two three four, five six seven eight
4672 1783　　four six seven two, one seven eight three

特殊情况：
1. 如果号码里面有数字 0，0 可以读成字母 O（oh）或者 zero。
　　1098 2014　　one oh/zero nine eight, two oh/zero one four
2. 如果有两个重复的数字，使用 double；如果有三个重复的数字，使用 triple。
　　2633 7488　　two six double three, seven four double eight
　　2333 4666　　two triple three, four triple six

场景对话 Conversation

A: Hello, Jack. May I have your phone number?
B: Yes, my phone number is 2333 4066.
A: Got it. See ya.
B: Take care.

A：你好，杰克。你能告诉我你的手机号码吗？
B：可以，我的手机号码是 2333 4066（two triple three, four oh/zero double six）。
A：记下了，再见。
B：保重。

Part 2　序数词 Ordinal Numbers

01　序数词的读法

（1）1，2，3 的序数词

one → first	英 /fɜːst/	美 /fɜːrst/	第一
two → second	英 /ˈsekənd/	美 /ˈsekənd/	第二
three → third	英 /θɜːd/	美 /θɜːrd/	第三

（2）大部分情况下，在基数词的基础上加 -th

four → fourth	英 /fɔːθ/	美 /fɔːrθ/	第四
six → sixth	英 /sɪksθ/	美 /sɪksθ/	第六
ten → tenth	英 /tenθ/	美 /tenθ/	第十

（3）8 去 t，9 去 e

eight → eighth	英 /eɪtθ/	美 /eɪtθ/	第八
nine → ninth	英 /naɪnθ/	美 /naɪnθ/	第九

（4）以 -ve 结尾的，替换成 f，加 -th

five → fifth	英 /fɪfθ/	美 /fɪfθ/	第五
twelve → twelfth	英 /twelfθ/	美 /twelfθ/	第十二

（5）以 -ty 结尾的，把 y 替换成 i，加 -eth

twenty → twentieth	英 /ˈtwentiəθ/	美 /ˈtwentiəθ/	第二十
thirty → thirtieth	英 /ˈθɜːtiəθ/	美 /ˈθɜːrtiəθ/	第三十
forty → fortieth	英 /ˈfɔːtiəθ/	美 /ˈfɔːrtiəθ/	第四十

（6）两位数及以上（基数词 + 序数词）

twenty-one → twenty-first	英 /ˌtwenti 'fɜːst/	美 /ˌtwenti 'fɜːrst/	第二十一
twenty-two → twenty-second	英 /ˌtwenti 'sekənd/	美 /ˌtwenti 'sekənd/	第二十二
twenty-three → twenty-third	英 /ˌtwenti 'θɜːd/	美 /ˌtwenti 'θɜːrd/	第二十三
two hundred and twenty → two hundred and twentieth			第二百二十
three hundred and twenty-one → three hundred and twenty-first			第三百二十一

02 序数词的应用场景

（1）顺序

I like the <u>first</u> one. 我喜欢第一个。

> **Notes:** 两位数字只需要把个位数变成序数词，中间加上连字符；三位数字及以上需要把最后两位数字变成序数词，若十位数为 0，则只把个位数变成序数词。

（2）楼层

I live on the <u>third</u> floor. 我住在三楼。

（3）生日

He held a party for his <u>eightieth</u> birthday. 他举办了一个派对来庆祝自己的 80 岁大寿。

（4）世纪

We're living in the <u>twenty-first</u> century. 我们生活在 21 世纪。

（5）国王或女王的名字

Elizabeth II（Elizabeth the second）伊丽莎白二世

场景对话 Conversation

A: Hey, Emma, there are two cakes. Which one do you prefer?
B: I like the first one.

A：嘿，艾玛，这有两个蛋糕，你更喜欢哪一个？
B：我喜欢第一个。

Lesson 7　星期与日期
Week and Date

Part 1　星期 Week

句型一：

What day is it today? 今天星期几？
It's Friday. 今天星期五。

句型二：

What day is today? 今天星期几？
Today is Friday. 今天星期五。

词汇补充 Word Supplement

the day before yesterday 前天

单词	英	美	中文
yesterday	/ˈjestədeɪ/	/ˈjestərdeɪ/	昨天
today	/təˈdeɪ/	/təˈdeɪ/	今天
tomorrow	/təˈmɒrəʊ/	/təˈmɑːroʊ/	明天

the day after tomorrow 后天

working days 工作日：

Monday	/ˈmʌndeɪ/	/ˈmʌndeɪ/	星期一
Tuesday	/ˈtjuːzdeɪ/	/ˈtuːzdeɪ/	星期二
Wednesday	/ˈwenzdeɪ/	/ˈwenzdeɪ/	星期三
Thursday	/ˈθɜːzdeɪ/	/ˈθɜːrzdeɪ/	星期四
Friday	/ˈfraɪdeɪ/	/ˈfraɪdeɪ/	星期五

weekend 周末：

Saturday	/ˈsætədeɪ/	/ˈsætərdeɪ/	星期六
Sunday	/ˈsʌndeɪ/	/ˈsʌndeɪ/	星期日

场景对话 Conversation

A: What day is it today?
B: It's Friday.
A: Weekend's coming!
B: Hooray!

A：今天是星期几？
B：今天星期五。
A：到周末啦！
B：万岁！

Part 2 日期 Date

提问

What's today's date?=What's the date today? 今天几月几号?

词汇精讲 Word Study

date
英 /deɪt/
美 /deɪt/

n. 1. 日期；日子
What's the date today? 今天几号?

2. 约会
I wanna ask her out on a date. 我想和她出去约会。

3. 约会对象
My date isn't going to show. 我的约会对象不会出现了。

回答

It's May 8 (, 2024). (2024年) 5月8号。

词汇补充 Word Supplement

季节和月份

spring 春 英 /sprɪŋ/ 美 /sprɪŋ/	March 三月 英 /mɑːtʃ/ 美 /mɑːrtʃ/	April 四月 英 /'eɪprəl/ 美 /'eɪprəl/	May 五月 英 /meɪ/ 美 /meɪ/
summer 夏 英 /'sʌmə(r)/ 美 /'sʌmər/	June 六月 英 /dʒuːn/ 美 /dʒuːn/	July 七月 英 /dʒʊ'laɪ/ 美 /dʒʊ'laɪ/	August 八月 英 /'ɔːgəst/ 美 /'ɔːgəst/
autumn 秋 英 /'ɔːtəm/ 美 /'ɔːtəm/	September 九月 英 /sep'tembə(r)/ 美 /sep'tembər/	October 十月 英 /ɒk'təʊbə(r)/ 美 /ɑːk'toʊbər/	November 十一月 英 /nəʊ'vembə(r)/ 美 /noʊ'vembər/
winter 冬 英 /'wɪntə(r)/ 美 /'wɪntər/	January 一月 英 /'dʒænjuəri/ 美 /'dʒænjueri/	February 二月 英 /'februəri/ 美 /'februeri/	December 十二月 英 /dɪ'sembə(r)/ 美 /dɪ'sembər/

场景对话 Conversation

A: What day is it today?
B: It's Friday.
A: Oh, and what's the date today?
B: May 8, 2024.

A：今天是星期几？
B：今天星期五。
A：哦，今天几号？
B：2024年5月8日。

A: Thank you.
B: You are welcome.

A：谢谢。
B：不客气。

1. 日期的读法：月份 + 日（序数词）+ 年
   May 8—May（the）eighth（口语，最常用）
   　　　　the eighth（day）of May（英式，较为正式）
2. 年份的读法
   （1）一般两组数字为一组，用基数词
   　　1467—fourteen sixty-seven
   （2）当第三个数字为 0 时
   　　1305—thirteen oh five（更常用）
   　　　　 thirteen hundred and five
   （3）当第三和第四个数字都为 0 时
   　　1900—nineteen hundred
   （4）2000—2010 年
   　　2000—(the year) two thousand
   　　2001—two thousand（and）one
   　　2002—two thousand（and）two
   　　……
   　　2010—two thousand（and）ten
   （5）2010 年及以后
   　　2011—two thousand and eleven；twenty eleven
   　　2012—two thousand and twelve；twenty twelve

Lesson 8　时间
Time

提 问

What time is it? =Do you have/know the time?
　　　　　　　=May/Could I have the time?
（请问）现在几点？

回 答

01 整点

It's seven o'clock. = It's seven.
　　　　　　　　　= Seven.
　　　　　　　　七点。

02 几点几分

（1）顺读法（点钟数 + 分钟数）

It's three ten. 三点十分。
It's seven twenty. 七点二十。

（2）逆读法（分钟数 +past/to+ 点钟数）

a. 小于 30 分用 past，表示"几点过几分"

　　It's twenty past seven. 七点二十。

b. 大于 30 分用 to，表示"差几分钟几点"

　　It's twenty to seven. 六点四十。

03 半点

It's eight thirty.
=It's half past eight.
=It's half to nine.
八点半。

> **Notes:** "30 分"在逆读法中读作 half，而不读作 thirty。

04 15 分

It's ten fifteen. 十点十五。
It's a quarter past ten. 十点十五。

> **Notes:** "15 分"在逆读法中读作 a quarter，而不读作 fifteen。

It's a quarter to ten. 九点四十五。

词汇精讲 Word Study

quarter
英 /ˈkwɔːtə(r)/
美 /ˈkwɔːrtər/

n. 1. 四等份之一
He cut the watermelon into quarters. 他把西瓜切成四等份。
2. 15 分钟，一刻钟
It's a quarter to ten. 九点四十五。
3. 季度
I get an electricity bill every quarter. 我每季度都会收到一张电费单。

05 强调上午 / 下午

It's seven a.m. 上午七点。
It's six p.m. 下午六点。

06 12 点

It's noon. =It's 12 p.m. 中午 12 点。
It's midnight. =It's 12 a.m. 午夜 12 点。

07 大约的时间

It's almost ten. 快十点了。
It's a little before ten. 还差一点儿到十点。
It's a little after ten. 十点过了一点儿。

词汇精讲 Word Study

almost
英 /ˈɔːlməʊst/
美 /ˈɔːlmoʊst/

ad. 几乎；差不多 =nearly
It's almost time to go.
是差不多该走的时候了。
Dinner's almost ready.
饭就要做好了。

💬 场景对话 Conversation

A: What time is it?
B: It's twenty to eight.
A: Oh! I gotta go!
B: Why are you so hurry?
A: I am gonna be late for class!
B: OK, bye!
A: See ya!

A：现在几点？
B：七点四十分。
A：啊！我要走了！
B：你为什么这么着急？
A：我上课要迟到了！
B：好的，再见！
A：再见！

Lesson 9　天气和气温
Weather and Temperature

Part 1　天气 Weather

提问

How's the weather today/tomorrow?
=What's the weather like today/tomorrow?
今天 / 明天天气如何？

How's the weather in Beijing?
=What's the weather like in Beijing?
北京天气如何？

How's the weather outside/out there?
=What's the weather like outside/out there?
外面的天气如何？

What's the weather forecast/report for tomorrow?
=What does the weather forecast/report say for tomorrow?
天气预报说明天的天气如何？

词汇精讲 Word Study

forecast
英 /ˈfɔːkɑːst/
美 /ˈfɔːrkæst/

n. 预测，预报
The weather forecast said it was gonna be very cold tomorrow.
天气预报称明天会很冷。
I don't think these sales forecasts are realistic.
我认为这些销量预测并不现实。

回答

01 天气的好坏

It's a lovely/terrible day.
天气好 / 不好。

02 具体的天气

It's sunny.
=It's a sunny day.
是晴天。

03 关于下雨

It looks like it's going to rain.
看起来要下雨了。

It's raining.
正在下雨。

It's supposed to rain tomorrow.
明天可能会下雨。

词汇补充 Word Supplement

表达"天气好"的形容词：

lovely	英 /ˈlʌvli/	美 /ˈlʌvli/	宜人的
good	英 /ɡʊd/	美 /ɡʊd/	好的
beautiful	英 /ˈbjuːtɪf(ə)l/	美 /ˈbjuːtɪf(ə)l/	美好的

表达"天气不好"的形容词：

terrible	英 /ˈterəb(ə)l/	美 /ˈterəb(ə)l/	糟糕的
awful	英 /ˈɔːf(ə)l/	美 /ˈɔːf(ə)l/	糟糕的
horrible	英 /ˈhɒrəb(ə)l/	美 /ˈhɔːrəb(ə)l/	可怕的

描述具体天气的形容词：

sunny	英 /ˈsʌni/	美 /ˈsʌni/	阳光充足的
clear	英 /klɪə(r)/	美 /klɪr/	晴朗的
cloudy	英 /ˈklaʊdi/	美 /ˈklaʊdi/	多云的
windy	英 /ˈwɪndi/	美 /ˈwɪndi/	多风的；风大的
rainy	英 /ˈreɪni/	美 /ˈreɪni/	阴雨的；多雨的
snowy	英 /ˈsnəʊi/	美 /ˈsnoʊi/	下雪多的
foggy	英 /ˈfɒɡi/	美 /ˈfɑːɡi/	有雾的
smoggy	英 /ˈsmɒɡi/	美 /ˈsmɑːɡi/	有雾霾的

Unit 2 基本信息 Basic Information

词汇精讲 Word Study

suppose
英 /sə'pəʊz/
美 /sə'poʊz/

v. 1. 认为，推断
Do you suppose he will come? 你认为他会来吗？
2. be supposed to do sth. 应当，应该
You're not supposed to park here. 你不应该把车停在这里。

场景对话 Conversation

A: Hey, Tom, where are you now?
B: I am in Beijing.
A: How's the weather in Beijing?
B: It's a terrible day. It's raining right now.
A: Oh, sorry to hear that.

A：嘿，汤姆，你现在在哪里？
B：我在北京。
A：北京的天气如何？
B：天气不好。现在正在下雨。
A：噢，很遗憾听到这个消息。

Part 2 气温 Temperature

提问
What's the temperature?
=Do you know what the temperature is?
温度是多少？

回答
It's (really) hot today. 今天（非常）热。
It's (about) 20 degrees. (大约) 20 度。
It's –10 (minus ten) degrees. 零下 10 度。

词汇补充 Word Supplement

描述气温的形容词：
boiling hot 极热的
(boiling 英 /'bɔɪlɪŋ/ 美 /'bɔɪlɪŋ/ 炽热的)
hot 英 /hɒt/ 美 /hɑːt/ 热的
warm 英 /wɔːm/ 美 /wɔːrm/ 温暖的
cool 英 /kuːl/ 美 /kuːl/ 凉爽的
chilly 英 /'tʃɪli/ 美 /'tʃɪli/ 冷的
cold 英 /kəʊld/ 美 /koʊld/ 寒冷的
freezing (cold) 极冷的
(freezing 英 /'friːzɪŋ/ 美 /'friːzɪŋ/ 冰冷的)

场景对话 Conversation

A: What's the weather like out there?
B: It's clear and sunny.
A: What's the temperature?
B: It's about 38 degrees.
A: That's really hot!
B: Yeah! I am gonna stay at home for a whole day!
A: Me too!

A：外面天气怎么样？
B：晴朗且阳光充足。
A：温度是多少？
B：大约 38 度。
A：真是太热了！
B：是的！我要在家待一整天！
A：我也是！

Lesson 10 建议、看法和重复
Suggestions, Opinions and Repetition

Part 1　建议 Suggestions

◇ Why don't you do sth. ?
　Why don't you come together? 你为什么不一起来呢？

◇ How about (doing) sth. ?
　How about joining us? 加入我们怎么样？

◇ I suggest + that 从句
　I suggest we go on a hike on the weekend. 我建议我们周末去徒步旅行。

◇ If I were you, I would do sth.
　If I were you, I would talk to her about it. 如果我是你，我会和她说这件事。

◇ It might be a good idea to do sth.
　It might be a good idea to book a table in advance. 提前预订桌位比较好。

◇ Maybe we could do sth.
　Maybe we could watch a movie tonight. 或许我们今晚可以看电影。

◇ I would advise you to do sth.
　I would advise you to give him a call. 我建议你给他打个电话。

◇ I think you should do sth.
　I think you should finish the work today. 我觉得你应该在今天把工作完成。

◇ You'd better do sth.
　You'd better get up early. 你最好早起。

词汇精讲 Word Study

suggest
英 /sə'dʒest/
美 /sə'dʒest/

v. 1. 建议，提议
　　 I suggest we go out to eat. 我提议我们出去吃吧。
2. 推荐；举荐
　　 Can you suggest some good books? 你能推荐一些好书吗？
3. 使认为；表明
　　 All the evidence suggests he's innocent. 所有证据都表明他是无辜的。
4. 暗示
　　 Are you suggesting I'm fat? 你是在暗示我胖吗？

Unit 2　基本信息 Basic Information

场景对话 Conversation

A: What are we going to do during the weekend?
B: Maybe we could go hiking.
A: I don't really want to go outside. Why don't we throw a party at home?
B: That's a good idea!

A：周末我们要做什么呢？
B：也许我们可以去远足。
A：我不太想出去。我们为什么不在家举办聚会呢？
B：是个好主意！

Part 2　看法 Opinions

提问

◇ What do you think (of sth.) ?
　What do you think of this movie? 你觉得这部电影怎么样？

◇ What's your opinion (of/on/about sth.) ?
　What's your opinion on this issue? 你对这个问题怎么看？

◇ How do you feel about sth. ?
　How do you feel about this car? 你觉得这辆车怎么样？

回答

◇ I think/believe + that 从句
　I think he is a good guy. 我觉得他人不错。

◇ In my opinion, ...
　In my opinion, it's a great movie. 在我看来，这是一部很棒的电影。

◇ As far as I'm concerned, ...
　As far as I'm concerned, he should be responsible for the accident.
　就我而言，他应该对事故负责。

◇ If you ask me, ...
　If you ask me, you shouldn't buy that car. 要我说的话，你不该买那辆车。

场景对话 Conversation

A: What do you think of this movie?
B: I think it's a great movie.

A：你觉得这部电影怎么样？
B：我觉得这是一部很棒的电影。

031

Part 3 重复 Repetition

Sorry? 你说什么?
Pardon? / Pardon me? / May I beg your pardon? 请再说一遍?
Sorry, I didn't catch you. 抱歉,我没听清你说的。
Sorry, I didn't hear what you said. 抱歉,我没听清你说的。
Sorry, could you repeat that, please? 抱歉,你可以再说一遍吗?
Sorry, could you say that again, please? 抱歉,你可以再说一遍吗?

场景对话 Conversation

A: Hi, Alex. How's it going?
B: Hi, Jack. I'm good. You?
A: The same as usual. Oh, may I have your e-mail address?
B: Yeah. It's alex123@gmail.com.
A: Sorry, could you say that again, please?
B: alex123@gmail.com.
A: OK, got it. Bye.
B: See you.

A:嗨,亚历克斯,最近怎么样?
B:嗨,杰克,我挺好的,你呢?
A:还是老样子。对了,你能告诉我你的邮箱地址吗?
B:当然,我的邮箱是 alex123@gmail.com。
A:抱歉,你能再说一遍吗?
B:alex123@gmail.com。
A:好的,我记下了。再见。
B:再见。

Unit 3　人际交往 Interpersonal Communication

Lesson 11　邀请
Invitations

提　问

01 非正式邀请

（1）询问是否有空

◇ Are you free...?

　　Are you free on Saturday night? 你周六晚上有空吗？

◇ Are you doing anything...?

　　Are you doing anything on Saturday night? 你周六晚上有安排吗？

词汇精讲 Word Study **free** 英 /friː/ 美 /friː/	a. 1. 能随自己意愿的；随心所欲的 　　　Please feel free to contact me. 请随时与我联系。 　　2. 不收费的 　　　Admission is free. 免费入场。 　　3. 未使用的；空着的 　　　Is this seat free? 这个座位空着吗？ 　　4. 没有安排活动的；空闲的 　　　What do you like to do in your free time? 你有空的时候喜欢干什么？

（2）非正式邀请句式

◇ Why don't we...?

　　Why don't we go climbing together? 我们为什么不一起去爬山呢？

◇ How about...?

　　How about going for a drink? 去喝一杯怎么样？

◇ Do you wanna...?

　　Do you wanna have dinner with me? 你想和我一起吃晚饭吗？

◇ Let's...

　　Let's go hiking tomorrow. 我们明天去远足吧。

◇ Are you up for...?

　　Are you up for going shopping? 你想去购物吗？

◇ **Are you in the mood to...?**

Are you in the mood to <u>go to the party</u>? 你想去参加派对吗？

◇ **What do you say we...?**

What do you say we <u>play badminton on the weekend</u>? 周末我们去打羽毛球怎么样？

◇ **Do you feel like...?**

Do you feel like <u>watching a movie together</u>? 你想一起去看电影吗？

02 正式邀请

◇ **Would you like to...?**

Would you like to <u>have dinner with me</u>? 你愿意与我共进晚餐吗？

◇ **I'd like to ask you to...**

I'd like to ask you to <u>have dinner with me next week</u>.
我想邀请你下周和我一起共进晚餐。

◇ **May we have the pleasure of your company... ?**

May we have the pleasure of your company <u>at dinner</u>?
我们能有幸邀请您共进晚餐吗？

词汇精讲 Word Study

pleasure
英 /ˈpleʒə(r)/
美 /ˈpleʒər/

n. 1. 高兴，愉快；乐事
   It's a pleasure to meet you. 很高兴认识你。
2. 玩乐；休闲
   Are you in London for business or pleasure? 你来伦敦是出差还是游玩？

回　答

01 接受邀请

Sure. 当然了。
Great. 好的。
Sounds great. 听起来不错。
Why not? 为什么不呢？
I'd love to. 我愿意。

02 建议改天

May I take a rain check? 下次吧，好吗？
Maybe next time. 或许下次吧。

03 表示不确定

Maybe. 可能吧。
I'm not sure. 我不太确定。
It depends. 看情况。

04 委婉拒绝

I'd love to, but I can't. I have to prepare for the exam.
我想去来着，但是去不成。我得准备考试。
I'm not really in the mood to go out, actually. 我其实没什么心情出去。
I'm really sorry. I need to do my homework. 真不好意思，我得做作业。
I'm afraid I can't. I'd like to finish my work. 恐怕不行，我得完成工作。
I really wish I could, but I have to see the dentist. 真希望我能去，但我得去看牙医。
Thank you for asking me, but I have other plans. 谢谢你邀请我，但我有别的安排了。

回应：

Oh, I see. 啊，我知道了。
That's OK. 没关系。
OK, maybe next time. 好吧，下次再约。

场景对话 Conversation

A: It was nice talking with you. Are you free on Saturday night?
B: Well, I think so.
A: Would you like to have dinner with me on Saturday night?
B: Yeah, why not?

A：和你聊天真开心。你周六晚上有空吗？
B：嗯，有空。
A：你想周六晚上和我共进晚餐吗？
B：好啊，为什么不呢？

Lesson 12　电话用语
Phone Calls

Part 1　电话用语 Phone Calls

01 接电话先说

（1）认识号码

Hi, Peter. What's up? 嗨，彼得，怎么了？

（2）不认识号码

Hello, this is Jack speaking. 喂，我是杰克。

Who is this?
Who's calling?　　　您是哪位？
Who am I talking to?

02 打电话先说

（1）确定是本人接电话

Hi, Jack. It's Peter. How are you doing? 喂，杰克，我是彼得。最近怎么样？

（2）不确定是本人接电话

Hello, this is Peter speaking. May/Can I speak to Jack?
喂，我是彼得，能让杰克接电话吗？

Hi, it's Peter here. May/Can I speak to Jack?
喂，我是彼得。能让杰克接电话吗？

03 要找的人在

（1）是本人

Hi, Peter. It's me. 喂，彼得，是我。

Hi, Peter. What's up? 喂，彼得，怎么了？

（2）不是本人

OK, I will put him/her on the phone. 好的，我让他/她来接电话。

04 要找的人不在

He/She is not here. 他/她不在这儿。

He/She is out. 他/她出去了。

A: Yeah. This is Jack. Could you ask her to call me back?
B: Sure!
A: Thank you.
B: Bye!
A: Bye!

A: 好啊。我是杰克，你能让她待会儿给我回个电话吗？
B: 当然！
A: 谢谢。
B: 再见！
A: 再见！

Part 2 短信用语 Messages

are=r 是
are you=r u 是你
be=b 有；是
for=4 对；为了
want to=wanna 想要
thanks=thx 谢谢
OK=K 好的
BTW=by the way 顺便说说
ASAP=as soon as possible 尽快
BRB=be right back 马上回来

you=u 你
to=2 向，朝
to be=2b 存在
for you=4 u 为了你
going to=gonna 将要
tonight=2nite 今晚
TTYL=talk to you later 以后再谈
LOL=laugh out loud 大声笑
FYI=for your information 供参考
CYA=see you 再见

场景对话 Conversation

A: Hey, Jack. How r u doing?
B: Good. What's up, man?
A: Not much. R u free 2nite for a drink? I passed all my exams. Finally!
B: Lol, good 4 u, man. Btw where r we gonna meet?
A: Sky Bar. Let's say 7 p.m. OK?
B: K, CYA then!
A: CYA!

A: 嘿，杰克，最近怎么样？
B: 挺好的。兄弟你怎么样？
A: 没什么。你今晚有空喝一杯吗？我终于通过了所有的考试！
B: 哈哈哈，祝贺你。那我们在哪里见呢？
A: 天空酒吧。我们晚上七点见，可以吗？
B: 好的，到时候见！
A: 再见！

Lesson 13 帮助
Asking for and Offering Help

Part 1 请求帮助 Asking for Help

提 问

01 请求帮助

Excuse me, could you help me? 打扰一下，你能帮帮我吗？
Sorry to bother/interrupt you, could you do me a favor? 抱歉打扰一下，你能帮我个忙吗？
Sorry for interrupting, could you give me a hand? 抱歉打扰一下，你能帮我个忙吗？
Hey, man, you got a moment? 嘿，兄弟，你有空吗？

02 具体事项

Could you open the window for me? 你能帮我把窗户打开吗？
Could you pass me the salt? 你能把盐递给我吗？
Could you lend me some money? 你能借我点钱吗？
May I borrow your car? 我能借你的车吗？
Would you mind helping me with these bags? 你介意帮我搬一下这些行李吗？

回 答

01 答应提供帮助

Sure. /Shoot. 当然。
No problem. 没问题。
Yeah, why not. 当然可以。

Go ahead. 说吧。
With pleasure. 当然可以。
What's up? 怎么了？

02 拒绝提供帮助

◇ I'd love/like to, but+ 具体理由
　I'd love to, but I'm in the same boat with you. 我也想，但我的处境和你一样。

◇ Sorry, but+ 具体理由
　Sorry, but I'm broke. 抱歉，我也没钱了。

回应：
It's all right/OK. 没关系。
Thank you anyway. 不管怎么样，还是谢谢你。

Unit 3　人际交往 Interpersonal Communication

03 表达忙 / 有事

Sorry, I'm kinda busy right now. Can I talk to you later?
抱歉，我现在有点忙，能待会儿再和你说吗？

Sorry, I have to go right now. Can I talk to you later?
抱歉，我现在得走了，能待会儿再和你说吗？

回应：

OK, talk to you later. 好，那待会儿再说。

场景对话 Conversation

A: Hey, Jack, could you give me a hand?
B: Shoot. What's up?
A: Could you lend me some money?
B: Yeah, why not. How much do you want?
A: 50 dollars will be enough. Thank you.
B: OK, here you are.

A：嘿，杰克，你能帮我个忙吗？
B：当然，怎么了？
A：你能借我点钱吗？
B：当然可以，你想借多少？
A：50 美元就可以了，谢谢。.
B：好，给你。

A: Hey, Jack, could you do me a favor?
B: Sure, what's up?
A: Could you lend me some money?
B: Sorry, but I'm broke.
A: It's OK.

A：嘿，杰克，你能帮我个忙吗？
B：当然，怎么了？
A：你能借我点钱吗？
B：抱歉，我也没钱了。
A：没关系。

A: Hey, Jack, could you do me a favor?
B: Sorry, I'm kinda busy right now. Can I talk to you later?
A: OK, talk to you later.

A：嘿，杰克，你能帮我个忙吗？
B：抱歉，我现在有点儿忙，能待会儿再和你说吗？
A：好，那待会儿再谈。

Part 2　提供帮助 Offering Help

提　问

01 提供帮助

What can I do for you? 我能为你做什么？

What do you need? 你需要什么帮助吗？
May I help you? 我可以帮你吗？
How can I help? 有什么可以帮忙的吗？

02 随时帮忙

Just let me know if you need anything. 如果你有任何需要，就告诉我。
Just give me a call if you need any help. 如果你需要任何帮助，就给我打电话。

03 具体事项

I can call a taxi for you. 我可以帮你叫辆车。
I'd be happy to collect the package for you. 我很乐意帮你去取快递。
Do you need me to pick you up? 你需要我去接你吗？
Would you like me to reserve a seat for you? 您需要我为您预订位子吗？

回 答

01 接受别人的帮助

Thank you so much. 太感谢了。
That would be great. 那太好了。
Sure, I'd appreciate that. 当然，我会很感激。
That's very nice/kind of you. 你真好。

词汇精讲 Word Study	
appreciate 英 /əˈpriːʃieɪt/ 美 /əˈpriːʃieɪt/	v. 1. 重视，赏识 I really appreciate your paintings. 我真的很欣赏你的画作。 2. 领会，体会 I appreciate that it's a difficult decision for you to make. 我了解这对于你来说是一个艰难的决定。 3. 感谢 I really appreciate it. 我真的很感激。

02 拒绝别人的帮助

No, thanks. It's OK. 不用了，谢谢。没关系。
Thank you, but I can handle it by myself. 谢谢，我可以自己解决。

场景对话 Conversation

A: Hi, how are you doing?
B: I'm good. You?
A: Great. I'm Jack, by the way. What's your name?
B: My name is Peter. Nice to meet you.
A: Nice to meet you, too.
B: Are you new here?
A: Yeah, I just came here for a couple of days.
B: Okay, just let me know if you need anything.
A: Thank you so much.
B: You are welcome.

A：嗨，最近怎么样？
B：还不错。你呢？
A：我很好。顺便说一下，我是杰克，你叫什么名字？
B：我叫彼得。很高兴认识你。
A：我也很高兴认识你。
B：你是新来的吗？
A：是的，我刚来这里几天。
B：好的，如果你有任何需要，就告诉我。
A：非常感谢。
B：不客气。

Lesson 14 感谢
Gratitude

01 表达感谢

（1）一般感谢

Thanks. 谢谢。

Thank you. 谢谢你。

Thanks for helping me. 谢谢你的帮助。

Thank you for your help. 谢谢你的帮助。

（2）非常感谢

Thanks a lot. 非常感谢。

Thank you so/very much. 非常感谢。

Thank you for everything you have done for me. 感谢你为我做的一切。

I really appreciate it. 非常感谢。

I'm so grateful. 非常感谢。

It's very kind/nice of you. 你人真好。

I owe you one. 我欠你个人情。

词汇精讲 Word Study	
grateful 英 /ˈgreɪtf(ə)l/ 美 /ˈgreɪtf(ə)l/	a. 感激的；表示感谢的 I can't express how grateful I am. 我无法表达我的感激之情。
owe 英 /əʊ/ 美 /oʊ/	v. 1. 欠 He owes me 200 dollars. 他欠我 200 美元。 2. 应把……归功于 I owe everything to my family. 这一切都归功于我的家人。 3. 感激，感恩 I owe you one. 我欠你一个人情。

（3）无比感谢

I can't thank you enough. 我再怎么感谢你都不为过。

I can't express how grateful I am. 我无法表达我的感激之情。

I am forever in your debt. 我永远欠你一个人情。

词汇精讲 Word Study

debt
英 /det/
美 /det/

n. 1. 借款；欠款；债务
He has to repay the debt. 他不得不偿还这笔债务。
2. 负债情况
He is deep in debt. 他负债累累。
3. 人情债；恩情
I am forever in your debt. 我永远欠你一个人情。

02 回应感谢

Anytime. 随时效劳。
My pleasure. 我的荣幸。
It's OK/all right. 没事儿。
Glad to help. 能帮到你我很开心。
No problem. / No worries. / No big deal. 小事儿。
You're welcome. 别客气。
Don't mention it. 别客气。

词汇精讲 Word Study

mention
英 /'menʃ(ə)n/
美 /'menʃ(ə)n/

n. /v. 提及，说起
She made no mention of her family. 她没提及她的家庭。
I didn't mention it to her. 我没和她提过这件事。

🗨 场景对话 Conversation

A: Thank you for everything you have done for me, Jack.
B: It's my pleasure.
A: I owe you one.
B: Come on, man. No worries.

A：杰克，感谢你为我做的一切。
B：是我的荣幸。
A：我欠你个人情。
B：兄弟，别这样，都是小事儿。

Lesson 15　道歉
Apology

01　道歉"四步走"

（1）承认错误

It's my fault. 是我的错。

(It's) my bad. （是）我的错。

I screwed up. 我搞砸了。

I messed up. 我搞砸了。

> **短语精讲** Phrase Study
>
> ● screw (sb. /sth.) up
>   1. 搞糟；弄坏
>   I screwed up. 我搞砸了。
>   2. 使神经不正常
>   Losing his job really screwed him up. 失去工作让他万念俱灰。
>   3. 拧牢；旋紧
>   Will you please screw it up? 你能把它拧紧吗？
> ● mess (sb. /sth.) up
>   1. 弄脏，弄乱
>   Don't mess up my clean room. 不要把我干净的房间弄乱了。
>   2. 搞砸，弄糟
>   I really messed up this time. 这次我真的把事情搞砸了。
>   3. 使心情恶劣；使精神崩溃
>   That really messed me up. 这简直让我崩溃。

（2）正式道歉

a. sorry

　I'm sorry. 对不起。

　I'm sorry for being late. 真抱歉，我来晚了。

　I'm sorry about that. 我对此感到抱歉。

　I'm sorry that I forgot to notice you. 真抱歉，我忘记通知你了。

b. apology/apologize

　My apologies. 我道歉。

　I owe you an apology. 我欠你一个道歉。

　I would like to give you my apology for being late. 对于迟到，我深表歉意。

　I apologize for being late. 真抱歉，来晚了。

c. forgive

Please forgive me. 请原谅我。
Can you ever forgive me? 你能原谅我吗?
Please forgive me for being late. 请原谅我来晚了。

(3) 进一步解释

It was an accident. 这是个意外。
I didn't mean it/to do that. 我不是有意的。
I didn't do it on purpose. 我不是有意这么做的。

(4) 保证 & 解决方案

You have my word. 我向你保证。
It won't happen again. 以后不会再发生了。
I'll take care of this. 我会处理好这件事的。
To make up for it, I'd like to buy you a new one. 为了补偿，我给你买个新的吧。

02 回应道歉

That's OK/all right. 没事。
It doesn't matter（at all）.（完全）没关系。
Never mind. 没关系。
Forget about it. 别放在心上。
There's no need to apologize. =It's really not necessary. 你没必要道歉。
I forgive you. =Apology accepted. 我原谅你了。
It happens. 总会有这样的事发生。
Don't worry about it. 别担心。

场景对话 Conversation

A: I'm so sorry that I screwed up the whole thing.
B: Never mind. Just be careful next time.
A: It won't happen again.
B: OK, just forget about it.

A：真抱歉，我把整件事都搞砸了。
B：没关系，下次注意点就好。
A：下次不会再发生了。
B：好的，别放在心上了。

Unit 4　情绪态度 Emotions and Attitudes

Lesson 16　积极情绪
Positive Emotions

01　开心

（1）一般开心

I'm happy. 我是开心的。
I feel great. 我感觉很好。
I'm in a good mood. 我心情不错。

（2）非常开心

I'm so/really happy. 我真的很开心。
That really made my day. 这令我一天都很开心。
I'm walking on air now. 我现在非常开心。

（3）极其开心

I couldn't be happier. 我已经开心到极点了。
This is the happiest moment in my life. 这是我一生中最开心的时刻。
Nothing could please me more. 没有什么能让我更开心了。

02　兴奋 / 激动

This is really thrilling/exciting. 这真是令人激动。
It's breathtaking. 这真是激动人心。
I'm too excited to go to sleep/say a word. 我激动得睡不着觉 / 说不出话。

03　惊喜 / 惊讶

I'm really surprised!
我真的很惊讶！

Incredible/Unbelievable!
难以置信！

I can't believe it!
我不敢相信！

No way!
不是吧！

词汇精讲　Word Study

incredible
英 /ɪnˈkredəb(ə)l/
美 /ɪnˈkredəb(ə)l/

a. 不能相信的；难以置信的，不可思议的

I heard an incredible story.
我听到了一个不可思议的故事。
I think his new novel is incredible.
我认为他的新小说太棒了。

04 满足

I feel satisfied. 我很满意。
I am pleased. 我很满意。
This is good enough. 已经够好了。

05 期待

I can't wait to go to the concert.
我迫不及待想去看演唱会。

I'm counting down the days until I go on vacation.
我开始进行度假倒计时了。

I am looking forward to seeing you.
我盼望着见到你。

> **短语精讲** Phrase Study
> - look forward to (doing) sth. 期望，期待
> Looking forward to your reply.
> 期待您的回信。
> I am looking forward to going back to school.
> 我期待着回学校。

06 乐观

I've been hoping for the best. 我一直抱着最好的期盼。
I've been optimistic about it. 我一直对此持乐观态度。
I believe things will be going well. 我认为事情会变好的。

场景对话 Conversation

A: I am really happy now!
B: What's up?
A: I just got promoted!
B: Congratulations!

A：我现在真的很开心！
B：怎么了？
A：我升职了！
B：恭喜呀！

Lesson 17 消极情绪
Negative Emotions

01 紧张 / 焦虑 / 压力

I'm really nervous. 我真的很紧张。

I'm very anxious. 我非常焦虑。

I'm stressed out. 我焦虑不安。

词汇精讲 Word Study

anxious
英 /ˈæŋkʃəs/
美 /ˈæŋkʃəs/

a. 1. 忧虑的，令人焦急的
I am very anxious about the interview. 我对这次面试感到焦虑。
2. 渴望的
I am anxious to open my birthday presents. 我很想打开我的生日礼物。

02 难过

I'm not happy/unhappy. 我不开心。

I'm feeling down. 我心情不好。

That upsets me. / It makes me upset. 这令我难过。

词汇精讲 Word Study

upset
英 /ʌpˈset/
美 /ʌpˈset/

v. 1. 使心烦意乱，使苦恼，使不适
Don't upset yourself about it. 别为这件事苦恼了。
2. 搅乱
It has upset my original plan. 这打乱了我原本的计划。

a. 1. 心烦的，苦恼的
I am so upset about it. 我对此感到非常难过。
2. （肠胃等）不适的
I have an upset stomach. 我肠胃不适。

03 生气

I'm (really) angry. 我（真的）生气。

That pisses me off. 气死我了。

I'm blowing up! 我气炸了！

04 受够了

That's it! 够了！

I can't take it anymore. 我受不了了。

I've had enough. 我受够了。

05 害怕

I'm scared. 我害怕。

I'm terrified. 我害怕。

It chilled me to the bones. 这让我毛骨悚然。

词汇精讲 Word Study

chill
英 /tʃɪl/
美 /tʃɪl/

v. 1. （使）变冷，（使）感到冷
I put the beer into the fridge to chill. 我把啤酒放进冰箱里冷藏。

2. 使恐惧；恐吓
Her words chilled me to the bone. 她的话让我毛骨悚然。

3. （非正式）放松；休息
I decided to stay home and chill. 我决定待在家里休息。

n. 1. 寒冷，寒气
There was a chill in the air this morning. 今天早晨寒气袭人。

2. 害怕的感觉
Her words sent a chill down my spine. 她的话让我毛骨悚然。

06 担心

I'm worried. 我很担心。

I tossed and turned over it. 我为此辗转反侧。

It's been keeping me up at night. 这件事让我彻夜未眠。

07 失望

I'm very disappointed. 我很失望。

It's not what I expected. 这不是我期待的。

What a pity/shame! 真遗憾！

场景对话 Conversation

A: What's happening? You are not looking great.

B: I've been rejected by my dream school. It makes me really upset.

A：发生什么了？你看起来不太好。

B：我被我梦想中的学校拒绝了，这让我感到很难过。

Lesson 18　同意与反对
Agreement and Disagreement

Part 1　同意 Agreement

01 部分同意

I partly agree. 我部分同意。

I agree with you up to a point. 在某种程度上我同意你。

I understand that, but there're still some problems. 我理解，但还是有一些问题。

02 一般同意

Why not? 为什么不呢？
Of course. 当然。
No problem. 没问题。
I agree. 我同意。
You're right. 你是对的。
You said it. 你说对了。

Your opinion is reasonable. 你的观点有道理。
I'm for it. 我没意见。
I don't see why not. 为什么不这么做呢。
I feel the same way. 我也觉得。
I have no problem with that. 我没意见。

词汇精讲 Word Study

reasonable
英 /ˈriːznəbl/
美 /ˈriːz(ə)nəb(ə)l/

a. 1. 通情达理的，讲道理的
   She is a reasonable person. 她是一个通情达理的人。
2. 合理的
   I think it is a reasonable decision. 我认为这是一个合理的决定。
3. （价钱）公道的
   Apples are fairly reasonable at this time of year.
   这个时候苹果的价格还算公道。
4. 尚好的，过得去的
   She could read English with reasonable fluency.
   她英语读得还算流利。

---

03 非常同意

Sounds great! 听起来不错！
Good idea! 好主意！
Excellent advice! 绝佳的建议！
I totally/absolutely agree（with you）! 我完全同意！
Totally! /Absolutely! /Definitely! /Exactly! 当然！

You're dead right! 你说得太对了！
I couldn't agree more! 我非常赞同！

Unit 4　情绪态度 Emotions and Attitudes

🗨 场景对话 Conversation

A: I think his new album is so great!
B: I totally agree with you! I have been listening to this album on (a) loop recently.
A: I heard that he's gonna hold a concert this weekend. Would you like to come with me?
B: Absolutely!

A：我觉得他的新专辑太棒了！
B：完全赞同！我最近一直在循环听这张专辑。
A：我听说他这周末要举行演唱会。你想和我一起去吗？
B：当然了！

Part 2　反对 Disagreement

01 一般反对

Nope. 不。
Not really. 不见得。
Of course not. 当然不。
I disagree. 我不同意。
I don't agree. 我不同意。

I beg to differ. 我不敢苟同。
I'm against it. 我反对。
I don't think so. 我不这么认为。
I take a different view. 我持不同意见。
I don't feel the same way about it. 我不这么觉得。

02 非常反对

Absolutely not! 当然不！
I totally/completely disagree! 我完全不同意！
I have a completely different opinion on it. 我在这个问题上有完全不同的看法。

🗨 场景对话 Conversation

A: Hey, Robert, do you like movies? I think movies are so interesting.
B: I don't think so. I think movies are boring.
A: Why? You don't like stories?
B: I like stories. I just like reading better.
A: OK, I see.

A：嘿，罗伯特，你喜欢电影吗？我觉得电影可有意思了。
B：我不这么认为，我觉得电影很无聊。
A：为什么？你不喜欢故事吗？
B：我喜欢，只不过我更喜欢读故事。
A：好吧，我知道了。

Part 3 中立态度 Neutral Attitudes

01 无所谓

Whatever. 无所谓。
I don't care. 我不在乎。

02 不确定

I have no idea. 我不知道。
I'm not sure. 我不确定。

场景对话 Conversation

A: I think she is a difficult person to get along with. What do you think?
B: I'm not sure. I only met her once.

A：我认为她很难相处。你觉得呢？
B：我不确定。我就见过她一次。

Lesson 19　喜欢与讨厌
Likes and Dislikes

Part 1　喜欢 Likes

01 感兴趣

◇ I'm interested in...
I'm interested in reading.
我对阅读感兴趣。

◇ I take a (great) interest in...
I take a (great) interest in singing.
我对唱歌（很）感兴趣。

02 喜欢

◇ I like/love to do/doing sth.
I like/love playing basketball.
I like/love to play basketball.
我喜欢打篮球。

◇ I enjoy doing sth.
I enjoy listening to music.
我喜欢听音乐。

◇ I am crazy about...
I am crazy about football.
我非常喜欢踢足球。

◇ I am into...
I am into painting.
我很喜欢画画。

◇ I'm fond of...
I'm fond of cooking.
我喜欢做饭。

◇ I'm a (big) fan of...
I'm a (big) fan of badminton.
我（很）喜欢打羽毛球。

◇ I'm keen on...
I'm keen on music.
我喜欢听音乐。

◇ I adore...
I adore her.
我喜欢她。

词汇精讲 Word Study

keen
英 /kiːn/
美 /kiːn/

a. 1. 热心的
He was very keen to help. 他很热心，愿意帮忙。
2. 激烈的
I have a keen interest in literature. 我对文学有着强烈的兴趣。
3. 敏锐的，敏捷的
The cat has a keen sense of smell. 这只猫的嗅觉很灵敏。
4. 喜爱的；(对……)着迷的
I'm keen on music. 我对音乐着迷。

adore
英 /əˈdɔː(r)/
美 /əˈdɔːr/

v. 1. 崇拜，敬慕，爱慕（某人）
He adores you. 他爱慕你。
2. 喜爱，热爱（某事物）
I adore the movie. 我非常喜欢这部电影。

03 更喜欢

◇ I prefer... (to...).
I prefer coffee to tea.
比起茶，我更喜欢喝咖啡。

◇ I'd rather... than...
I'd rather stay at home than go out.
比起出门，我更喜欢待在家里。

04 最喜欢

◇ My favorite... is...
My favorite color is green.
我最喜欢的颜色是绿色。

◇ I like... the most.
Of all the sports, I like basketball the most.
所有运动中，我最爱篮球。

词汇精讲 Word Study

favorite
英 /'feɪvərɪt/
美 /'feɪvərɪt/

a. 最喜欢的
She is my favorite actress. 她是我最喜欢的女演员。
n. 最喜欢的人（或物）
Bubble tea is my favorite. 奶茶是我的最爱。

场景对话 Conversation

A: Do you like fruit?
B: Yeah! I like apples, bananas and strawberries.
A: Which one is your favorite?
B: I like strawberries the most.

A：你喜欢水果吗？
B：是的！我喜欢苹果、香蕉和草莓。
A：哪个是你最喜欢的？
B：我最喜欢草莓。

Part 2　讨厌 Dislikes

01 不喜欢

◇ I don't like... (at all).
I don't like cooking at all.
我一点儿也不喜欢做饭。

◇ I dislike...
I dislike doing sports.
我讨厌做运动。

02 讨厌 / 厌恶

◇ I hate...
I hate carrots. 我讨厌胡萝卜。

◇ I (really) loathe...
I really loathe him. 我真的很讨厌他。

◇ I detest...
I detest having to get up early.
我讨厌不得不早起。

词汇精讲 Word Study	v. 极不喜欢；厌恶
loathe 英 /ləʊð/ 美 /loʊð/	I loathe hypocrites. 我讨厌伪君子。 She loathes washing dishes. 她讨厌洗碗。

detest 英 /dɪˈtest/ 美 /dɪˈtest/	v. 厌恶；憎恨；讨厌 The brothers detest each other. 这俩兄弟互相讨厌对方。 I detest going to parties. 我讨厌参加派对。

03 最不喜欢

◇ My least favorite... is...
My least favorite color is blue.
我最不喜欢的颜色是蓝色。

◇ I don't like... the most.
I don't like traveling the most.
我最不喜欢旅行。

◇ I like... least in the world.
I like carrots least in the world.
我最不喜欢胡萝卜。

场景对话 Conversation

A: What do you think of this dish?
B: I don't like it. I hate carrots.

A：你觉得这道菜怎么样？
B：我不喜欢。我讨厌胡萝卜。

Part 3　中立态度 Neutral Attitudes

I don't mind doing housework. 我不介意做家务。
I don't really care about it. 我不怎么在乎。
It's all the same to me. 我都行。

场景对话 Conversation

A: Do you usually do housework?
B: Sometimes.
A: Do you like doing housework?
B: Well, I don't mind doing it.

A：你经常做家务吗？
B：有时做。
A：你喜欢做家务吗？
B：嗯，我不介意做。

Lesson 20　支持、鼓励和祝贺，宽慰，信任与怀疑
Support, Encouragement and Congratulations, Comfort, Trust and Doubt

Part 1　支持、鼓励和祝贺 Support, Encouragement and Congratulations

01 支持

I will support you. 我会支持你的。
I will back you up. 我会支持你的。
I've got your back. 我支持你。
I'm on your side. 我站在你这边。

I'm here for you. 有我呢。
I'll stand by you. 我会支持你的。
I am right behind you. 我支持你。

02 鼓励

You can do/make it! 你可以的！
Just go for it! 努力去争取吧！
You're doing a great job! 你做得很棒！

Don't give up! 别放弃！
Don't lose heart! 别丧失信心！
Keep your chin up! /Chin up! 打起精神来！

03 祝贺

Congratulations! /Congrats! 祝贺你！
Good for you! 为你开心！

I am happy for you! 真为你高兴！

场景对话 Conversation

A: What's wrong?
B: The task is too difficult.
A: Don't lose heart! You can make it!

A：发生了什么？
B：这个任务太难了。
A：别丧失信心！你可以的！

Part 2　宽慰 Comfort

01 会好的

It will be fine. 会好的。
Everything is gonna be OK. 一切都会好的。

Everything will work out in the end. 一切都会解决的。

02 放轻松

Take it easy. 放轻松。
Just relax. 放轻松。
Take your time. 别着急。

03 别担心

Don't worry. 别担心。
There is nothing to worry about. 没什么可担心的。
Don't let it bother you. 别为这事烦心。

04 不是你的错 / 不是什么事儿

It's not your fault. 这不是你的错。
It has nothing to do with you. 这和你没关系。
It's not a big deal. 不是什么大事儿。

场景对话 Conversation

A: I am so worried.
B: What happened?
A: I made a mistake in the test.
B: Don't worry. It's not a big deal.

A：我好担心啊。
B：发生什么了？
A：我在考试中犯了个错误。
B：别担心，不是什么大事儿。

Part 3 信任与怀疑 Trust and Doubt

01 信任某人

I (definitely) trust you. 我（绝对）相信你。
I have confidence/faith in you. 我对你有信心。
I think I can depend on you. 我觉得我可以指望你。

02 相信某人的话

I believe you. 我相信你。

I take your word for it. 我相信你的话。

I have no doubt about it. 我一点都不怀疑。

03 不信任某人

I don't trust you. 我不信任你。

I don't think I can trust you. 我觉得我不能信任你。

I don't feel like I can count on you. 我认为我不能指望你。

04 不相信 / 怀疑某人说的话

I won't buy your story. 我不相信你说的话。

I don't buy it. 我不相信。

I doubt it. 我表示怀疑。

It's doubtful! 这很可疑!

词汇精讲 Word Study

doubtful

英 /ˈdaʊtf(ə)l/
美 /ˈdaʊtf(ə)l/

a. 1. 难以预测的
It is doubtful whether he will get the job.
他能否得到这份工作还很难说。

2. 怀疑的
I am still doubtful about what he said.
我对他所说的话仍持怀疑态度。

🗨 场景对话 Conversation

A: Why didn't you come to class yesterday?
B: I...I was ill.
A: I don't buy it. Just tell me the truth.
B: Well, I woke up late.

A：你昨天怎么没来上课？
B：我……我病了。
A：我可不信。快告诉我真相。
B：那个，我起晚了。

场景对话

导　语

本章"场景对话"精心设计了 8 个单元，每个单元都围绕不同的生活场景展开，旨在提升你的英语口语能力，让你能够在各种情境中自如地交流。

- 第 5 单元：行——旅行是探索世界的窗口。从机场的值机、安检、登机，到交通工具的选择，你将学会如何在旅途中用英语进行有效沟通。
- 第 6 单元：住——住宿体验直接影响旅行的质量。本单元涵盖了预订酒店、入住、客房服务、投诉处理到退房等环节，让你能够在住宿期间保持流畅的交流。
- 第 7 单元：吃——餐饮体验是文化交流的重要部分。从餐厅预订、点餐到用餐和投诉，地道实用的对话将帮助你在不同餐饮场合中享受美食的同时也享受语言的乐趣。
- 第 8 单元：购——购物不仅是一种乐趣，也是了解一个地方文化的方式。本单元教你如何在购物时讨价还价、理解促销信息、处理结账以及享受售后服务。
- 第 9 单元：娱乐——休闲娱乐是生活的调味剂。无论是游乐园的尖叫，还是咖啡厅的悠闲，本单元的对话帮助你在娱乐活动中更好地交流和体验。
- 第 10 单元：紧急事件——面对紧急情况时，有效沟通至关重要。必备的英语表达将帮助你在问路、应对疾病、遭遇抢劫、办理护照或遗失物品时，能够保持冷静并寻求帮助。
- 第 11 单元：情感——情感表达是语言的核心。本单元深入探讨如何用英语进行介绍、约会、表白、分手和讨论婚姻，让情感交流变得更加真挚和深刻。
- 第 12 单元：节日——节日是庆祝和感恩的时刻。通过学习如何在圣诞节、感恩节、万圣节、情人节等节日中用英语表达祝福和分享喜悦，本单元将加深你对西方文化的理解。

通过本章的学习，你将能够在各种场景下使用英语进行有效沟通，不仅能促进语言能力的提升，还能增进文化理解，拓宽交际圈。现在，让我们一起进入到这些生动的场景中，用英语开启一段新的旅程吧！

Unit 5 交通 Transportation

Lesson 21 办理登机、安检与登机
Check-in, Security and Boarding

Part 1 办理登机 Check-in

词汇 Vocabulary

- 舱位：
  first class 头等舱   business class 商务舱   economy class 经济舱

- 航班时间：
  morning flight 上午航班   afternoon flight 下午航班   red-eye flight 夜间航班

- 单程 / 往返：
  one-way ticket 单程票   round-way ticket 往返票

- 直飞 / 转机：
  layover   英 /'leɪəʊvə(r)/   美 /'leɪoʊvər/
  =stopover   英 /'stɒpəʊvə(r)/   美 /'stɑːpoʊvər/   中途停留
  direct/non-stop flight 直飞   connecting flight 需要转机的航班

- 场所：
  domestic terminal 国内航站楼   international terminal 国际航站楼
  (terminal   英 /'tɜːmɪn(ə)l/   美 /'tɜːrmɪn(ə)l/   航站楼)
  check-in counter 值机柜台

> **词汇精讲 Word Study**
>
> **domestic**
> 英 /də'mestɪk/
> 美 /də'mestɪk/
>
> a. 1. 本国的
>   This newspaper focuses on domestic affairs. 这家报纸主要报道国内事务。
> 2. 家庭的
>   I need to buy some domestic appliances. 我需要买一些家用电器。
> 3. 驯养的
>   She is a domestic cat. 她是一只家猫。

- 携带物品：
  passport   英 /'pɑːspɔːt/   美 /'pæspɔːrt/   护照
  ticket   英 /'tɪkɪt/   美 /'tɪkɪt/   机票
  boarding pass 登机牌

- 座位类型：
  aisle seat   英 /aɪl siːt/   美 /aɪl siːt/   靠走道的座位
  window seat 靠窗的座位   exit seat 靠近紧急出口的座位
  middle seat 中间的位置

Unit 5 交通 Transportation

- 行李类型：
  baggage   英 /ˈbæɡɪdʒ/   美 /ˈbæɡɪdʒ/   （美）行李
  luggage   英 /ˈlʌɡɪdʒ/   美 /ˈlʌɡɪdʒ/   （英）行李
  suitcase   英 /ˈsuːtkeɪs/   美 /ˈsuːtkeɪs/   行李箱
  carry-on baggage（随身带上飞机的）手提行李

- 行李重量：
  (free) baggage allowance 行李（免费）托运的限度
  (allowance   英 /əˈlaʊəns/   美 /əˈlaʊəns/   限额；定量）
  overweight   英 /ˌəʊvəˈweɪt/ 美 /ˌoʊvərˈweɪt/ 超重的
  excess weight 超出限重的重量
  (excess   英 /ˈekses/   美 /ˈekses/   超额的）
  charge   英 /tʃɑːdʒ/   美 /tʃɑːrdʒ/
  =fee   英 /fiː/   美 /fiː/   收费

- 违禁物品：
  prohibited items 违禁物品
  (prohibited   英 /prəˈhɪbɪtɪd/ 美 /prəˈhɪbɪtɪd/ 被禁止的）
  lithium battery 锂电池
  (lithium   英 /ˈlɪθiəm/   美 /ˈlɪθiəm/   锂）

实用表达 Useful Expressions

01 询问值机柜台

A: Where is the check-in counter for United Airlines? 美国联合航空的值机柜台在哪儿？
B: That's in counter K. 在 K 柜台。

02 办理登机

A: I want to check in, please. 我想办理登机手续，谢谢。
B: May I see your passport, please? 请出示您的护照。

词汇精讲 Word Study

check
英 /tʃek/
美 /tʃek/

v. 1. + in 办理登机手续；酒店办理入住手续
I want to check in, please. 我想办理登机手续。
I'd like to check in, please. 我想办理入住手续。
2. + out 酒店办理退房
I'd like to check out, please. 我想办理退房手续。
3. 结账离开
Check, please. 请结账，谢谢。
4. 寄放，寄存
Do you want to check your coat? 您要寄放外套吗？

03 询问目的地

A: Hi, welcome to United Airlines. Where are you flying?
　　您好，欢迎来到联合航空，请问您要飞哪里？
B: I'm flying to New York. 我要飞纽约。

04 询问座位

A: I would like a/an window/aisle seat. 我喜欢靠窗/靠近走道的座位。
B: OK, let me check for you. 好的，我帮您查一下。

05 托运行李

A: Do you have any baggage to check in? 您有行李需要托运吗？
B: Yes, one suitcase. 有的，一个行李箱。

06 行李超重

A: Your luggage is (two kilos) overweight. 您的行李超重了（两公斤）。
B: How much do I have to pay for the excess weight? 我要为超重的行李付多少钱？
A: For excess luggage, we charge 30 dollars per kilo.
　　对于行李中超重的部分，每公斤收费 30 美元。

场景对话 Conversation

A: I want to check in, please.
B: May I have your passport?
A: Here you are. I'd like a window seat.
B: OK, let me check for you.

A：请帮我办理登机手续。
B：请出示您的护照。
A：给你。我想要一个窗边的座位。
B：好的，我帮您查询一下。

Part 2　安检 Security

词汇 Vocabulary

- 相关词汇：

security　　　　英/sɪˈkjʊərəti/　　美/sɪˈkjʊrəti/　　安检
pat-down　　　　英/ˈpæt daʊn/　　美/ˈpæt daʊn/　　全身检查
metal detector 金属检测器

- 相关物品：

tray　　　　　　英/treɪ/　　　　美/treɪ/　　　　托盘

| liquid | 英 /ˈlɪkwɪd/ | 美 /ˈlɪkwɪd/ | 液体 |
| lighter | 英 /ˈlaɪtə(r)/ | 美 /ˈlaɪtər/ | 打火机 |

flammable items 易燃物品
| （flammable | 英 /ˈflæməb(ə)l/ | 美 /ˈflæməb(ə)l/ | 易燃的） |

metallic items/objects 金属物品
| （metallic | 英 /məˈtælɪk/ | 美 /məˈtælɪk/ | 金属制的） |

electronic products/items 电子产品
| （electronic | 英 /ˌlekˈtrɒnɪk/ | 美 /ˌlekˈtrɑːnɪk/ | 电子的） |

实用表达 Useful Expressions

01 询问地点

A: Excuse me, do you know where the security is? 不好意思，请问安检在哪里？
B: Just go straight and turn left. 直走，然后左拐。

02 工作人员的指示

Do you have any liquids or flammable items in your suitcase?
您的行李箱中有液体或者易燃物吗？
Could you take off/remove your shoes/coat, please? 请脱掉您的鞋/外套。
Please stand here for a pat-down. 请站在这里接受身体检查。
Could you put all metallic objects into the tray? 请把所有的金属物品放进托盘中。
I'm afraid you can't take that through. 您恐怕不能带这件物品进去了。

Part 3　登机 Boarding

词汇 Vocabulary

departure/waiting lounge 候机室
| （lounge | 英 /laʊndʒ/ | 美 /laʊndʒ/ | 〈机场等的〉等候室） |

baggage trolley= baggage cart 手推车
（trolley	英 /ˈtrɒli/	美 /ˈtrɑːli/	手推车）
delay	英 /dɪˈleɪ/	美 /dɪˈleɪ/	=put off 延误
cancel	英 /ˈkæns(ə)l/	美 /ˈkæns(ə)l/	=call off 取消

（boarding）gate 登机口　　　　　boarding time 登机时间

实用表达 Useful Expressions

01 询问登机口

Is this the gate for the flight to New York? 前往纽约的航班是在这个登机口登机吗?
Could you tell me where Gate 211 is? 请问登机口 211 在哪里?

02 询问登机时间

What's the boarding time? 登机时间是什么时候?
Has the flight been called? 这趟航班开始呼叫了吗?

03 关于飞机延误

（1）关于时间

How long is the delay? =How long will the flight be put off? 飞机会延误多久?

（2）关于赔偿

How will I be compensated for this delay? 针对这次延误，你们将如何进行赔偿呢?

（3）关于投诉

How can I file/make a complaint about this? 我要如何投诉?

词汇精讲 Word Study

compensate
英 /'kɒmpenseɪt/
美 /'kɑːmpenseɪt/

v. 1. 补偿，弥补
How will you compensate for the loss? 你要如何弥补这次的损失?
2. 抵消
His enthusiasm compensates for his lack of skill.
他的热情弥补了技术上的不足。

场景对话 Conversation

A: Excuse me, may I ask what's the boarding time?
B: I'm sorry. The flight is late because of the heavy fog.
A: How long will the flight be put off?
B: Maybe three hours. Sorry for the inconvenience.

A：打扰了，请问什么时候登机?
B：很抱歉。因为大雾，航班误点了。
A：航班要延误多长时间?
B：大概三个小时吧。很抱歉给您带来不便。

Lesson 22 机舱服务 Plane Service

词汇 Vocabulary

- **物品：**

blanket	英 /ˈblæŋkɪt/	美 /ˈblæŋkɪt/	毛毯
pillow	英 /ˈpɪləʊ/	美 /ˈpɪloʊ/	枕头
headphones	英 /ˈhedfəʊnz/	美 /ˈhedfoʊnz/	（头戴式）耳机

  in-flight magazine 飞机上提供的杂志　　electronic devices 电子设备

- **设施：**

seatbelt	英 /ˈsiːtbelt/	美 /ˈsiːtbelt/	安全带
pedal	英 /ˈped(ə)l/	美 /ˈped(ə)l/	脚踏板

  seat back 座椅靠背　　overhead bin 舱顶行李柜
  seat pocket 座位袋　　tray table 小桌板　　window shade 遮光板

- **饮品：**

tea	英 /tiː/	美 /tiː/	茶
coffee	英 /ˈkɒfi/	美 /ˈkɔːfi/	咖啡
juice	英 /dʒuːs/	美 /dʒuːs/	果汁
Coke	英 /kəʊk/	美 /koʊk/	可口可乐
Pepsi	英 /ˈpepsi/	美 /ˈpepsi/	百事可乐
Sprite	英 /spraɪt/	美 /spraɪt/	雪碧

  (hot/cold) water（热/冷）水

- **紧急情况：**

parachute	英 /ˈpærəʃuːt/	美 /ˈpærəʃuːt/	降落伞
turbulence	英 /ˈtɜːbjələns/	美 /ˈtɜːrbjələns/	气流波动

  life vest 救生衣
  emergency exit 紧急出口

(emergency	英 /ɪˈmɜːdʒənsi/	美 /ɪˈmɜːrdʒənsi/	紧急情况)

  oxygen mask 氧气面罩

(oxygen	英 /ˈɒksɪdʒən/	美 /ˈɑːksɪdʒən/	氧气)

实用表达 Useful Expressions

01 关于座位

（1）找不到座位

Excuse me, I can't find my seat. Could you help me?
不好意思，我找不到我的座位。你能帮帮我吗？

Can you direct me to my seat, please? 请把我带到我的座位上，可以吗？

（2）发现有人坐在自己的座位上

Excuse me, but you're in my seat. 不好意思，但是您坐在了我的座位上。

（3）换座位

I wonder if I could switch to an aisle seat. 我想知道我可否换到一个靠过道的座位上。
Excuse me, would you mind if we swapped seats?
=Excuse me, would you mind exchanging seats with me?
打扰一下，您介意我们换一下座位吗？

词汇精讲 Word Study

switch
英 /swɪtʃ/
美 /swɪtʃ/

n. 1. 开关
Can you flip the switch? 你能按一下开关吗？
2. 转变
When did she make the switch from nurse to singer? 她什么时候从护士变成了歌手？
v. 1. 开/关电器等
Can you switch the TV off? 你能把电视关了吗？
2. （使）改变，转变
When did you switch jobs? 你们什么时候调动工作的？
3. 交换；调换
The dates of the last two exams have been switched. 最后两门考试的日期调换了。

swap
英 /swɒp/
美 /swɑːp/

n./v. 交换
Let's do a swap. 我们交换一下吧。
Can we swap places? 我能和你换一下位置吗？

exchange
英 /ɪksˈtʃeɪndʒ/
美 /ɪksˈtʃeɪndʒ/

n./v. 1. 交换；交流
We had an exchange of information. 我们进行了信息的交换。
We exchanged ideas with foreign students. 我们和留学生交流思想。
2. 兑换
I need to exchange some dollars. 我需要换些美元。
I need to exchange my currency into dollars. 我需要将我的货币兑换成美元。

02 温馨提示及提供服务（空乘人员）

（1）温馨提示

Please fasten your seatbelt. 请系好安全带。
Please return your seat back to the upright. 请调直座椅靠背。
Please lock your tray table in place. 请收起小桌板。
Please put up window shades. 请打开遮光板。

Please switch/turn off all electronic devices during take-off and landing.
请在起飞和降落的过程中关闭所有的电子设备。
We are experiencing some turbulence. Please remain in your seat and fasten your seatbelt.
飞机遇到气流颠簸，请勿离开座位并系好安全带。
Please remain in your seat until the plane has come to a complete stop.
飞机尚未完全停稳前请勿离开座位。

（2）提供服务

What can I do for you? 我能为您做些什么？
Can I get you anything? 您需要什么？
Would you like chicken or beef? 您要鸡肉饭还是牛肉饭？
What would you like to drink? 您要喝什么？

03 寻求服务

Can you help me put my luggage into the overhead bin?
您能帮我把行李放到舱顶行李柜里吗？
Can you help me adjust the seat? 您能帮我调节一下座椅吗？
Excuse me, can I have a blanket/pillow? 打扰一下，我能要一条毯子 / 一个枕头吗？
Can I have a Coke/some water, please? 能给我来一杯可乐 / 水吗？
Will food be served? / Will there be any food on the flight?（航班）会提供食物吗？
What time will the meal be served? 什么时候供餐呢？
Is there free Wi-Fi available on this flight? 这趟航班有免费的无线网络吗？
Where is the bathroom? 卫生间在哪里？

词汇精讲 Word Study

adjust
英 /əˈdʒʌst/
美 /əˈdʒʌst/

v. 1. 调整，调节
You can turn this knob to adjust the volume. 你可以转动这个旋钮来调节音量。
2. 适应；习惯
He quickly adjusted himself to student life. 他很快适应了学生生活。

场景对话 Conversation

A: Hi, would you like chicken or beef?
B: I'll have the beef, please.
A: OK, what would you like to drink?
B: Coke, please.
A: Here you are.
B: Thank you.

A：您好，您要鸡肉还是牛肉？
B：我要牛肉。
A：好的，您想喝点什么？
B：请给我可口可乐。
A：给您。
B：谢谢。

Lesson 23 过海关与领取行李
Customs and Reclaiming the Luggage

Part 1　过海关 Customs

实用表达 Useful Expressions

01 询问目的

A: What's the purpose of your visit? 您来这儿的目的是什么？
B: I'm here for tourism/business. 我来旅行 / 出差。

> **词汇精讲 Word Study**
> **purpose**
> 英 /ˈpɜːpəs/
> 美 /ˈpɜːrpəs/
>
> n. 意图；目的
> He talked about the purpose of his visit. 他谈了他来访的意图。
> You need a purpose. 你需要一个目标。

02 询问时间

A: How long do you plan to stay in the USA?
=How long will you be staying in the USA?
您计划在美国停留多久？
B: For about two weeks.
大约两周。

> **句型精讲 Sentence Structure**
> • plan to do sth. 打算 / 计划做某事
> I'm not planning to stay here much longer.
> 我没打算在这儿久留。
> How do you plan to spend your holiday?
> 你打算怎么度过你的假期？

03 询问目的地

A: Where will you be staying?
您要住在哪里？
B: I will be staying in Holiday Inn Hotel.
我会住在假日酒店。

04 询问国籍

A: Your nationality, please?
=Which country are you from?
请问您的国籍是哪儿？ /
您来自哪个国家？
B: I am from China.
我来自中国。

> **词汇精讲 Word Study**
> **nationality**
> 英 /ˌnæʃəˈnæləti/
> 美 /ˌnæʃəˈnæləti/
>
> n. 1. 国籍
> What's your nationality?
> 你的国籍是哪儿？
> 2.（构成国家一部分的）民族
> The country is home to five nationalities.
> 这个国家有五个民族。

场景对话 Conversation

A: What's the purpose of your visit?
B: I'm here for tourism.
A: How long will you be staying?
B: For about two weeks.
A: Where will you be staying?
B: I will be staying in Holiday Inn Hotel.
A: Okay. Nice trip!

A：您此行的目的是什么？
B：我是来旅游的。
A：您要待多久？
B：大约两周。
A：您要住在哪里？
B：我将住在假日酒店。
A：好的，祝您旅途愉快！

Part 2 领取行李 Reclaiming the Luggage

词汇 Vocabulary

conveyor belt 传送带
baggage claim/baggage reclaim 行李提取处
claim tag 行李提取票

实用表达 Useful Expressions

01 取行李

A: Sorry to bother you, where is the baggage claim?
不好意思打扰了，请问在哪儿取行李？
B: Go downstairs and turn right.
下楼，然后右转。
A: Thank you very much.
非常感谢。

02 丢行李

A: I lost a piece of luggage.
我丢了一件行李。
B: We'll attempt to assist you.
我们会尽力帮您找的。

> **词汇精讲 Word Study**
>
> **attempt**
> 英 /əˈtempt/
> 美 /əˈtempt/
> v./n. 努力；尝试；试图
> I attempted to finish my work before 7 p.m. 我努力在晚上7点前完成工作。
> I passed my driving test at the first attempt. 我考驾照一次就通过了。
>
> **assist**
> 英 /əˈsɪst/
> 美 /əˈsɪst/
> v. 援助，帮助，协助
> I will assist you in solving the problem. 我会帮助你解决这个问题的。
> The school tried to assist students in finding jobs. 学校努力帮助学生找工作。

场景对话 Conversation

A: Sorry to bother you, where is the baggage claim?
B: Go downstairs and turn right.
A: Thank you very much.

A：对不起，打扰你了，行李提取处在哪里？
B：下楼右转。
A：非常感谢。

Lesson 24　乘坐地铁与公交车
Taking the Subway and Taking a Bus

Part 1　乘坐地铁 Taking the Subway

词汇 Vocabulary

metro	英 /'metrəʊ/	美 /'metroʊ/	
=subway	英 /'sʌbweɪ/	美 /'sʌbweɪ/	（美）地铁
underground	英 /ˌʌndə'graʊnd/	美 /ˌʌndər'graʊnd/	
=tube	英 /tjuːb/	美 /tuːb/	（英）地铁
entrance	英 /'entrəns/	美 /'entrəns/	入口
exit	英 /'eksɪt/	美 /'eksɪt/	出口
change	英 /tʃeɪndʒ/	美 /tʃeɪndʒ/	
=transfer	英 /træns'fɜː(r)/	美 /træns'fɜːr/	换乘

subway station 地铁站　　　　transfer/interchange station 换乘站
ticket office/window 售票处　　ticket machine （自动）售票机

实用表达 Useful Expressions

01　询问地铁站的位置

Is there a subway station nearby? 这附近有地铁站吗？
Could you tell me where the nearest subway station is?
您能告诉我最近的地铁站在哪儿吗？
I can't find the subway entrance. Could you help me?
我找不到地铁站的入口，您能帮帮我吗？

02　乘几号线

Could you tell me how to get to Universal Studios? 您可以告诉我怎么去环球影城吗？
Which train stops at Times Square? 哪趟车在时代广场停？
Where is this train heading? 这辆车是开往哪儿的？

03　买地铁票

Excuse me, do you know where the ticket office is?
打扰一下，您知道售票处怎么走吗？

Excuse me, could you tell me where the ticket machine is?
打扰一下，您知道自动售票机在哪儿吗？
How much is one ticket? 一张票要多少钱？

04 询问时间

How often do the trains come?=How frequently do the trains come?
车多长时间来一趟？
How long does it take to get to the next stop?=How long until the next stop?
到达下一站要多久？

05 关于换乘

Where/At which station am I supposed to change for Line 4?
我该在哪里换乘四号线呢？
Where can I transfer if I want to go to Universal Studios?
如果我想去环球影城的话，我应该在哪里换乘？

06 出站

Which exit is for Empire State Building? 去帝国大厦应该走哪个出口？

场景对话 Conversation

A: Where is the train heading?
B: The train is bound for Victoria Station.

A：这班火车开往哪里？
B：这班火车开往维多利亚站。

A: Excuse me, could you tell me how to get to Universal Studios?
B: You should take Line 4.

A：打扰一下，您能告诉我去环球影城怎么走吗？
B：坐 4 号线。

Part 2　乘坐公交车 Taking a Bus

词汇 Vocabulary

fare　　　　　[英]/feə(r)/　　[美]/fer/　　车费 / 票价
bus stop 公交车站　　　　　　　　　　　bus pass = metro card 公交卡
airport shuttle bus 机场大巴　　　　　　front door 前门
rear door 后门

实用表达 Useful Expressions

01 询问车次

Could you tell me which bus I should take to go downtown?
请问，我到市中心该乘哪辆车？
Excuse me, is this the bus to the railway station? 打扰了，这是去火车站的车吗？
Where does this bus go? 这辆车是去哪儿的？

02 询问票价

How much is the bus fare? 车费多少？
How much is the fare to this station? 到这个站要多少钱？

03 询问时间

How long do I have to wait for the next bus? 下一趟公交车还要等多久？
Do you know how often the No.1 bus runs? 您知道1路车多久来一趟吗？
How long will it take to get downtown? 到市中心要多久？

04 询问座位

Is this seat taken?=Is anyone sitting here? 这儿有人坐了吗？

05 寻求帮助

Where are we? 我们到哪儿了？
What is the next stop? 接下来是哪一站？
Where should I get off? 我该在哪站下车？
Could you let me know when we get to Times Square? 到时代广场的时候请告诉我一声好吗？

场景对话 Conversation

A: Is this seat taken?
B: No, you can sit here.
A: Do you know what the next stop is?
B: Universal Studios.
A: Oh, thank you very much!

A：这个座位有人吗？
B：没有，你可以坐在这里。
A：您知道下一站是哪儿吗？
B：环球影城。
A：哦，非常感谢！

Lesson 25　乘坐出租车与租车
Taking a Taxi and Renting a Car

Part 1　乘坐出租车 Taking a Taxi

词汇 Vocabulary

taxi	英 /'tæksi/	美 /'tæksi/	出租车
trunk	英 /trʌŋk/	美 /trʌŋk/	（美）后备厢
boot	英 /buːt/	美 /buːt/	（英）后备厢
fare	英 /feə(r)/	美 /fer/	车费
receipt	英 /rɪˈsiːt/	美 /rɪˈsiːt/	收据
change	英 /tʃeɪndʒ/	美 /tʃeɪndʒ/	零钱

taxi stand 出租车候车处　　　　　　　　　air conditioner 空调

实用表达 Useful Expressions

01　路边招呼出租车

Hi, taxi! 嗨，出租车！
Excuse me, taxi! 出租车！
Where can I get/catch a taxi? 我可以在哪里打到出租车？
Is there a taxi stand around here? 这附近哪里有出租车招呼站？

02　预约出租车服务

Hello, could I get a taxi to pick me up <u>at the hotel</u>? 你好，我能叫辆出租车来我的酒店吗？
I would like to book a taxi for <u>three o'clock this afternoon</u>. 我想预约今天下午 3 点的出租车。

03　把行李放入后备厢

Can you open the trunk, please? 能开一下后备厢吗？
Could you help me to put the baggage into the trunk? 您能帮我把行李放进后备厢吗？

04　目的地的询问与回答

提问

Where to?=Where are you going?
　　　　　=Where would you like to go?
　　　　　（您想）去哪儿？

075

回答

To this address, please. 请到这个地址。(地址写在纸上或者显示在手机上)
I need to go to the airport. 我需要到机场。
Take me to the airport, please. 请把我送到机场。

05 询问距离和时间

How long before we get there? 我们还有多久能到?
Is that place far from here? 那个地方离这儿远吗?

06 车内服务

Could you please turn up the air conditioner a little? 可以麻烦你把冷气调强一点吗?
Could you please turn off the air conditioner and open the window?
可以麻烦你把空调关了,然后把窗户打开吗?
Could you please turn down the music? 可以麻烦你把音乐调小声一点吗?

07 关于车速

Could you speed up/slow down a little? 你能开快/慢一点儿吗?
I'm in a hurry. Please take a shortcut. 我赶时间,请抄捷径。

08 下车

Please drop me off at the building over there. 请让我在那边的楼前下车。
Let me off here. 让我在这儿下车吧。

09 询问车费

What's the fare? 车费多少?
May I have a receipt, please? 我可以要一张收据吗?
Keep the change. 零钱不用找了。

场景对话 Conversation

A: Where would you like to go?
B: Take me to the airport, please.
A: Okay.
B: How long before we get there?
A: About 20 minutes.

A:您要去哪里?
B:请送我去机场。
A:好的。
B:我们要多久才能到那里?
A:大约20分钟。

Part 2 租车 Renting a Car

词汇 Vocabulary

- 证件：

  passport　　　　　英 /'pɑːspɔːt/　　　　美 /'pæspɔːrt/　　　　护照

  international driver's license 国际驾驶证

  (license　　　　　英 /'laɪs(ə)ns/　　　　美 /'laɪs(ə)ns/　　　　许可证)

- 车的规格：

  mid-size car 中型车　　　　　　　full-size car 标准规格车

  compact car 小型车

  (compact　　　　英 /kəm'pækt/　　　　美 /kəm'pækt/　　　　紧凑的，小巧的)

- 车的类型：

  sedan　　　　　　英 /sɪ'dæn/　　　　　美 /sɪ'dæn/

  =saloon　　　　　英 /sə'luːn/　　　　　美 /sə'luːn/　　　　普通轿车

  van　　　　　　　英 /væn/　　　　　　美 /væn/　　　　　面包车

  pick-up　　　　　英 /'pɪk ʌp/　　　　　美 /'pɪk ʌp/　　　　皮卡

  sport utility vehicle（SUV）运动型多功能汽车

  (utility　　　　　英 /juː'tɪləti/　　　　美 /juː'tɪləti/　　　　多用途的)

  (vehicle　　　　英 /'viːəkl/　　　　　美 /'viːəkl/　　　　车辆)

实用表达 Useful Expressions

01 租车

A: How can I rent a car? 我要怎么租车呢?

I would like to rent a car for <u>five days</u>, please. 我想租辆车，租五天。

B: Please fill out/complete this form. 请填写这个表格。

02 选车

A: What size are you looking for? 您想租什么规格的车呢?

B: I need a <u>sedan</u> that can fit <u>four</u> people. 我需要一辆能容下四个人的轿车。

A: Automatic or manual?　自动挡还是手动挡?

B: Automatic/manual, please.　自动挡 / 手动挡，谢谢。

03 价格

A: What's the daily rate? 日租金多少？
B: 300 dollars a day. 一天 300 美元。

04 取车

Hello, I'd like to pick up my rental car, please. 你好，我想来取我租的车。
I rented a car from you. Could I pick it up now? 我从你们这里租了辆车，我现在能取了吗？
When should I drop it off? 我应该什么时候还车呢？

场景对话 Conversation

A: How can I rent a car?
B: Please fill out this form.
A: OK.
B: What size are you looking for?
A: I need a sedan that can fit four people.
B: Automatic or manual?
A: Automatic, please. And what's the daily rate?
B: 300 dollars a day.
A: Okay, here you are.

A：我要怎么租车呢？
B：请填写这个表格。
A：好的。
B：您想租什么规格的车呢？
A：我需要一辆能容下四个人的轿车。
B：自动挡还是手动挡？
A：自动挡，谢谢。日租金多少？
B：一天 300 美元。
A：好的，给你。

Unit 6 酒店 Hotel

Lesson 26 预订酒店
Making Reservations

词汇 Vocabulary

- 房间类型：

single room 单人间   double room 双人间（一张双人床）
standard=twin room 标准间（两张单人床）

- 套房类型：

superior suite	英 /suːˈpɪərɪə(r) swiːt/	美 /suːˈpɪrɪər swiːt/	高级套房
deluxe suite	英 /dɪˈlʌks swiːt/	美 /dɪˈlʌks swiːt/	豪华套房
business suite	英 /ˈbɪznəs swiːt/	美 /ˈbɪznəs swiːt/	商务套房
executive suite	英 /ɪgˈzekjətɪv swiːt/	美 /ɪgˈzekjətɪv swiːt/	行政套房
presidential suite	英 /ˌprezɪˈdenʃl swiːt/	美 /ˌprezɪˈdenʃl swiːt/	总统套房
family suite	英 /ˈfæməli swiːt/	美 /ˈfæməli swiːt/	家庭套房

- 床的大小：

king-sized bed 特大号床   queen-sized bed 次特大号床

实用表达 Useful Expressions

01 关于时间

A: Which dates would you like to reserve? 您想预订哪天的房间？
B: I would like to book a double room on April 2. 我想预订4月2日的一个双人间。
A: How many nights do you wish to stay? =How long will you be staying for?
   您打算住几晚？
B: Two nights. 两个晚上。

词汇精讲 Word Study

reserve
英 /rɪˈzɜːv/
美 /rɪˈzɜːrv/

v. 1. 保留，留存
I'd prefer to reserve my judgement on the proposal. 我保留对这个提案的意见。
2. 预订
I have reserved a table for two under the name of Jack.
我用杰克的名字预订了一张两人桌。

n. 1. 储备（物）
I have a reserve of food and water in case of emergency.
我储备了食物和水，以防发生紧急情况。
2. 保留
She trusted him without reserve. 她毫无保留地信任他。

3. 替补队员，后备部队
The team has three reserves in case anyone is injured.
该队有三名替补队员，以防有人受伤。
4. 自然保护区
They did some voluntary work in the nature reserve.
他们在自然保护区做一些志愿工作。

02 有无房间

提问

I want to book a room from May 1 to 4. Are there any vacant rooms? / Do you have any rooms available?
我想预订一间房，从 5 月 1 号到 4 号。你们有空房间吗？

回答

（1）有房间

Yes, we have vacancy on those dates. 有的，我们在那几天有空房间。

（2）没有房间

I'm sorry, we are fully booked/we are all booked up. 很抱歉，我们已经预订满了。

词汇精讲 Word Study

vacant
英 /ˈveɪkənt/
美 /ˈveɪkənt/

a. 1. 空着的；未被占用的
Are there any vacant rooms? 还有空房吗？
2. （职位）空缺的
The position has been vacant for a month. 该职位空缺了一个月。
3. 无神的；呆滞的
He has a vacant look on his face. 他的脸上呈现出呆滞的表情。

vacancy
英 /ˈveɪkənsi/
美 /ˈveɪkənsi/

n. 1. （职位的）空缺；空职；空额
We have a vacancy for a sales manager. 我们有一个销售经理的职位空缺。
2. （旅馆等的）空房，空间
I'm sorry, we have no vacancies. 对不起，我们这里客满。

available
英 /əˈveɪləbl/
美 /əˈveɪləbl/

a. 1. 可获得的，可得到的
Is there free Wi-Fi available? 这有免费的无线网络吗？
2. 有空的
She is not available. 她现在没空。

03 关于房间类型

A: What type/kind of room would you like to reserve? 您想预订什么类型的房间呢？

B: I would like to reserve/book a single/double/standard room.
我想预订一间单人房 / 双人房 / 标准间。
I would like a room with a view of the city/river.
我想要看得到城市 / 河流景观的房间。

04 关于房费

What's the price? 房费多少钱？
Is there a deposit? 需要交押金吗？
Is there any charge for an extra bed? 外加床铺要收费吗？

词汇精讲 Word Study

deposit
英 /dɪˈpɒzɪt/
美 /dɪˈpɑːzɪt/

v. 1. 使沉淀
Layers of mud were deposited by the flood.
洪水过后，泥土淤积了好几层。

2. 存放
You can deposit your valuables in a safe.
你可以把你的贵重物品存放在一个保险柜中。

3. 储蓄
She deposited 200 dollars in her account.
她把 200 美元存入了她的账户。

n. 1. 定金，押金
I put a deposit of 1,000 dollars on the car.
我支付了 1000 美元作为车的押金。

2. 存款
He made a large deposit at the bank yesterday.
他昨天在银行存了一大笔钱。

3. 矿
They found a lot of gold deposits in this area.
他们在这个地区发现了很多金矿。

场景对话 Conversation

A: Hello, this is Holiday Inn Hotel. What can I do for you?
A：您好，这里是假日酒店。我能为您做些什么？

B: I'd like to book a standard room, please.
B：我想订一间标准间。

A: Which dates would you like to reserve?
A：您想预订什么日期的？

B: From May 1 to 4.
B：从 5 月 1 日到 4 日。

A: Okay, no problem.
A：好的，没问题。

Lesson 27　办理入住
Check-in

词汇 Vocabulary

- 相关物品：

passport　英/ˈpɑːspɔːt/　美/ˈpæspɔːrt/　护照
ID card 身份证　　　　　　　　room card/room key/key card 房卡

- 其他：

reservation　英/ˌrezəˈveɪʃn/　美/ˌrezərˈveɪʃn/　预订
check in 办理入住手续　　　　under the name of 以……的名义

实用表达 Useful Expressions

01　办理入住

A: Welcome to Holiday Inn Hotel. What can I do for you?
欢迎来到假日酒店。我能为您做什么？

B: I would like to check in. 我想办理入住。

02　关于预订

A: Have you made the reservation?
=Do you have a reservation with us? 您有预订吗？

B: Yeah, we have a reservation for two standard rooms for four nights.
是的，我们预订了两间标准间，入住四晚。

A: What name is the reservation under? 您预订的名字是什么？

B: Jack. /I have a reservation under the name of Jack.
杰克。/ 我用杰克的名字预订了房间。

词汇精讲 Word Study

reservation
英/ˌrezəˈveɪʃn/
美/ˌrezərˈveɪʃ(ə)n/

n. 1.（住处、座位等的）预订
I would like to make a reservation for Friday night.
我想预订周五晚上的晚餐。

2. 保留；犹豫
I have reservations about letting her travel alone.
我对让她独自旅行持保留意见。

03　查看证件

A: May I see some IDs? 请出示您的身份证明。

B: Here you are/There you go. 给你。

04 关于会员

A: I have a membership card of your hotel. Can I get a room upgrade?
我有贵酒店的会员，请问可以给我升级房型吗？

B: Let me check for you. 让我为您查一下。

词汇精讲 Word Study

upgrade
v. 英 /ˌʌpˈɡreɪd/
美 /ˌʌpˈɡreɪd/
n. 英 /ˈʌpɡreɪd/
美 /ˈʌpɡreɪd/

v. 1. 提升；提拔
She has been upgraded to deputy manager. 她晋升为副经理了。

2. 改善；使升级
The system has been upgraded. 系统已经升级了。

3. 使升舱；使（旅馆房间等）升级
I was upgraded from economy to business class. 我从经济舱升到了商务舱。

n. 1. 升级
The upgrade to the latest version will cost 200 dollars.
升级到最新版本将花费 200 美元。

2. 升舱；（旅馆房间等）升级
Can I get a room upgrade? 可以给我升级房间吗？

---

05 其他问题

Could you please bring my baggage up to my room? 能帮我把行李拿到房间吗？
How can we get to our room? 我们怎么去房间呢？

场景对话 Conversation

A: Hi, what can I do for you?
B: I would like to check in. I have a reservation.
A: Okay. May I see some IDs, please?
B: Here you are.

A：您好，我能为您做些什么吗？
B：我要办理入住手续。我预订了房间。
A：好的。请出示您的身份证明。
B：给你。

Lesson 28　客房服务 Room Service

词汇 Vocabulary

shampoo	英 /ʃæm'puː/	美 /ʃæm'puː/	洗发水
Wi-Fi	英 /'waɪ faɪ/	美 /'waɪ faɪ/	无线网络
password	英 /'pɑːswɜːd/	美 /'pæswɜːrd/	密码
laundry service	英 /'lɔːndri 'sɜːvɪs/	美 /'lɔːndri 'sɜːrvɪs/	洗衣服务
iron	英 /'aɪən/	美 /'aɪərn/	
=press	英 /pres/	美 /pres/	熨
dry-clean	英 /ˌdraɪ 'kliːn/	美 /ˌdraɪ 'kliːn/	干洗
wake-up call 叫醒电话		body wash 沐浴露	

实用表达 Useful Expressions

01　寻求服务

I'd like a wake-up call at 7 o'clock. 请在早上 7 点钟打电话叫醒我。
Can I get more shampoo and body wash? 可以提供更多的洗发水和沐浴露吗？
What's the Wi-Fi code/password? 无线网络的密码是多少？
Do you offer laundry service? 你们提供洗衣服务吗？
Where can we have our laundry done? 衣服送到哪里洗？
I want to have this shirt ironed/pressed. 请帮我熨一下这件衬衫。
Can you dry-clean this coat for me? 你能帮我干洗一下这件大衣吗？

词汇精讲 Word Study

laundry
英 /'lɔːndri/
美 /'lɔːndri/

n. 1. 洗衣房，洗衣店
She sent the clothes to the laundry. 她把衣服送到了洗衣店。
2. 待洗的衣服；洗好的衣服
There is a pile of dirty laundry on the chair. 椅子上有一堆脏衣服。

iron
英 /'aɪən/
美 /'aɪərn/

n. 1. 铁
She had a will of iron. 她有钢铁般的意志。
2. 熨斗
I bought a steam iron. 我买了一个蒸汽熨斗。
v. 熨烫
I need to iron that dress before I can wear it. 我得先把那件连衣裙熨平再穿。

press
英 /pres/
美 /pres/

n. 1. 报章杂志；印刷媒体
The story was reported in the press. 这件事已在报刊上报道了。
2. 新闻记者
Christie looked relaxed and calm as he faced the press.
面对记者的时候，克里斯蒂显得放松而镇静。

3. 印刷机
We were able to watch the books rolling off the presses.
我们可以看到书本从印刷机上源源不断地印出。

4. 报道，评论
The airline got a bad press recently. 这家航空公司最近受到了媒体的批评。

v. 1. （被）压，挤
He pressed a handkerchief to his nose. 他用手绢捂住了鼻子。

2. 将……塞进；把……按入
He pressed a coin into her hand. 他把一枚硬币塞进她手里。

3. 坚持；反复强调
I don't want to press the point , but you do owe me 200 dollars.
我不想总提这一点，但你确实欠我 200 美元。

4. 熨平
My suit needs pressing. 我的西服该熨了。

02 点餐

Is room service available around the clock?
客房送餐服务是全天都有吗？

What time is breakfast served?
早餐几点供应？

I would like to order two burgers.
Please send them to Room 233.
我要点两个汉堡。请送到 233 房间。

短语精讲 Phrase Study

- around the clock 全天候；夜以继日
They worked around the clock to save people.
他们夜以继日地工作来救人。
The police watched the house around the clock.
警方全天候地监视着这座房子。

场景对话 Conversation

A: Hello, can I get more shampoo and body wash?
B: Sure. Anything else?
A: I would like to order two burgers.
B: Right away.

A：你好，能再给我一些洗发水和沐浴露吗？
B：当然。还有其他的需要吗？
A：我想点两个汉堡。
B：马上给您送到。

Lesson 29　投诉
Filing Complaints

词汇 Vocabulary

television	英 /ˈtelɪvɪʒ(ə)n/	美 /ˈtelɪvɪʒ(ə)n/	电视
toilet	英 /ˈtɔɪlət/	美 /ˈtɔɪlət/	抽水马桶
shower	英 /ˈʃaʊə(r)/	美 /ˈʃaʊər/	淋浴器
hairdryer	英 /ˈheədraɪə(r)/	美 /ˈherdraɪər/	吹风机

air conditioner 空调
power socket/outlet 电源插座

(socket	英 /ˈsɒkɪt/	美 /ˈsɑːkɪt/	〈电源〉插座）
(outlet	英 /ˈaʊtlet/	美 /ˈaʊtlet/	〈电源〉插座）

electric kettle 电水壶

(electric	英 /ɪˈlektrɪk/	美 /ɪˈlektrɪk/	用电的）
(kettle	英 /ˈket(ə)l/	美 /ˈket(ə)l/	〈烧水用的〉壶）

实用表达 Useful Expressions

01　开头

I have a complaint. 我有事要投诉。
I want to complain to your manager. 我要向你们的经理投诉。

> **词汇精讲 Word Study**
>
> **complaint**
> 英 /kəmˈpleɪnt/
> 美 /kəmˈpleɪnt/
>
> n. 抱怨；埋怨；投诉；控告
> I'd like to make a complaint.
> 我有事要投诉。
>
> **complain**
> 英 /kəmˈpleɪn/
> 美 /kəmˈpleɪn/
>
> v. 抱怨；埋怨；发牢骚
> He never complains. 他从不抱怨。
> You are always complaining! 你总是在抱怨！

02　投诉事项

（1）通用句型

The air conditioner isn't working. 空调用不了。
There's something wrong with the TV. 电视出了点问题。

（2）具体表达

I can't open the door with the room key. 这个房卡打不开房门。
The toilet is blocked. 马桶堵住了。

The water won't drain from the shower. 淋浴排不出水。
There is no hot water. 没有热水。
The Internet is so slow. 网很慢。
It's very noisy in the next room. 隔壁房间很吵。
The food I ordered one hour ago still hasn't arrived. 我一个小时前点的食物还没有送来。
My laundry hasn't been sent back yet. 我送洗的衣服还没有送还。

词汇精讲 Word Study

block
英 /blɒk/
美 /blɑːk/

n. 1. （方形平面）大块；立方体
We need a block of wood. 我们需要一大块木头。
2. 大楼；（成组建筑中的）一栋楼房
She showed me around the office block. 她带我参观了办公大楼。
3. 街区
We live on the same block. 我们住在同一个街区。
4. （东西的）一批，一组；（时间的）一段
I deleted several blocks of text in the document. 我删除了文件中的几段文字。

v. 1. 堵塞；阻塞
The toilet is blocked. 马桶堵住了。
2. 堵住（某人的路等）；挡住（某人的视线等）
A fallen tree is blocking the road. 倒下来的树把路给挡住了。
3. 妨碍；阻碍
They tried to block the acquisition. 他们试图阻止这次的收购。

drain
英 /dreɪn/
美 /dreɪn/

v. 排去，放水
Drain the swimming pool. 把游泳池的水放掉。

n. 1. 耗竭
Raising two kids is a big drain on their resources.
抚养两个孩子对于他们来说是巨大的消耗。
2. 排水沟，排水管
They are in charge of cleaning drains. 他们负责清理下水道。

03 结尾

Can you send someone to fix it? 你能派人过来修一下吗?
Can you solve this for me? 你能帮我解决一下吗?

场景对话 Conversation

A: My air conditioner is not working. Can you send someone to fix it?
B: Okay, right away.

A：我的空调坏了，你能派人来修一下吗?
B：好的，马上去。

Lesson 30　退房及后续服务
Check-out

词汇 Vocabulary

cash	英/kæʃ/	美/kæʃ/		现金
receipt	英/rɪˈsiːt/	美/rɪˈsiːt/		收据
invoice	英/ˈɪnvɔɪs/	美/ˈɪnvɔɪs/		发票

hotel reception/front desk 宾馆接待处 / 前台
check out 办理退房手续　　　　　　room key/key card 房卡
extra fee 额外的费用　　　　　　　credit card 信用卡

实用表达 Useful Expressions

01　续住

A: Excuse me, sir, are you ready to check out?
先生，打扰了，请问您准备退房了吗？
B: I would like to extend my stay for another day, please. 我想续住一晚。
A: Okay, no problem. 好的，没问题。

> **词汇精讲 Word Study**
> **extend**
> 英/ɪkˈstend/
> 美/ɪkˈstend/
>
> v. 1. 延长，扩大
> Don't worry. The deadline has been extended. 别担心，截止日期延长了。
> 2. 提供，给予
> I would like to extend my thanks to you. 我想向你表示感谢。
> 3. （使）伸展，（使）达到
> She extended her hand to greet me. 她伸出手和我打招呼。

02　退房时间

What's the latest checkout time? 请问最晚什么时候必须退房？
May I check out at 14:00? 我可以下午两点退房吗？
I'll be ready to leave in ten minutes. 10 分钟后我就可以准备退房了。

03　其他服务

（1）行李

I would like to have someone pick up my luggage. 我想请人来帮我提一下行李。

> **短语精讲 Phrase Study**
>
> • pick (sb./sth.) up
>   1. 接电话
>   I'll pick up the phone. 我来接这个电话。

> 2. （开车）接某人
>   I'll pick you up at the airport. 我开车去机场接你。
> 3. 增加，增强
>   The wind is picking up now. 现在风越刮越大了。
> 4. 搭讪
>   He goes to clubs to pick up girls. 他到夜店去找女生搭讪。

Can you send someone for my luggage, please? 可以麻烦你派人来帮我搬行李吗？

（2）出租车和机场巴士

Can you book a taxi for me? I'm going to the airport.
你可以帮我预订一辆出租车吗？我要去机场。

Could you book me on the airport shuttle bus? 可以帮我预订一下机场大巴吗？

04 突发情况

（1）丢房卡

I believe I lost my key card. I can't seem to find it now.
我觉得我把房卡弄丢了，现在好像找不到它。

（2）落东西

I lost my shirt in my room. Can you mail it to me?
我把我的衬衫落在屋里了。你能邮寄给我吗？

（3）额外消费

Why am I being charged this extra fee in my bill? I don't remember using the minibar.
为什么我的账单里有额外消费？我不记得自己用过迷你吧。

05 退房结账

I would like to check out. 我想退房结账。
I am checking out now. Give me the bill, please. 我想退房。请给我账单，谢谢。
Can I pay by credit card/in cash? 我可以刷卡/用现金支付吗？
Can I get a receipt? 你能给我一个收据吗？
Can you make out an invoice for me? 你能给我开张发票吗？

场景对话 Conversation

A: I would like to check out.
B: Okay. Please wait a minute.
A: Can you make out an invoice for me?
B: Sure.

A：我想退房。
B：好的，请稍等。
A：能给我开一张发票吗？
B：当然可以。

Unit 7　餐厅 Restaurant

Lesson 31　预订餐厅和到店
Making a Reservation and Arriving at the Restaurant

> **Part 1**　预订餐厅 Making a Reservation

词汇 Vocabulary

- 预订：
  reservation　　　英 /ˌrezəˈveɪʃn/　　　美 /ˌrezərˈveɪʃ(ə)n/　　　预订
  be booked up=be fully booked（酒店、餐馆等）订满，被订完

- 座位类型：
  terrace　　　英 /ˈterəs/　　　美 /ˈterəs/　　　露天平台
  non-smoking/smoking area 无烟区 / 吸烟区　　　private room 包厢

实用表达 Useful Expressions

01　是否有座

提问

I would like to make a <u>dinner</u> reservation for <u>Saturday night</u>. 我想预订周六晚上的晚餐。
May I book a table for <u>four</u>, please? 我可以预订一个四人座的桌位吗？

回答

（1）没有位置
I'm sorry, we are fully booked.＝I'm sorry, we are all booked up.
很抱歉，我们已经预订满了。

（2）有位置
How many people are in your party/group? 请问您一共几位呢？
回应：There are <u>five</u> of us. 我们一共五个人。

02　座位类型

Can I book a table <u>on the terrace</u>? 我可以预订一个露天阳台的桌位吗？
We prefer a table <u>in the non-smoking/smoking area</u>. 我想要无烟区 / 吸烟区的座位。
I want a table <u>by the window</u>. 我想要窗边的座位。
I would like to book <u>a private room for 10 people</u>. 我想订一个 10 个人的包厢。

03 修改预订

Please postpone my reservation to 8:00 p.m. 请把我的预约延迟到晚上 8 点。
I would like to make my reservation one hour earlier than the original time.
我想把我的预约时间提前一个小时。
Please change my reservation from tomorrow to Sunday next week.
请把我的预约从明天改到下星期日。

> **词汇精讲 Word Study**
>
> **postpone**
> 英 /pəˈspəʊn/
> 美 /poʊˈspoʊn/
>
> v. 延迟，延期
> We had to postpone the event due to the bad weather.
> 由于天气恶劣，我们不得不推迟活动。
> They decided to postpone the meeting until next week.
> 他们决定将会议推迟到下周。

04 取消预订

I'm sorry. I need to cancel my reservation for Saturday.
很抱歉，我需要取消周六的预订。

场景对话 Conversation

A: I would like to make a reservation for Saturday night.
B: How many people are in your group?
A: There are five of us.
B: Okay, no problem.

A：我想预订周六晚上的晚餐。
B：您有多少人？
A：我们有五个人。
B：好的，没问题。

Part 2　到店 Arriving at the Restaurant

实用表达 Useful Expressions

01 有预订

Hello, I have a reservation under the name of Jack. 你好，我有预订，名字叫杰克。

02 没有预订

（1）无需等位

A: Good evening. Table for two, please? 晚上好，能给我们一张两人桌吗？

B: Sure, right this way. 当然，这边请。

（2）需要等位

How long do I need to wait? 我需要等多久？

How many people are there ahead of us? 在我们前面还有多少人？

Could I take a look at the menu while we are waiting, please?
等待的时候我可以看看菜单吗？

词汇精讲 Word Study

ahead
英 /əˈhed/
美 /əˈhed/

ad. 1.（时间、空间）向前面，在前面
How many people are there ahead of us? 在我们前面还有多少人？

2. 提前；预先；提早
You need to check in two hours ahead. 您需要提前两个小时办理登机手续。

3. 占优势；领先
You need to work hard to keep ahead. 你要努力才能保持领先优势。

场景对话 Conversation

A: Good evening. Do you have a reservation?
B: Yes, I have a reservation under the name of Jack.
A: OK, right this way.

A: Good evening. What can I do for you?
B: Good evening. Table for two, please?
A: I'm sorry. We are all booked up.
B: How long do I need to wait?
A: Maybe half an hour.
B: OK, could I take a look at the menu while we are waiting?
A: Of course. Here you are.
B: Thank you.

A：晚上好，请问您有预订吗？
B：有，我用杰克的名字预订的。
A：好的，这边请。

A：晚上好，我能为您做些什么？
B：晚上好，能给我们一张两人桌吗？
A：很抱歉，我们这儿都订满了。
B：我需要等多久？
A：大概半个小时吧。
B：好的，等的时候我能看一下菜单吗？
A：当然可以，给您。
B：谢谢。

Lesson 32 点餐 Ordering Food

词汇 Vocabulary

- **特色菜：**

specialty	英 /ˈspeʃəlti/	美 /ˈspeʃəlti/	特色菜

  local dishes 地方菜　　　　　　　　chef's special 主厨特选（主厨特别推荐的菜品）

- **开胃菜：**

appetizer	英 /ˈæpɪtaɪzə(r)/	美 /ˈæpɪtaɪzər/	（美）开胃菜
starter	英 /ˈstɑːtə(r)/	美 /ˈstɑːrtər/	（英）开胃菜
salad	英 /ˈsæləd/	美 /ˈsæləd/	沙拉

  chicken wings 鸡翅　　　　　　　crab cakes 蟹肉饼

- **主菜：**

entrée	英 /ˈɒntreɪ/	美 /ˈɑːntreɪ/	(main course)主菜
steak	英 /steɪk/	美 /steɪk/	牛排
chicken	英 /ˈtʃɪkɪn/	美 /ˈtʃɪkɪn/	鸡肉
salmon	英 /ˈsæmən/	美 /ˈsæmən/	三文鱼

  pork/lamb chop 猪/羊排　　　　　(barbecued) ribs（烤）肋排

- **甜品：**

dessert	英 /dɪˈzɜːt/	美 /dɪˈzɜːrt/	甜品
cheesecake	英 /ˈtʃiːzkeɪk/	美 /ˈtʃiːzkeɪk/	芝士蛋糕
pie	英 /paɪ/	美 /paɪ/	派
waffle	英 /ˈwɒfl/	美 /ˈwɑːfl/	华夫饼
pancake	英 /ˈpænkeɪk/	美 /ˈpænkeɪk/	薄饼

  bread pudding 面包布丁

- **汤：**

soup	英 /suːp/	美 /suːp/	汤

  the soup of the day 每日特色汤　　　onion soup 洋葱汤

lobster bisque	英 /ˈlɒbstə(r) bɪsk/	美 /ˈlɑːbstər bɪsk/	龙虾浓汤

- **配菜：**

cabbage	英 /ˈkæbɪdʒ/	美 /ˈkæbɪdʒ/	卷心菜

  side dish 配菜　　　baked potatoes 烤土豆　　　baked beans 烤豆角

- **牛排：**

rare	英 /reə(r)/	美 /rer/	生的

  medium-rare 三分熟

medium	英 /ˈmiːdiəm/	美 /ˈmiːdiəm/	五分熟

  medium-well 七分熟　　　　　well-done 全熟

- 鸡蛋：

scrambled egg	英 /'skræmb(ə)ld eg/	美 /'skræmbld eg/	炒蛋
hard-boiled egg	英 /ˌhɑːd 'bɔɪld eg/	美 /ˌhɑːrd 'bɔɪld eg/	全熟煮蛋
poached egg	英 /pəʊtʃt eg/	美 /poʊtʃt eg/	水煮荷包蛋
fried egg 煎蛋	sunny-side up 单面煎的	over easy 双面煎的	

- 口味：

salty	英 /'sɔːlti/	美 /'sɔːlti/	咸的
sour	英 /'saʊə(r)/	美 /'saʊər/	酸的
sweet	英 /swiːt/	美 /swiːt/	甜的
bitter	英 /'bɪtə(r)/	美 /'bɪtər/	苦的
spicy	英 /'spaɪsi/	美 /'spaɪsi/	辣的
light	英 /laɪt/	美 /laɪt/	口味清淡的
heavy	英 /'hevi/	美 /'hevi/	口味重的

实用表达 Useful Expressions

01 要菜单

A: Could I have the menu, please? 我能看一下菜单吗？
B: No problem. Here you are. 没问题，给您。

02 点餐

提问

Excuse me, may I take your order now? 打扰一下，我可以现在为您点餐吗？
Hello, are you ready to order? 您好，您准备好要点餐了吗？

回答

（1）还未决定

No, not yet. Give us a moment, please. 还没有，给我们几分钟，谢谢。
I'm not sure what to order. 我不确定要点什么。

（2）寻求推荐

What's your specialty? 你们餐厅的特色菜是什么？
What's the chef's special? 你们的主厨特选是什么？
What do you recommend?=Do you have any recommendations? 能推荐一些菜吗？

词汇精讲 Word Study

recommend
英 /ˌrekə'mend/
美 /ˌrekə'mend/

v. 1. 推荐；举荐
   Can you recommend a good restaurant? 你能推荐一家好的餐厅吗？
2. 劝告；建议
   I recommend you should see a doctor. 我建议你去看看医生。
3. 使受欢迎
   The hotel has much to recommend it. 这家酒店有很多值得称道的地方。

recommendation

英 /ˌrekəmen'deɪʃn/
美 /ˌrekəmen'deɪʃ(ə)n/

n. 1. 正式建议；提议
We decided to accept his recommendation. 我们决定接受他的提议。

2. 推荐；介绍
I bought this phone on his recommendation.
我是根据他的推荐买的这部手机。

3. 推荐信；求职介绍信
I need three letters of recommendation to support my application.
我的申请需要三封推荐信。

（3）针对具体菜品的问题和要求

How is this dish cooked? 这道菜是如何烹饪的？
Does the dish contain shrimp? I'm allergic to seafood. 这道菜含有虾肉吗？我对海鲜过敏。
What do the lamb chops come with? 羊排的配菜是什么？
I don't want it too spicy.
我不想这道菜做得太辣。
No garlic, please. 请不要放大蒜。
Don't put pepper in it, please.
不要放胡椒，谢谢。

词汇精讲 Word Study

allergic
英 /ə'lɜːdʒɪk/
美 /ə'lɜːrdʒɪk/

a. 1. 过敏的
I am allergic to cat hair.
我对猫毛过敏。

2. （对……）十分反感的
She is allergic to horror movies. 她很不喜欢恐怖片。

（4）关于酒水

A: What would you like to drink? 您要喝点什么？
B: I'd like a cup of coffee. 我要一杯咖啡。(Pepsi, please. 百事可乐，谢谢。)

（5）关于牛排

A: How would you like your steak/meat cooked? 您希望牛排几分熟？
B: Medium. 五分熟。

（6）关于鸡蛋

A: How would you like your eggs cooked? 您的鸡蛋要怎么做？
B: Sunny-side up, please. 单面煎蛋，谢谢。

💬 场景对话 Conversation

A: Hi, are you ready to order?
B: Yes, I'd like a steak and a potato salad.
A: OK. How would you like your meat cooked?
B: Medium-well, please.
A: No problem. What would you like to drink?
B: Pepsi, please.
A: Alright.

A：嗨，您准备好点菜了吗？
B：是的，我要一份牛排和一份土豆沙拉。
A：好的，牛排要几分熟？
B：七分熟。
A：没有问题。您想喝点什么？
B：百事可乐，谢谢。
A：好的。

Lesson 33 用餐和投诉
During the Meal and Making Complaints

Part 1 　用餐 During the Meal

词汇 Vocabulary

spoon	英/spuːn/	美/spuːn/	勺	
plate	英/pleɪt/	美/pleɪt/	盘子	
knife	英/naɪf/	美/naɪf/	刀	
fork	英/fɔːk/	美/fɔːrk/	叉	
bowl	英/bəʊl/	美/boʊl/	碗	

chopsticks	英/'tʃɒpstɪks/	美/'tʃɑːpstɪks/	筷子	
saucer	英/'sɔːsə(r)/	美/'sɔːsər/	茶碟	
napkin	英/'næpkɪn/	美/'næpkɪn/	餐巾	
serving spoon 公共汤勺				

实用表达 Useful Expressions

01　招呼服务员

A: Excuse me, could you come here, please? 劳驾，你可以过来一下吗？
B: Right away. 马上就来。

02　续杯

A: Could I please have my water refilled? 麻烦帮我加一下水，好吗？
B: Okay, right away. 好的，这就来。

A: Do you charge for refills? 续杯要收费吗？
B: Nope, refills are free/on the house.
续杯是免费的。

词汇精讲 Word Study

refill
英/ˌriːˈfɪl; ˈriːfɪl/
美/ˌriːˈfɪl; ˈriːfɪl/

v. 再装满；重新装满
He refilled her glass.
他又给她倒满了一杯。

n. 又一份同种饮料
Would you like a refill?
你再来一杯吗？

短语精讲 Phrase Study

- on the house（酒吧或饭店）免费提供的
It's on the house.
这是免费招待的。
All the drinks are on the house.
所有的酒水都免费提供。

03　换菜

Excuse me, can I change my order, please?
不好意思，请问我可以更改我点的餐吗？
May I change my order from whiskey to beer?
可以把我点的威士忌换成啤酒吗？

04 加菜

Could I have one more serving/helping of this dish? 这道菜我们可以再点一份吗?

We would like to have one more order of barbecued ribs. 我们想再点一份烤肋排。

05 催菜

Would you please serve us quicker? 可以请你上菜快一点吗?

Excuse me, what happened to our order? 不好意思,但是我们的菜怎么还没来?

Can you speed up our order? We're in a hurry. 可以快点上菜吗?我们赶时间。

06 增加餐具和座位

Could we please have one more plate? 我们能再要一个盘子吗?

Please give us some napkins. 请给我们一些餐巾纸。

Could you please add another chair here? I have another friend joining us for dinner. 可以在这里加一把椅子吗?我有朋友要过来和我们共进晚餐。

场景对话 Conversation

A: Excuse me, could you come here, please?
B: Coming right away.
A: Could you please add another chair here? I have another friend joining us for dinner.
B: Okay, wait a minute.

A:不好意思,你能过来一下吗?
B:马上就来。
A:能在这里再加一把椅子吗? 我还有一个朋友要来和我们一起吃晚饭。
B:好的,请稍等。

Part 2　投诉 Making Complaints

词汇 Vocabulary

	英	美	
stale	/steɪl/	/steɪl/	不新鲜的,变味的
soggy	/'sɒgi/	/'sɑːgi/	湿而软的;受潮的
overdone	/ˌəʊvə'dʌn/	/ˌoʊvər'dʌn/	
=overcooked	/ˌəʊvə'kʊkt/	/ˌoʊvər'kʊkt/	煮得过度的
underdone	/ˌʌndə'dʌn/	/ˌʌndər'dʌn/	
=undercooked	/ˌʌndə'kʊkt/	/ˌʌndər'kʊkt/	未煮透的,半生不熟的
tough	/tʌf/	/tʌf/	不嫩的,老的

实用表达 Useful Expressions

01 关于食物本身

It tastes/looks/smells weird/strange. 这道菜吃 / 看 / 闻起来很奇怪。

The dish is stale/not fresh at all. 这道菜一点儿也不新鲜。

I didn't expect my steak to be this salty. 我没想到我的牛排会这么咸。

The chicken is undercooked. 这鸡肉还没熟。

The steak is overcooked and tough. 这份牛排煎得太老了。

02 上错菜

This is not what I ordered. 这不是我点的菜。

What is this? I didn't order it. 这是什么？我没点这道菜。

03 其他问题

This place is too noisy. 这地方太吵了。

The people at the next table are smoking. 隔壁桌的客人在抽烟。

I was badly treated by a rude waiter. 你们的一个服务员态度非常恶劣。

场景对话 Conversation

A: Excuse me, the steak is overcooked and tough.

B: I really apologize for that. Allow me to replace it with a better one.

A: Alright.

A：打扰一下，这份牛排煎得太老了。

B：真的很抱歉，请允许我为您换一份更好的。

A：好吧。

Lesson 34 打包和结账
Paying the Check

词汇 Vocabulary

leftovers	英 /ˈleftəʊvə(r)z/	美 /ˈleftoʊvərz/	剩菜
bill	英 /bɪl/	美 /bɪl/	（英）账单
check	英 /tʃek/	美 /tʃek/	（美）账单
tip	英 /tɪp/	美 /tɪp/	小费
coupon	英 /ˈkuːpɒn/	美 /ˈkuːpɑːn/	优惠券

takeout bag=doggy/doggie bag 打包袋 　　　service charge 服务费

实用表达 Useful Expressions

01 打包

Can you please pack/wrap up the leftovers for me to go?
你可不可以帮我打包这些剩菜？
Can I get it to go?
我能打包带走吗？
Can you give me a doggie bag?
你可以给我拿个打包袋吗？

词汇精讲 Word Study

pack
英 /pæk/
美 /pæk/

v. 1. 捆扎，把……打包
I haven't packed yet.
我还没收拾行李呢。
2. 使挤在一起，塞满
Fans packed the stadium to watch the concert. 体育场挤满了观看演唱会的粉丝。

n. 包，小盒
He bought a pack of gum.
他买了一盒口香糖。

短语精讲 Phrase Study

- wrap（sth.）up
  1. 打包，包裹
  Can you please wrap up the leftovers for me to go?
  你可不可以帮我打包这些剩菜？
  2. 住口；闭嘴；别再捣乱
  You two, wrap it up!
  你们两个，别说话了！
  3. （使）穿得暖和
  Wrap up warm. It's cold outside.
  穿暖和点儿，外面冷。
  4. 完成，结束（协议或会议等）
  It's getting late. Let's wrap it up.
  时间不早了，我们结束今天的会议吧。

02 结账

Check, please. 我想结账。
How much is the bill? 多少钱？

03 AA 制

Let's go Dutch. 我们各付各的吧。

Let's split the bill. 我们平分账单吧。
Let's go fifty-fifty. 我们平分账单吧。

04 请客

Let me pick up/grab the check today. 今天由我来付钱。
I'll take care of it. /I'll get it this time. 我来买单就好了。
It's on me. =It's my treat. =I'll treat you. 我请客。

05 支付

I would like to pay in cash/by credit card. 我想用现金／信用卡支付。
May I have a receipt, please?
能开收据吗？
Can I use these coupons?
我可以使用这些优惠券吗？

> **词汇精讲 Word Study**
>
> **coupon**
> 英 /'ku:pɒn/
> 美 /'ku:pɑ:n/
>
> *n.* 1. （购物）票证；（购物）优惠券
> I have a lot of discount coupons.
> 我有很多打折优惠券。
> 2. （报纸、杂志附的）传单
> Please fill out the coupon and send it to us.
> 请填写传单并寄回给我们。

06 关于小费

（1）现金
Keep the change. 不用找了。

（2）刷卡
有些餐厅是由顾客自己在账单上写想要支付的小费金额。有些餐厅会提供选项，一般是账单金额的 10%~20%，顾客可以自由选择。

💬 场景对话 Conversation

A: Excuse me, can I get it to go, please?
B: Okay, let me get you a takeout bag.
A: Thank you.

A：对不起，我可以打包带走吗？
B：好的，我给您拿个打包袋。
A：谢谢。

A: Check, please.
B: Coming right away.
A: How much is the bill?
B: The total comes to 80 dollars.
A: Here you are.

A：我想结账。
B：马上就来。
A：多少钱？
B：总共是 80 美元。
A：给你。

Lesson 35 快餐店
Fast-food Restaurants

词汇 Vocabulary

- 常见的快餐店：
  KFC（Kentucky Fried Chicken）肯德基　　McDonald's 麦当劳
  Subway 赛百味　　　　　　　　　　　　Pizza Hut 必胜客
  Burger King 汉堡王　　　　　　　　　　Domino's Pizza 达美乐披萨

- 套餐类型：
  value meal 超值套餐　　　　　　　　　　kid's meal 儿童套餐
  bucket meal 全家桶套餐　　　　　　　　 Combo A/B/C A/B/C 套餐

- 主食：

sandwich	英 /ˈsænwɪtʃ/	美 /ˈsænwɪtʃ/	三明治
hamburger	英 /ˈhæmbɜːgə(r)/	美 /ˈhæmbɜːrgər/	汉堡包
cheeseburger	英 /ˈtʃiːzbɜːgə(r)/	美 /ˈtʃiːzbɜːrgər/	芝士汉堡

  pizza（6-inch/9-inch/12-inch）（6 寸/9 寸/12 寸）披萨

- 小食及甜品：

chips	英 /tʃɪps/	美 /tʃɪps/	（英）薯条
pie	英 /paɪ/	美 /paɪ/	派
sundae	英 /ˈsʌndeɪ; ˈsʌndi/	美 /ˈsʌndeɪ; ˈsʌndi/	圣代
salad	英 /ˈsæləd/	美 /ˈsæləd/	沙拉
doughnut	英 /ˈdəʊnʌt/	美 /ˈdoʊnʌt/	甜甜圈
cheesecake	英 /ˈtʃiːzkeɪk/	美 /ˈtʃiːzkeɪk/	芝士蛋糕

  hot dog 热狗　　　　　　　　　　　　　chicken wing 鸡翅
  French fries（美）薯条　　　　　　　　　mashed potato 土豆泥
  egg tart 蛋挞　　　　　　　　　　　　　(ice-cream) cone 圆筒
  milk shake 奶昔

- 饮品：

Coke	英 /kəʊk/	美 /koʊk/	可口可乐
Pepsi	英 /ˈpepsi/	美 /ˈpepsi/	百事可乐
Sprite	英 /spraɪt/	美 /spraɪt/	雪碧
coffee	英 /ˈkɒfi/	美 /ˈkɔːfi/	咖啡
milk	英 /mɪlk/	美 /mɪlk/	牛奶
soda	英 /ˈsəʊdə/	美 /ˈsoʊdə/	苏打水

  iced tea 冰茶　　　　　　　　　　　　　orange juice 橙汁

milk/bubble tea 奶茶

- 杯子大小：

small	英 /smɔːl/	美 /smɔːl/	小杯
middle	英 /ˈmɪd(ə)l/	美 /ˈmɪd(ə)l/	
=medium	英 /ˈmiːdiəm/	美 /ˈmiːdiəm/	中杯
large	英 /lɑːdʒ/	美 /lɑːrdʒ/	大杯

- 其他：

ketchup	英 /ˈketʃəp/	美 /ˈketʃəp/	番茄酱
straw	英 /strɔː/	美 /strɔː/	吸管
napkin	英 /ˈnæpkɪn/	美 /ˈnæpkɪn/	餐巾纸

实用表达 Useful Expressions

01 点餐

提问

May I help you? 我能为您做什么？
What can I do for you? 我能为您做什么？
Can I take your order? 我能为您点餐吗？

回答

A sandwich, please. 一个三明治，谢谢。
I'd like（to order）a cheeseburger, please. 我想要一个芝士汉堡，谢谢。
I'll take/have two value meals. 我要两份超值套餐。

02 薯条

A: What size fries do you want? 你要多大号的薯条？
B: Large/Medium/Small size. 大号 / 中号 / 小号。

03 饮料

A: What kind of drink would you like?
   =What would you like to drink? 你想喝什么饮料？
B: A small Sprite, please. 一小杯雪碧，谢谢。

A: Would you like Coke with ice? 你的可乐要加冰吗？
B: Yes, please. 加冰，谢谢。
  （No ice, please. 不加冰，谢谢。）

04 在这儿吃还是带走

A:（Will that be）For here or to go? 在这儿吃还是带走？
B: For here/to go, please. 在这儿吃 / 带走，谢谢。

05 辅助餐具和配料

Could I have extra ketchup? 我能再要一包番茄酱吗？
Do you have any straws? 你们有吸管吗？
Can I have some napkins? 我能要一些餐巾纸吗？

06 询问时间

When will that be ready? 什么时候能做好？
How long will it be? 需要多长时间？

场景对话 Conversation

A: Can I take your order, please?
B: I'd like a Combo A.
A: For here or to go?
B: To go.
A: Anything else?
B: And a chocolate sundae. That's it.
A: That will be 10 dollars.
B: Okay. Here you are.

A：您要点餐吗？
B：我要套餐 A。
A：在这儿吃还是带走？
B：带走。
A：还需要别的吗？
B：一个巧克力圣代，就是这些。
A：一共 10 美元。
B：好的，给你。

Unit 8　购物 Shopping

Lesson 36　选购 Shopping Around

词汇 Vocabulary

- 商店类型：

  supermarket　　　英 /ˈsuːpəmɑːkɪt/　　美 /ˈsuːpərmɑːrkɪt/　　超市
  shopping mall/center 购物中心　　department store 百货商场
  outlet（store）奥特莱斯店（经销店，折扣店）
  convenience store 便利店　　grocery store 杂货店

- 商场设施：

  exit　　　　　英 /ˈeksɪt/　　　　美 /ˈeksɪt/　　　　出口
  directory　　英 /dəˈrektəri/　　美 /dəˈrektəri/　　商店目录
  bathroom　　英 /ˈbɑːθruːm/　　美 /ˈbæθruːm/
  =restroom　　英 /ˈrestruːm/　　美 /ˈrestruːm/　　厕所
  escalator　　英 /ˈeskəleɪtə(r)/　美 /ˈeskəleɪtər/　　手扶电梯
  elevator　　英 /ˈelɪveɪtə(r)/　　美 /ˈelɪveɪtər/　　（美）升降梯
  lift　　　　　英 /lɪft/　　　　　美 /lɪft/　　　　（英）升降梯
  stairs　　　英 /steəz/　　　　美 /sterz/　　　　楼梯
  main entrance 大门
  information desk 服务台
  fitting room 试衣间

- 商品类型：

  cosmetics　　英 /kɒzˈmetɪks/　　美 /kɑːzˈmetɪks/　　化妆品
  jewelry　　　英 /ˈdʒuːəlri/　　　美 /ˈdʒuːəlri/　　　珠宝
  electronics　英 /ˌlekˈtrɒnɪks/　　美 /ˌlekˈtrɑːnɪks/　电子产品
  sporting goods 体育用品　　women's clothing 女装
  men's clothing 男装　　children's clothing 童装
  women's shoes 女鞋　　men's shoes 男鞋

- 衣服的名称：

  （1）上身
  coat　　　　英 /kəʊt/　　　　美 /koʊt/　　　　外套
  sweater　　英 /ˈswetə(r)/　　美 /ˈswetər/　　毛衣
  shirt　　　　英 /ʃɜːt/　　　　　美 /ʃɜːrt/　　　　衬衫

T-shirt	英 /'ti: ʃɜːt/	美 /'ti: ʃɜːrt/	T 恤
hoodie	英 /'hʊdi/	美 /'hʊdi/	卫衣
jacket	英 /'dʒækɪt/	美 /'dʒækɪt/	夹克

（2）下身

skirt	英 /skɜːt/	美 /skɜːrt/	半身裙
dress	英 /dres/	美 /dres/	连衣裙
pants	英 /pænts/	美 /pænts/	（美）裤子
trousers	英 /'traʊzəz/	美 /'traʊzərz/	（英）裤子
jeans	英 /dʒiːnz/	美 /dʒiːnz/	牛仔裤
shorts	英 /ʃɔːts/	美 /ʃɔːrts/	短裤
sock	英 /sɒk/	美 /sɑːk/	袜子

- 其他：

suit	英 /suːt/	美 /suːt/	西装
swimming suit/trunks	英 /trʌŋks/	美 /trʌŋks/	泳衣 / 泳裤
pyjamas/pajamas	英 /pə'dʒɑːməz/	美 /pə'dʒɑːməz/	睡衣

- 尺码：

XS=extra small 特小码
S=small	英 /smɔːl/	美 /smɔːl/	小码
M=medium	英 /'miːdiəm/	美 /'miːdiəm/	中码
L=large	英 /lɑːdʒ/	美 /lɑːrdʒ/	大码

XL=extra large 特大码

- 领子：

V-neck	英 /'viː nek/	美 /'viː nek/	V 领
crew-neck	英 /ˌkruː 'nek/	美 /ˌkruː 'nek/	圆领

- 材质：

cotton	英 /'kɒtn/	美 /'kɑːt(ə)n/	棉
wool	英 /wʊl/	美 /wʊl/	羊毛
linen	英 /'lɪnɪn/	美 /'lɪnɪn/	亚麻布
leather	英 /'leðə(r)/	美 /'leðər/	皮革
silk	英 /sɪlk/	美 /sɪlk/	丝绸

实用表达 Useful Expressions

01 进入商店

A: Hi, what can I do for you? 您好，我能为您做些什么吗？
B: I'm just looking around. 我随便看看。

02 关于尺码

Do you have this coat in my size? 这外套有适合我的尺码吗？

Can you get me a size L? 能给我拿一个大号的吗？

This size doesn't fit me. Can I have a smaller/larger one?
这个尺寸不合适，能给我拿一件小/大一码的吗？

A: What's your size? 您穿什么尺码？
B: Small/Medium/Large. 小码/中码/大码。

03 关于材质

提问

What material is it made of?
这个是什么材料做的？

回答

It's 100% pure cotton. 这是百分之百纯棉的。
It's pure wool. 这是纯羊毛的。
It's real leather. 这是真皮的。

> **短语精讲** Phrase Study
>
> - make of 指看得出原材料，原材料的性质没有变化
>   The chair is made of wood.
>   这把椅子是由木头制成的。
> - make from 指看不出原材料，原材料的性质发生了变化
>   Paper is made from wood.
>   纸是由木头制成的。

04 关于颜色

Do you have this jacket in black? 这件夹克衫有黑色的吗？
Is this the only color? 这是唯一的颜色吗？
Do you have another color? 还有别的颜色吗？

05 关于其他

Could I get one with a V-neck/crew-neck? 拿件 V 字领/圆领的可以吗？
Will it shrink? 这个会缩水吗？
Will this sweater pill? 这件毛衣会起球吗？
Will the color fade? 会褪色吗？

词汇精讲 Word Study

shrink
英 /ʃrɪŋk/
美 /ʃrɪŋk/

v. 1. （使）收缩
My pants shrank after washed in water. 水洗后我的裤子缩水了。

2. 退缩，畏缩
I shrank back against the wall when he was shouting at me.
当他冲我大喊大叫时，我退到了墙根。

pill
英 /pɪl/
美 /pɪl/

v. 起球；结绒
Will this sweater pill? 这件毛衣会起球吗？

n. 药丸
You should take three pills a day. 你应该一天吃三片药。

06 试穿

Can I try it on? 我可以试穿一下吗？
Where are the fitting rooms? 试衣间在哪儿？

07 做决定

买：
I'll take it/them. 我要买这个/这些。
Give me two, please. 请给我两个。

不买：
I'll try another place. Thank you. 我再去其他地方看看，谢谢。
I think I'll pass. Thank you very much. 我想我还是不要了，非常感谢。

犹豫：
I haven't decided yet. 我还没有做好决定。
I'll think about it. Thanks, though. 我还要再考虑一下，不过还是要谢谢。

场景对话 Conversation

A: What's your size?
B: Can you get me a size L?
A: Okay, here you are.
B: Thank you. Can I try it on?
A: Of course.
B: Where are the fitting rooms?
A: They are just over there.

A：您穿多大号？
B：能给我一件大号的吗？
A：好的，给您。
B：谢谢。我可以试穿吗？
A：当然可以。
B：试衣间在哪里？
A：就在那边。

Lesson 37　讨价还价和打折促销
Bargaining and Sales

Part 1　讨价还价 Bargaining

词汇 Vocabulary

budget　　　英 /ˈbʌdʒɪt/　　　美 /ˈbʌdʒɪt/　　预算
discount　　英 /ˈdɪskaʊnt/　　美 /ˈdɪskaʊnt/　折扣
price range 价格范围　　　　lowest price 最低价
best offer 最低价

实用表达 Useful Expressions

01　表明态度

It's beyond my price range. 这超出我愿意支付的价格范围了。
That's over my budget. 这超出我的预算了。
It's a bit too much. 太贵了一点。

词汇精讲 Word Study

beyond
英 /bɪˈjɒnd/
美 /bɪˈjɑːnd/

ad.　在更远处；再往后
　　It's hard to tell what lies beyond. 往后很难说。
prep. 1. 在……的那边，远于
　　The village is beyond the river. 村庄在河的那边。
　　2. 迟于
　　We cannot allow the work to continue beyond the end of the year.
　　该工作必须在年前完成。
　　3. 超出；越出
　　The situation is beyond my control. 我已经无法控制这一局面。

02　讲价

Is there any discount? =Can I have a discount?=Would you give me a discount?
能给我打个折吗？

Can you give me a deal on this? 这能卖得便宜一点吗？

I'll consider it if you cut down/lower the price.
如果你把价钱降低点的话，我会考虑的。

What's the lowest price you are willing to go to?=What's your best offer?
你能给的最低价格是多少？

Would you take/accept <u>50 dollars</u>? 你接受 50 美元这个价格吗？

场景对话 Conversation

A: How much is it?
B: 200 dollars.
A: It's a bit too much. Can you give me a deal on this?
B: 180 dollars then.
A: Would you take 150 dollars?
B: Ummm... Alright.

A：多少钱？
B：200 美元。
A：有点太贵了。你能给我打折吗？
B：那 180 美元吧。
A：你能接受 150 美元吗？
B：嗯……好吧。

Part 2　打折促销 Sales

词汇 Vocabulary

sale	英 /seɪl/	美 /seɪl/	大减价

sales drive/campaign/promotion 促销活动
（campaign　英 /kæm'peɪn/　美 /kæm'peɪn/　活动）
（promotion　英 /prə'məʊʃ(ə)n/　美 /prə'moʊʃ(ə)n/　促销活动）
clearance sale 清仓大甩卖
（clearance　英 /'klɪərəns/　美 /'klɪrəns/　清除；排除）
BOGO（=buy one get one free）/two-for-one 买一赠一
on sale 廉价出售；促销　　　　　special offer 特价优惠

实用表达 Useful Expressions

01 询问是否有折扣或促销活动

Does your store have a clearance sale? 你们店有清仓甩卖的东西吗？
I'm curious if you have any deals or promotions going on?
我想知道你们有什么处理品或者促销活动吗？
Are all the goods on sale? 所有的商品都打折吗？

词汇精讲
Word Study

clearance
英 /'klɪərəns/
美 /'klɪrəns/

n. 1. 净空；余隙
　　 Make sure you allow enough clearance on each side.
　　 确保在两侧留有足够的间隙。
　 2. 许可（证），批准
　　 The plane will be taking off as soon as it gets clearance.
　　 一旦获得许可，飞机就会起飞。

3. （银行）票据交换，清算
   Clearance can take up to five days. 支票的兑现可能需要最多 5 天的时间。
4. 清除，清理
   Does your store have a clearance sale? 你们店有清仓甩卖的东西吗？

02 折扣的表达方式

75% off/20% off 打 2.5 折 / 打 8 折

Club members get a 15% discount. 会员可享受 8.5 折优惠。

These items are BOGO. 这些商品买一送一。

场景对话 Conversation

A: Are all the goods on sale?
B: No. Only these items are BOGO.
A: Okay. Oh, I like this one. How much is it?
B: It's 100 dollars.
A: Can I have a discount?
B: Well, I can give you a 20% discount.
A: Great. I'll take it.

A：所有的商品都打折吗？
B：不是，只有这些东西是买一送一的。
A：好的。噢，我喜欢这个。多少钱？
B：100 美元。
A：能给我打个折吗？
B：好吧，我可以给你打 8 折。
A：太好了。我就要它了。

知识拓展 More to Know

1. 百分数
   方法：基数词 +percent
   75%   seventy-five percent
   25%   twenty-five percent

2. 分数
   方法：分子用基数词表示，分母用序数词表示（当分子 >1 时，分母加 s）

   $\frac{1}{2}$ one half/a half

   $\frac{1}{3}$ one-third $\frac{2}{3}$ two-thirds

   $\frac{1}{4}$ one-fourth/one quarter/a quarter $\frac{3}{4}$ three-fourths/three quarters

   $3\frac{1}{4}$ three and one fourth $2\frac{5}{8}$ two and five-eighths

3. 小数
   0.2   point two   0.02   point zero/oh two
   0.002   point zero/oh zero/oh two   1.2   one point two
   1.22   one point twenty-two/one point two two
   1.223   one point two hundred and twenty-three/one point two two three

4. 钱的数量
   $5   five dollars
   $5.50   five dollars and fifty cents/five point fifty dollars/five, fifty

Lesson 38 结账
Paying

词汇 Vocabulary

checkout counter=cashier（desk）收银台
（cashier　　　英 /kæˈʃɪə(r)/　　　美 /kæˈʃɪr/　　　出纳员）
installment　　英 /ɪnˈstɔːlmənt/　　美 /ɪnˈstɔːlmənt/　　分期付款
cash　　　　　英 /kæʃ/　　　　　　美 /kæʃ/　　　　　现金
credit card 信用卡　　　　　　　　　paper/plastic bag 纸袋 / 塑料袋
delivery charge 运输费用

实用表达 Useful Expressions

01 询问地点

Where do I pay? 我在哪里结账？
Where is the checkout counter? 收银台在哪里？

02 询问价钱

How much is it? 这个多少钱？
What's the total?=How much are they? 一共多少钱？

03 分期付款

A: Can I pay by installments? 我可以分期付款吗？
B: Sorry, you must pay them in full. 抱歉，您必须全款支付。
　　Yes, you can purchase this TV in installments over 12 months.
　　可以，您可以按 12 个月分期付款购买这台电视。

> **词汇精讲 Word Study**
>
> **installment**
> 英 /ɪnˈstɔːlmənt/
> 美 /ɪnˈstɔːlmənt/
>
> n. 1. 分期付款，分期交付
> I paid for the computer in installments.
> 我以分期付款的方式买了这台电脑。
> 2.（分期连载的）部分
> The final installment in her trilogy will be adapted into a TV series.
> 她的三部曲的最后一部将被改编成电视连续剧。

04 支付方式

A: Are you paying in cash or by credit card? 您付现金还是用信用卡？
B: I will pay in cash/by credit card. 用现金 / 信用卡支付。

05 打包

A: Do you prefer paper or plastic bags? 你更喜欢纸袋还是塑料袋？

B: Paper/Plastic bag, please. 纸袋/塑料袋，谢谢。

A: Do you want it gift-wrapped? 需要精致包装吗？

B: Please wrap it with a ribbon. 请帮我用丝带包装。

A: Do you want them to be packed separately? 您需要分开包装吗？

B: Please wrap them individually. 请把它们分开包装。
Pack them together, please. 请把它们包在一起。

词汇精讲 Word Study

wrap
英 /ræp/
美 /ræp/

v. 裹，包，捆
Do you need to wrap the gift? 您需要把礼物包裹起来吗？

n. 披肩
He gave me a silk wrap as my birthday present. 他给了我一条丝绸披肩作为生日礼物。

06 送货

Please deliver it for me. 请替我送货。

Is there a delivery charge? 送货到家要另外收费吗？

How much is the delivery charge? 送货费用是多少？

词汇精讲 Word Study

deliver
英 /dɪˈlɪvə(r)/
美 /dɪˈlɪvər/

v. 1. 递送；投递；运送
We promise to deliver within 48 hours. 我们承诺在48小时内送到。

2. 发表；宣布；发布
The president will deliver a speech about schools. 总统将就学校问题发表讲话。

3. 履行诺言；不负所望；兑现
She always delivers on her promises. 她总是信守诺言。

4. 接生（婴儿）
The baby was delivered safely on Tuesday night. 婴儿在周二晚上平安出生。

delivery
英 /dɪˈlɪvəri/
美 /dɪˈlɪvəri/

n. 1. 投递；交付
Please pay for goods on delivery. 请货到付款。

2. 分娩
The delivery room is on the second floor. 产房在二楼。

3. 讲话方式
The politician's delivery is dull. 这个政客的演讲方式很无聊。

场景对话 Conversation

A: How much are they?
B: 200 dollars in total.
A: Okay.
B: Are you paying in cash or by credit card?
A: By credit card, please.
B: Do you want them to be packed separately?
A: Pack them together, please.
B: No problem.

A：这些多少钱？
B：总共 200 美元。
A：好的。
B：您是付现金还是用信用卡？
A：用信用卡，谢谢。
B：您要分开包装吗？
A：请打包在一起吧。
B：没问题。

Lesson 39 售后服务
After-Sales Service

词汇 Vocabulary

warranty　　英 /ˈwɒrənti/　　美 /ˈwɔːrənti/　　保修期
after-sales service 售后服务　　after-sales service department 售后服务部门

实用表达 Useful Expressions

01 取得联系

How can I contact the after-sales service department? 我如何才能与售后服务部门联系？
Where can I make a complaint? 我该去哪里投诉呢？

02 关于保修期

How long is the warranty (period)? 保修期多长时间？
Is it still under warranty? 它还在保修期内吗？
What about repairing after expiry? 保修期过了需要维修该怎么办？

> **词汇精讲 Word Study**
>
> **expiry**（UK）
> 英 /ɪkˈspaɪəri/　　美 /ɪkˈspaɪəri/
> **=expiration**（US）
> 英 /ˌekspəˈreɪʃ(ə)n/　美 /ˌekspəˈreɪʃ(ə)n/
>
> n.（文件、协议等的）满期，届期，到期
> The license can be renewed on expiry.
> 执照期满时可延期。

03 具体问题

提问

What's the matter with the product? 商品出了什么问题？

回答

（1）家电类

It's broken. 它已经坏了。
It doesn't work at all. 它根本就不能运转/工作。

（2）衣帽类

There is a huge tear in <u>this shirt</u>. 这件衬衫上有一个大裂口。
<u>The jeans</u> fade seriously. 这条牛仔裤褪色严重。
I found a stain here. 我在这儿发现一个污点。
It doesn't fit. 这件衣服不合身。

It's the wrong size. 尺码错了。

词汇精讲 Word Study

fade
英 /feɪd/
美 /feɪd/

v. 1. 褪色
The jeans fade seriously. 这条牛仔裤褪色严重。
2. 凋谢
The flower has faded. 这朵花已经凋谢了。
3. 逐渐消失
My memory of childhood fades as time goes by.
我的童年记忆随着时间的流逝慢慢消失。

04 退换货

Can I replace it if it doesn't fit? 如果不合适，可以来换吗？
I want to return this. 我想退了这件商品。
I would like a refund on this coat. 我想退了这件大衣。

词汇精讲 Word Study

replace
英 /rɪˈpleɪs/
美 /rɪˈpleɪs/

v. 1. 代替，取代
Do you think robots will replace all the workers in the future?
你觉得机器人会在未来取代所有的工人吗？
2. 更换，调换
All the old computers need replacing. 所有的旧电脑都需要更换。
3. 把……放回原处
I replaced the cup on the table. 我把杯子放回桌上了。

refund
英 /ˈriːfʌnd; rɪˈfʌnd/
美 /ˈriːfʌnd; rɪˈfʌnd/

n. 退款
I would like a refund on this T-shirt. 我想退了这件T恤。
v. 退还（钱款）
We cannot refund you in full. 我们不会全额退还给您。

💬 场景对话 Conversation

A: What's the matter with the product?
B: It's broken.
A: Is it still under warranty?
B: Yes, it is.
A: Then you can come to our after-sales service department for repairing.
B: Okay. Thanks.

A：产品有什么问题？
B：它坏了。
A：还在保修期内吗？
B：是的。
A：那么您可以到我们的售后服务部来修理。
B：好的，谢谢。

A: Hi, how can I help you?
B: I want to return this. It doesn't fit. It's the wrong size.
A: Oh, let me check it for you.

A：您好，我能为您做什么？
B：我想退掉这个。它不适合，尺寸不对。
A：哦，让我检查一下。

Lesson 40　网上购物
Online Shopping

词汇 Vocabulary

- 网站相关：

account	英 /ə'kaʊnt/	美 /ə'kaʊnt/	账户
password	英 /'pɑːswɜːd/	美 /'pæswɜːrd/	密码
login	英 /'lɒgɪn/	美 /'lɔːgɪn/	登录
logout	英 /'lɒgaʊt/	美 /'lɔːgaʊt/	退出登录

- 配送相关：

package	英 /'pækɪdʒ/	美 /'pækɪdʒ/	包裹
compensation	英 /ˌkɒmpen'seɪʃ(ə)n/	美 /ˌkɑːmpen'seɪʃ(ə)n/	赔偿金

shipping fee 运费　　　　　　　　delivery service 送货服务
shipping address 收货地址　　　　shipping range 配送范围

- 运输类型：

by air 空运　　　by ship 水运　　　by train 铁路运输

实用表达 Useful Expressions

01　创建账号

I want to set up an account on eBay.
我想注册一个易趣网的账户。
I'd like to create an account on Amazon.
我想创建一个亚马逊的账号。

短语精讲 Phrase Study

- set sth. up
  1. 创建；建立；开办
     He's set up his own business.
     他创办了自己的公司。
  2. 安排；策划
     I've set up a meeting for Monday.
     我已安排好在周一开会。
  3. 安装好，装配好，调试好（设备或机器）
     You need to set up the equipment in advance. 你需要提前调试好设备。

02　关于运费

How much is the shipping fee?
运费是多少？
The shipping fee is ridiculous/too expensive.
这个运费太离谱了/太贵了。
The seller offers free delivery.
卖家提供免费送货服务。

03　关于派送时间

When will the product be delivered? 产品什么时候送达？
How long does it take <u>by air</u>? 这个寄空运要多久？

Can the product be delivered on the same day? 我订的产品能当天送达吗?

04 没有收到快递

Have my goods been shipped? 我的货发出了吗?
I haven't received my package for 15 days. Is it lost?
我半个月了还没有收到包裹,它是丢了吗?
Can you help me track my package? 你能帮忙追查一下我的快递到哪儿了吗?
Can I get compensation if my package is lost? 如果我的包裹丢失了,有没有赔偿金?

词汇精讲 Word Study

ship
英 /ʃɪp/
美 /ʃɪp/

v. 1. 船运;运输,运送
These products are gonna be shipped around the world.
货物将被运往世界各地。
2. 上市,把……推向市场
The software is due to ship next month. 这个软件定于下月上市。

track
英 /træk/
美 /træk/

v. 1. 跟踪;追踪
They tracked the tiger for miles. 他们追踪了这只老虎数英里。
2. 跟踪(进展情况)
The study tracked 100 patients for five years.
该研究对 100 名患者进行了五年的跟踪调查。
3. 跟踪摄影;移动摄影
The camera eventually tracked away. 摄影机最终将镜头推远。

n. 1. 小道,小径
We set off over a mountain track. 我们沿着一条山间小路出发。
2. (人、动物或车辆留下的)足迹,踪迹;车辙
We followed the bear's tracks in the snow.
我们跟着熊在雪地上留下的足迹走。
3. (火车)轨道
You'll find your train at track 8. 你将在 8 号轨道找到你的列车。
4. 赛道,跑道
The running track needs to be lengthened. 这条跑道需要加长。
5. (移动的)路径,路线,方向
The police are on the track of the thieves. 警察正在追踪窃贼。

compensation
英 /ˌkɒmpenˈseɪʃ(ə)n/
美 /ˌkɑːmpenˈseɪʃ(ə)n/

n. 补偿(或赔偿)物;(尤指)赔偿金,补偿金
He's still fighting for compensation after the accident.
他还在力争事故后的赔偿。
If you're still not satisfied, you can ask for compensation.
如果你仍然不满意的话,你可以索要赔偿金。

场景对话 Conversation

A: I haven't received my package yet. Could you help me track it?

B: Sure. May I have your order number, please?

A: Let me see. It's 599577809.

B: I'm sorry. Your goods haven't been shipped due to our carelessness.

A: Can I get compensation for the delay?

B: We will return your shipping fee.

A: OK, thanks.

B: No problem.

A：我还没有收到我的包裹。你能帮我追踪一下吗？

B：当然可以。请问您的订单号是多少？

A：让我看看。是599577809。

B：很抱歉。由于我们的疏忽，您的货物还没有发货。

A：我能得到延迟发货的赔偿吗？

B：我们会退还您的运费。

A：好的，谢谢。

B：没问题。

Unit 9　娱乐 Entertainment

Lesson 41　游乐园
Going to the Amusement Park

词汇 Vocabulary

- 相关词汇：

  amusement park 游乐园　　　theme park 主题乐园
  Disneyland 迪士尼乐园　　　Universal Studios 环球影城
  Lego Land 乐高乐园

- 游乐设施：

  carousel　　　　英/ˌkærə'sel/　　　美/ˌkærə'sel/　　　旋转木马
  roller coaster 过山车　　　　　　　Ferris wheel 摩天轮
  pirate ship 海盗船　　　　　　　　cable car 缆车
  bumper car 碰碰车

- 票的类型：

  adult ticket 成人票　　　child ticket 儿童票　　　senior ticket 老人票
  student ticket 学生票　　all-inclusive ticket 通票　full-price ticket 全价票
  half-price ticket 半价票

- 相关地点：

  entrance　　　　英/'entrəns/　　　　美/'entrəns/　　　入口
  bathroom　　　　英/'bɑːθruːm/　　　美/'bæθruːm/
  =restroom　　　 英/'restruːm/　　　 美/'restruːm/　　　厕所
  ticket office 售票处　　　　　　　 gift shop =souvenir shop 纪念品店
  (souvenir　　　英/ˌsuːvə'nɪə(r)/　　美/ˌsuːvə'nɪr/　　　纪念品)

- 相关表演：

  parade　　　　　英/pə'reɪd/　　　　美/pə'reɪd/　　　　游行
  fireworks show/display 烟火表演
  (firework　　　英/'faɪəwɜːk/　　　美/'faɪərwɜːrk/　　　烟火；烟花)

实用表达 Useful Expressions

01 买票

（1）询问位置

Where can I buy a ticket? 请问在哪里可以买票？

119

Where is the ticket office? 售票处在哪里?

(2) 询问票价

How much is the admission ticket? 入场券/门票多少钱?
Can I get a student discount? 我可以享受学生折扣吗?
Can kids/seniors get admitted for free? 小孩/老人可以免费进入吗?

词汇精讲
Word Study

admission
英 /əd'mɪʃ(ə)n/
美 /əd'mɪʃ(ə)n/

n. 1. (机构、组织等的)准许加入,进入权
How many students will gain admission to MIT this year?
今年有多少学生会被麻省理工学院录取?
2. (尤指对过错、罪行的)承认,招认,招供
He is a thief by his own admission. 他自己供认是小偷。
3. 入场费;门票费
How much is the admission ticket? 门票多少钱?

admit
英 /əd'mɪt/
美 /əd'mɪt/

v. 1. 承认,供认
I admit that you were right. 我承认你之前是对的。
2. 准许……进入
Can kids get admitted for free? 小孩可以免费进入吗?

(3) 正式买票

I would like to buy two adult tickets and one child ticket. 我要买两张成人票和一张儿童票。
Admission for one, please. 请给我一张门票。

02 存包

Where can I store my bag/baggage? 我可以在哪里存放包/行李?
May I store my bag? 我可以存包吗?

03 进入园区

Where is the entrance of the ride? 这个游乐设施的入口在哪里?
Do you know where the bathroom/restroom is? 你知道厕所在哪儿吗?
Is there a fireworks show/display tonight? 今晚有烟火表演吗?
Is the roller coaster open today? 过山车今天开放吗?

04 拍照留念

(1) 询问是否允许拍照

A: Are we allowed to take pictures here? 这里允许拍照吗?
　　Can I take a picture here? 我能在这儿拍照吗?

B：Yes, pictures are allowed here. 可以，这里允许拍照。
No, cameras are not allowed right now. 不行，现在不允许拍照。

（2）请求别人帮自己拍照

Would you take a picture for us? 您能给我们拍张照吗？
Just press here, please. 按这里就行了。
Say cheese！说茄子！

05 购买纪念品

Is there a gift shop nearby? 这儿附近有礼品店吗？
Could you pack and ship these souvenirs for me? 你可以帮我把这些纪念品打包运走吗？

词汇精讲 Word Study

nearby
英 /ˌnɪəˈbaɪ/
美 /ˌnɪrˈbaɪ/

a. 附近的
We had dinner in a nearby restaurant. 我们在一个附近的餐厅吃了晚餐。
ad. 在附近
She lived nearby. 她住在附近。

场景对话 Conversation

A: Excuse me, how much is the admission ticket?
B: 80 dollars for an adult.
A: Can kids get admitted for free?
B: No, but kids can enjoy 50% off on the ticket.
A: Alright, I would like two adult tickets and one child ticket.
B: That will be 200 dollars.
A: OK, here you are.

A：请问，门票多少钱一张？
B：成人 80 美元。
A：儿童可以免费入场吗？
B：不可以，但是儿童可以享受 5 折的票价。
A：好的，我要两张成人票和一张儿童票。
B：一共 200 美元。
A：好的，给你。

Lesson 42 酒吧
Going to the Bar

词汇 Vocabulary

- 酒的类型：

  beer 啤酒

  draft beer 生啤酒　　　　　　　bottled beer 瓶装啤酒
  light beer 淡啤酒，低度啤酒　　dark beer 黑啤酒，高度啤酒

  liquor 烈酒

brandy	英 /ˈbrændi/	美 /ˈbrændi/	白兰地
whiskey	英 /ˈwɪski/	美 /ˈwɪski/	威士忌
scotch	英 /skɒtʃ/	美 /skɑːtʃ/	苏格兰威士忌
vodka	英 /ˈvɒdkə/	美 /ˈvɑːdkə/	伏特加

  wine 葡萄酒

  red wine 红酒　　　　　　　　white wine 白葡萄酒

  others 其他

  | cocktail | 英 /ˈkɒkteɪl/ | 美 /ˈkɑːkteɪl/ | 鸡尾酒 |
  | sake | 英 /ˈsɑːki/ | 美 /ˈsɑːki/ | 日本清酒 |

- 相关人员：

bouncer	英 /ˈbaʊnsə(r)/	美 /ˈbaʊnsər/	门卫 / 保安
bartender	英 /ˈbɑːtendə(r)/	美 /ˈbɑːrtendər/	酒保
designated driver 代驾			
(designated	英 /ˈdezɪɡneɪtɪd/	美 /ˈdezɪɡneɪtɪd/	指定的)

实用表达 Useful Expressions

01　点酒

（1）点烈酒

I want my scotch on the rocks. 我的苏格兰威士忌要加冰。
I want a straight whiskey. 我要一杯不加冰的威士忌。

（2）点啤酒

A: Can I get a beer, please? 请给我来杯啤酒好吗？
B: Sure, bottled or draft? 当然可以，要瓶装的还是生啤？

A: Draft, please. 生啤，谢谢。

02 倒酒

A: Say when. 够了就说。
B: Enough/Thanks/Stop. 够了。

03 请别人喝酒

Can I buy you a drink? 我能请你喝一杯吗？

Can I interest you in a glass of red wine? 能赏脸喝一杯红酒吗？

04 举杯庆祝

Cheers! / Bottoms up! 干杯！

I'd like to propose a toast to the new couple!
我提议为这对新婚夫妇干杯！

Here's to Tom for his new job / our friendship!
为汤姆的新工作干杯！/ 为我们的友谊干杯！

All the best!
一切顺利，万事如意！（用于表示祝愿）

> **短语精讲** Phrase Study
>
> - propose a toast（to sb.）（为某人）祝酒 / 干杯
>   I want to propose a toast to my mother!
>   我想为我的母亲干杯！

词汇精讲 Word Study

propose
英 /prəˈpəʊz/
美 /prəˈpoʊz/

v. 1. 提议，建议，提出
What would you propose? 你想提什么建议？

2. 提名，推荐
He was proposed as manager. 他被推荐为经理。

3. 打算，计划
How do you propose solving the problem? 你打算怎么解决这个问题？

4. 求婚
He proposed to me! 他向我求婚了！

toast
英 /təʊst/
美 /toʊst/

n. 1. 烤面包
She had two pieces of toast and a cup of milk for breakfast.
她早餐吃了两片烤面包和一杯牛奶。

2. 祝酒；祝酒词
I'd like to propose a toast to the bride and groom!
我提议为新娘新郎的幸福干杯！

v. 1. 烘，烤
Do you want this bread toasted? 你要吃烤面包吗？

2. 向……祝酒，为……干杯
We toasted the success of the program. 我们为这个项目的成功干杯。

场景对话 Conversation

A: Hi, what can I get you?
B: Can I get a beer, please?
A: Sure, bottled or draft?
B: Draft, please.

A: Hi, can I have a drink?
B: Sure, what would you like to drink?
A: I want a straight whiskey.
B: Okay, wait a minute.

A：您好，您要点什么？
B：能给我来杯啤酒吗？
A：当然，瓶装的还是生的？
B：生啤酒，谢谢。

A：您好，给我来杯喝的好吗？
B：当然可以，您想喝点什么？
A：我要一杯不加冰的威士忌。
B：好的，请稍等。

Lesson 43 咖啡厅
Going to the Café

词汇 Vocabulary

- 咖啡类型：

espresso	英 /eˈspresəʊ/	美 /eˈspresoʊ/	意式浓缩咖啡
latte	英 /ˈlɑːteɪ/	美 /ˈlɑːteɪ/	拿铁
mocha	英 /ˈmɒkə/	美 /ˈmoʊkə/	摩卡
cappuccino	英 /ˌkæpuˈtʃiːnəʊ/	美 /ˌkæpuˈtʃiːnoʊ/	卡布奇诺
Americano	英 /əˌmerɪˈkɑːnəʊ/	美 /əˌmerɪˈkɑːnoʊ/	美式咖啡
macchiato	英 /ˌmækiˈɑːtəʊ/	美 /ˌmɑːkiˈɑːtoʊ/	玛奇朵

- 配料：

foam	英 /fəʊm/	美 /foʊm/	泡沫
cream	英 /kriːm/	美 /kriːm/	奶油
sugar	英 /ˈʃʊɡə(r)/	美 /ˈʃʊɡər/	糖
caramel	英 /ˈkærəmel/	美 /ˈkærəml/	焦糖
chocolate	英 /ˈtʃɒklət/	美 /ˈtʃɔːklət/	巧克力

- 牛奶：

non-fat/skimmed milk 脱脂牛奶　　low-fat milk 低脂牛奶
whole milk 全脂奶　　soy milk 豆奶

- 是否含有咖啡因：

caffeine	英 /ˈkæfiːn/	美 /kæˈfiːn/	咖啡因
caffeinated	英 /ˈkæfɪneɪtɪd/	美 /ˈkæfɪneɪtɪd/	含咖啡因的
decaf	英 /ˈdiːkæf/	美 /ˈdiːkæf/	低咖
decaffeinated	英 /diːˈkæfɪneɪtɪd/	美 /diːˈkæfɪneɪtɪd/	脱咖啡因的

- 糖浆：

syrup	英 /ˈsɪrəp/	美 /ˈsɪrəp/	糖浆
vanilla	英 /vəˈnɪlə/	美 /vəˈnɪlə/	香草口味
hazelnut	英 /ˈheɪzlnʌt/	美 /ˈheɪzlnʌt/	榛果口味
caramel	英 /ˈkærəmel/	美 /ˈkærəml/	焦糖口味
almond	英 /ˈɑːmənd/	美 /ˈɑːmənd/	杏仁口味
peppermint	英 /ˈpepəmɪnt/	美 /ˈpepərmɪnt/	胡椒薄荷口味

- 咖啡杯的大小：

small	英 /smɔːl/	美 /smɔːl/	小杯

medium　　　英 /ˈmiːdiəm/　　　美 /ˈmiːdiəm/　　　中杯
large　　　　英 /lɑːdʒ/　　　　美 /lɑːrdʒ/　　　　大杯
extra large 超大杯

- 星巴克咖啡杯的大小：

Starbucks　　英 /ˈstɑːbʌks/　　美 /ˈstɑːrbʌks/　　星巴克
Tall　　　　　英 /tɔːl/　　　　 美 /tɔːl/　　　　　中杯
Grande　　　 英 /ˈgrɑːndeɪ/　　美 /ˈgrɑːndeɪ/　　 大杯
Venti　　　　英 /ˈventɪ/　　　 美 /ˈventɪ/　　　　超大杯

- 浓缩咖啡的份数：

single　　　英 /ˈsɪŋ(ə)l/　　　美 /ˈsɪŋ(ə)l/　　　单份
double　　　英 /ˈdʌb(ə)l/　　 美 /ˈdʌb(ə)l/　　 双份
triple　　　 英 /ˈtrɪp(ə)l/　　 美 /ˈtrɪp(ə)l/　　 三份

- 在店里喝还是带走：

for here 在店里喝　　　　　　to go 带走

实用表达 Useful Expressions

01 邀请别人

Hey, do you want to grab a cup of coffee later? 嘿，一会儿想去喝杯咖啡吗？
Want to go with me to get some coffee later? 一会儿想和我去喝点咖啡吗？

词汇精讲 Word Study

grab
英 /græb/
美 /græb/

v. 1. 抓取，攫取
He grabbed my arm. 他抓住了我的手臂。
2. 赶紧做
I grabbed a quick bite. 我匆忙吃了点东西。
3. 抓住（机会）
You should grab this opportunity. 你应该抓住这次机会。
n. 抓，夺
They made a grab for the same rope. 他们抓住了同一根绳子。

02 点咖啡

（一般情况：杯子大小 + 咖啡种类 + 牛奶类型和额外加的东西 + 在店里喝 / 外带。）
I'd like a grande mocha for here. 我要一大杯摩卡，在店里用。
I want a small latte with vanilla syrup to go. 我要一小杯外带的拿铁咖啡配香草糖浆。
I'll have a hot latte with whole milk for here. 我想要一杯热拿铁，加全脂牛奶，在这里喝。

场景对话 Conversation

A: What can I get you?
B: I'll have an iced Americano.
A: What size would you like?
B: Medium, please.
A: Is that for here, or to go?
B: For here.
A: Would you like anything else?
B: No, thanks.
A: That will be 6 dollars.
B: Here you go.

A: May I take your order?
B: I would like a large iced latte to go.
A: Will that be all?
B: Yes.
A: Your total is 8 dollars.
B: Here you are.

A：您要点什么？
B：我要一杯冰美式。
A：您要多大杯的？
B：中杯，谢谢。
A：在这里喝还是带走？
B：在这儿喝。
A：您还要点别的吗？
B：不了，谢谢。
A：一共是6美元。
B：给你。

A：您要点单吗？
B：我要一杯大杯的冰拿铁带走。
A：就这些吗？
B：是的。
A：一共是8美元。
B：给你。

Lesson 44 健身房
At the Gym

词汇 Vocabulary

- 相关词汇：

gym	英 /dʒɪm/	美 /dʒɪm/	健身房
fitness	英 /'fɪtnəs/	美 /'fɪtnəs/	健康
instructor	英 /ɪn'strʌktə(r)/	美 /ɪn'strʌktər/	教练
coach	英 /kəʊtʃ/	美 /koʊtʃ/	教练

work out 锻炼

- 健身目标：

fit	英 /fɪt/	美 /fɪt/	健康的
toned	英 /təʊnd/	美 /toʊnd/	健壮的，结实的

bulk up 变得壮硕　　　　slim down 变得修长
build muscle 增肌　　　　burn fat 减脂

- 身材问题：

muffin top 腰间赘肉　　　　love handles 腰两侧的赘肉
beer belly 啤酒肚　　　　bingo wings 蝴蝶袖；上臂赘肉

- 运动类型：

weights	英 /weɪts/	美 /weɪts/	举重
curl	英 /kɜːl/	美 /kɜːrl/	弯举
cardio	英 /'kɑːdiəʊ/	美 /'kɑːrdioʊ/	有氧运动
crunch	英 /'krʌntʃ/	美 /'krʌntʃ/	仰卧卷腹
squat	英 /skwɒt/	美 /skwɑːt/	深蹲
stretch	英 /stretʃ/	美 /stretʃ/	拉伸

bench press 仰卧推举　　　　push-up 俯卧撑
pull-up 引体向上　　　　sit-up 仰卧起坐

- 身体部位：

chest	英 /tʃest/	美 /tʃest/	胸部
abs	英 /æbz/	美 /æbz/	
=abdominals	英 /æb'dɒmɪn(ə)lz/	美 /æb'dɑːmɪn(ə)lz/	腹部
back	英 /bæk/	美 /bæk/	背部
bottom	英 /'bɒtəm/	美 /'bɑːtəm/	臀部
leg	英 /leg/	美 /leg/	腿

thigh	英 /θaɪ/	美 /θaɪ/	大腿
calf	英 /kɑːf/	美 /kæf/	小腿肚
arm	英 /ɑːm/	美 /ɑːrm/	手臂

- 运动器材：

treadmill	英 /ˈtredmɪl/	美 /ˈtredmɪl/	跑步机
dumbbell	英 /ˈdʌmbel/	美 /ˈdʌmbel/	哑铃
barbell	英 /ˈbɑːbel/	美 /ˈbɑːrbel/	杠铃
bench	英 /bentʃ/	美 /bentʃ/	长凳
elliptical trainer	英 /ɪˈlɪptɪk(ə)l ˈtreɪnə(r)/	美 /ɪˈlɪptɪk(ə)l ˈtreɪnər/	椭圆机

实用表达 Useful Expressions

01 办理会员

（1）报名

I wanna sign up for a membership.
=I would like to apply for a gym membership.
我想申请健身房的会员。

（2）费用和营业时间

How much is the membership?
会费是多少？
What are the opening hours?
营业时间是什么时候？

> **短语精讲** Phrase Study
>
> - sign up（for sth.）报名（参加课程）
>   Can I sign up for this course in advance?
>   我能提前报名这门课程吗？
>   We highly recommend you sign up for this course.
>   我们强烈推荐您报名参加这个课程。
> - apply for sth. 申请
>   I am continuing to apply for jobs.
>   我在继续申请工作。
>   She applied for a passport.
>   她申请了一个护照。

02 健身目标

提问

Do you have any goals? 您的目标是什么？
What do you want to accomplish? 您想达成什么样的效果？

回答

I wanna get fit. 我想变得健康。
I wanna bulk up. 我想变得壮硕。
I wanna get rid of this muffin top. 我想减掉腰间的赘肉。

03 具体部位

提问

What are you working on today?=What part(s) do you do today? 您今天锻炼哪里?

回答

Today is my cardio day. 今天是我的有氧日。
I'd like to do weights. 我想做一些举重的运动。

04 使用器材

（1）还剩几组

How many more sets do you have left on this one?=How many sets left? 你还剩几组?

（2）换着来

Could I jump in?=Could I rotate with you? 我能和你轮着来吗?

词汇精讲 Word Study

rotate
英 /rəʊˈteɪt/
美 /ˈroʊteɪt/

v. 1.（使）旋转，转动
Rotate the wheel through 180 degrees. 将方向盘转动180度。
2.（工作）由……轮值；（人员）轮换，轮值
We rotate the night shift so no one has to do it all the time.
我们轮流值夜班，这样就不会有人总是上夜班了。

（3）是否用完

Are you using the dumbbell? 你在用这个哑铃吗?
Have you finished the barbell? 你用完这个杠铃了吗?

场景对话 Conversation

A: Hello, how can I help you?
B: I wanna sign up for a membership.
A: Great. Please fill out this application form.
B: Okay. How much is the membership?
A: It's 30 dollars per month.
B: Okay. And what are the opening hours?
A: We are open from 8 a.m. to 10 p.m.
B: Great. I will sign up for a month.
A: No problem.

A：您好，我能为您做什么吗？
B：我想注册会员。
A：太好了，请填写这张申请表。
B：好的。会员费是多少？
A：一个月30美元。
B：好的。营业时间是什么时候？
A：从早上8点到晚上10点。
B：太好了，我要注册一个月。
A：没有问题。

A: Hi, I'm Alex. I'm new to the gym.
B: Hi, I'm John, an instructor here. How can I help you?
A: I don't know how to use these machines. Can you help me out?
B: Do you have any goals?
A: I wanna slim down and get rid of this muffin top.
B: No problem. I can set up a workout routine for you.
A: What exactly do I need to do?
B: Running and some weight training. That will help you to burn fat.
A: Sounds great.

A：嗨，我是亚历克斯。我之前没来过健身房。
B：嗨，我是约翰，是这里的教练。我能为您做什么吗？
A：我不知道如何使用这些器材。你能帮我吗？
B：您有什么目标吗？
A：我想瘦下来，减掉腰间赘肉。
B：没问题，我可以为您制定一个锻炼计划。
A：我具体需要做些什么？
B：跑步和一些举重训练，这将帮助您燃烧脂肪。
A：听起来不错。

Lesson 45 野营
Camping

词汇 Vocabulary

- 野营装备：

tent	英 /tent/	美 /tent/	帐篷
flashlight	英 /ˈflæʃlaɪt/	美 /ˈflæʃlaɪt/	手电筒
backpack	英 /ˈbækpæk/	美 /ˈbækpæk/	背包
raincoat	英 /ˈreɪnkəʊt/	美 /ˈreɪnkoʊt/	雨衣
hammock	英 /ˈhæmək/	美 /ˈhæmək/	吊床
tackle	英 /ˈtæk(ə)l/	美 /ˈtæk(ə)l/	钓具

fishing rod 鱼竿　　　　　　　　　sleeping bag 睡袋
warm clothes 保暖的衣服　　　　　first aid kit 急救箱
camp chair 营地椅　　　　　　　　insect repellent 驱虫剂
（repellent　　英 /rɪˈpelənt/　　　美 /rɪˈpelənt/　　　驱虫剂）

实用表达 Useful Expressions

01 准备

Have you taken sleeping bags and insect repellent? 你带睡袋和驱虫剂了吗？
Remember to bring your tent and warm clothes. 记得带上帐篷和暖和的衣服。
I'll take a fishing rod and tackle. 我要带上钓竿和钓具。
We'll need a first aid kit. 我们需要一个急救箱。

02 扎营

（1）选址

We should camp on flat and dry ground. 我们应该在平坦干燥的地上露营。
How about we camp near the river? 我们在河边露营怎么样？
If we camp in the open, we will have a good view of stars.
如果我们露天露营，我们就能很好地看到星星。

（2）搭帐篷

Let's put/set up the tents. 咱们搭帐篷吧。
It's so hard to set up a tent. Could anybody help me?
搭个帐篷太难了。有人能帮我吗？
These two trees are perfect to hang the hammock.
这两棵树很适合挂吊床。

短语精讲 Phrase Study

- put/set up a tent =pitch a tent 搭帐篷

Should I set up a tent under a tree?
我应该在树下搭帐篷吗？
My father taught me how to put up a tent.
我父亲教会我怎么搭帐篷。

Unit 9　娱乐Entertainment

03 生火

It's getting dark soon. We should start a campfire to keep us warm.
天很快就要黑了，我们应该生起营火保暖。

Let's collect some wood to make a fire. 让我们收集一些木材生火吧。

Could you tell me how to build a campfire? 你能告诉我怎样生火吗？

词汇精讲 Word Study

campfire
英 /ˈkæmpfaɪə(r)/
美 /ˈkæmpfaɪər/

n. 篝火，营火
We sit around a campfire at night.
到了夜里，我们坐在篝火周围。
The campfire died out. 篝火熄灭了。

04 其他情况

Oh no! I think I forgot my sleeping bag. What am I gonna do now?
噢，不！我想我忘了带睡袋，我现在该怎么办？

I'm quite hungry now. Shall we have something to eat?
我现在很饿，我们吃点东西吧？

It's quite dark now. Let me turn on my flashlight. That'll help.
现在天很黑了，打开手电筒吧，会亮一些。

语法点睛 Grammar Notes

- be going to do sth. 打算做某事；要去做某事
What am I gonna do now?
我现在要怎么办？
What are you going to do?
你要去干什么？
I am going to watch TV.
我打算去看电视。
She is going to get some coffee.
她打算去喝咖啡。

💬 场景对话 Conversation

A: This looks like a good camping spot. What do you say?
A：这看起来像是个露营的好地方。你说呢？

B: I love the view from here. Let's set up the tents!
B：我喜欢这里的风景。我们把帐篷搭起来吧！

A: Okay.
A：好的。

B: Oh no! I think I forgot my sleeping bag. What am I gonna do now?
B：噢，不！我想我忘了带睡袋。我现在该怎么办？

A: Guess what? I have two.
A：你猜怎么着？ 我有两个。

B: That's great.
B：太好了。

Unit 10　紧急事件 Emergency

Lesson 46　问路和指路
Asking for and Giving Directions

词汇 Vocabulary

- 交通设施：

英文	英式音标	美式音标	中文
block	英 /blɒk/	美 /blɑːk/	街区
signpost	英 /ˈsaɪnpəʊst/	美 /ˈsaɪnpoʊst/	路标
intersection	英 /ˌɪntəˈsekʃn/	美 /ˌɪntərˈsekʃ(ə)n/	
=crossing	英 /ˈkrɒsɪŋ/	美 /ˈkrɔːsɪŋ/	十字路口
crosswalk	英 /ˈkrɒswɔːk/	美 /ˈkrɔːswɔːk/	人行横道
pedestrian crossing	英 /pəˌdestriən ˈkrɒsɪŋ/	美 /pəˌdestriən ˈkrɔːsɪŋ/	人行横道
tunnel	英 /ˈtʌn(ə)l/	美 /ˈtʌn(ə)l/	地下通道
roundabout	英 /ˈraʊndəbaʊt/	美 /ˈraʊndəbaʊt/	（交叉路口的）环岛

traffic circle（交叉路口的）环岛　　　traffic light 红绿灯

- 指路相关词汇：

英文	英式音标	美式音标	中文
left	英 /left/	美 /left/	左边
right	英 /raɪt/	美 /raɪt/	右边
beside	英 /bɪˈsaɪd/	美 /bɪˈsaɪd/	在旁边

go straight 直走　　　around the corner 在附近

- 常见建筑物名称：

英文	英式音标	美式音标	中文
square	英 /skweə(r)/	美 /skwer/	广场/购物区
hospital	英 /ˈhɒspɪt(ə)l/	美 /ˈhɑːspɪt(ə)l/	医院
supermarket	英 /ˈsuːpəmɑːkɪt/	美 /ˈsuːpərmɑːrkɪt/	超市
bank	英 /bæŋk/	美 /bæŋk/	银行
library	英 /ˈlaɪbrəri/	美 /ˈlaɪbreri/	图书馆
museum	英 /mjuˈziːəm/	美 /mjuˈziːəm/	博物馆
restaurant	英 /ˈrestrɒnt/	美 /ˈrestrɑːnt/	餐馆
school	英 /skuːl/	美 /skuːl/	学校
drugstore	英 /ˈdrʌgstɔː(r)/	美 /ˈdrʌgstɔːr/	药店
café	英 /ˈkæfeɪ/	美 /kæˈfeɪ/	咖啡厅

post office 邮局　　　　　　　shopping mall 商场
cinema/movie theater 电影院　　subway station 地铁站
police station 警察局　　　　　parking lot 停车场

Unit 10 紧急事件 Emergency

实用表达 Useful Expressions

01 关于地点

问路：

Do you know where the supermarket is? 你知道超市在哪儿吗？
Could you tell me the way to the drugstore? 可以告诉我去药店怎么走吗？
How can I get to the subway station? 我怎样才能去地铁站？
Could you direct me to the shopping mall? 你能告诉我去购物中心的路吗？

指路：

（1）直走 / 沿着走

Go straight on. 直走。
Go straight for two blocks. 往前直走两个街区。
It's right down this way. /Go along this street. 沿着这条路 / 街走下去就好。

（2）左右

It's on the left/right. 在你的左边 / 右边。
Turn left/right at the intersection. 在十字路口左转 / 右转。

（3）其他

It's across the street from the hospital. 就在医院对面。
It's around the corner. 就在附近。
It's right beside the school. 就在学校附近。

02 关于距离

提问

How far is the movie theater from here? 电影院离这里有多远呢？
Is it far from here? 离这儿远吗？
How long will it take to get there on foot/by subway?
步行 / 坐地铁到那里要花多长时间？

回答

Not far. /It's not far at all. 不远。/ 一点儿也不远。
It takes about ten minutes on foot/by subway. 走路 / 坐地铁大约要 10 分钟。
It's a couple of streets away. 隔着几条街吧。
It's two blocks from here. 离这儿有两个街区。

场景对话 Conversation

A: Could you please tell me how I can get to the nearest café?

B: Sure. There is a Starbucks Coffee around here. Go along this street and turn right at the second crossing.

A: Thank you.

B: You are welcome.

A：请问你能告诉我怎么去最近的咖啡厅吗？

B：当然。这附近有一家星巴克。沿着这条街走，在第二个十字路口右转。

A：谢谢。

B：不客气。

Lesson 47　突发疾病
Sudden Illnesses

词汇 Vocabulary

- **挂号相关：**

register	英 /'redʒɪstə(r)/	美 /'redʒɪstər/	挂号
registration	英 /ˌredʒɪ'streɪʃ(ə)n/	美 /ˌredʒɪ'streɪʃ(ə)n/	注册；挂号

registration office 挂号处　　registration card 挂号卡

- **医生类型：**

surgeon	英 /'sɜːdʒən/	美 /'sɜːrdʒən/	外科医生
physician	英 /fɪ'zɪʃ(ə)n/	美 /fɪ'zɪʃ(ə)n/	内科医生
dentist	英 /'dentɪst/	美 /'dentɪst/	牙科医生

- **科室名称：**

pharmacy	英 /'fɑːməsi/	美 /'fɑːrməsi/	药房
ward	英 /wɔːd/	美 /wɔːrd/	病房

consulting room 诊疗室　　waiting room 候诊室
emergency room 急诊室　　operating room 手术室

- **身体部位：**

head	英 /hed/	美 /hed/	头部
eye	英 /aɪ/	美 /aɪ/	眼睛
eyelid	英 /'aɪlɪd/	美 /'aɪlɪd/	眼睑
nose	英 /nəʊz/	美 /noʊz/	鼻子
tooth	英 /tuːθ/	美 /tuːθ/	
(pl. teeth	英 /tiːθ/	美 /tiːθ/)	牙齿
chest	英 /tʃest/	美 /tʃest/	胸腔
hand	英 /hænd/	美 /hænd/	手
wrist	英 /rɪst/	美 /rɪst/	手腕
finger	英 /'fɪŋɡə(r)/	美 /'fɪŋɡər/	手指
leg	英 /leɡ/	美 /leɡ/	腿
ankle	英 /'æŋk(ə)l/	美 /'æŋk(ə)l/	脚踝
skin	英 /skɪn/	美 /skɪn/	皮肤

- **具体病症：**

cold	英 /kəʊld/	美 /koʊld/	普通感冒
flu	英 /fluː/	美 /fluː/	流行性感冒
fever	英 /'fiːvə(r)/	美 /'fiːvər/	发烧
cough	英 /kɒf/	美 /kɔːf/	咳嗽

toothache	英 /ˈtuːθeɪk/	美 /ˈtuːθeɪk/	牙疼
headache	英 /ˈhedeɪk/	美 /ˈhedeɪk/	头疼
stomachache	英 /ˈstʌməkeɪk/	美 /ˈstʌməkeɪk/	胃痛
backache	英 /ˈbækeɪk/	美 /ˈbækeɪk/	背痛，腰痛
asthma	英 /ˈæsmə/	美 /ˈæzmə/	哮喘
diarrhea	英 /ˌdaɪəˈrɪə/	美 /ˌdaɪəˈriːə/	腹泻
allergy	英 /ˈælədʒi/	美 /ˈælərdʒi/	过敏症
rash	英 /ræʃ/	美 /ræʃ/	皮疹

- 症状表现：

dizzy	英 /ˈdɪzi/	美 /ˈdɪzi/	
=light-headed	英 /ˌlaɪt ˈhedɪd/	美 /ˌlaɪt ˈhedɪd/	头晕的
swollen	英 /ˈswəʊlən/	美 /ˈswoʊlən/	肿胀的
bloodshot	英 /ˈblʌdʃɒt/	美 /ˈblʌdʃɑːt/	布满血丝的
bleed	英 /bliːd/	美 /bliːd/	流血，失血
cavity	英 /ˈkævəti/	美 /ˈkævəti/	（龋齿的）洞
tight	英 /taɪt/	美 /taɪt/	不适的；憋气的
nauseous	英 /ˈnɔːziəs/	美 /ˈnɔːʃəs/	恶心的；想呕吐的
vomit	英 /ˈvɒmɪt/	美 /ˈvɑːmɪt/	呕吐
allergic	英 /əˈlɜːdʒɪk/	美 /əˈlɜːrdʒɪk/	（对……）过敏的
itchy	英 /ˈɪtʃi/	美 /ˈɪtʃi/	发痒的
dislocate	英 /ˈdɪsləkeɪt/	美 /ˈdɪsloʊkeɪt/	使脱臼
scald	英 /skɔːld/	美 /skɔːld/	
=burn	英 /bɜːn/	美 /bɜːrn/	烫伤
fracture	英 /ˈfræktʃə(r)/	美 /ˈfræktʃər/	断裂，折断
twist	英 /twɪst/	美 /twɪst/	
=sprain	英 /spreɪn/	美 /spreɪn/	扭伤

running nose 流鼻涕　　　　　　　　stuffy nose 鼻塞

- 与药物有关：

prescription	英 /prɪˈskrɪpʃn/	美 /prɪˈskrɪpʃ(ə)n/	处方
medicine	英 /ˈmedsn/	美 /ˈmedɪs(ə)n/	药，药物
tablet	英 /ˈtæblət/	美 /ˈtæblət/	
=pill	英 /pɪl/	美 /pɪl/	药片
dosage	英 /ˈdəʊsɪdʒ/	美 /ˈdoʊsɪdʒ/	（药的）剂量，服用量

prescription drug 处方药　　　　　OTC（over-the-counter）drug 非处方药
side effect 副作用

实用表达 Useful Expressions

01 挂号

Where is the registration office? 挂号处在哪里?
How can I apply for a registration card? 我要怎么申请一张挂号卡?
How much do you charge for the registration card? 挂号卡多少钱?

02 具体的病症描述

提问

What seems to be the trouble?=What's your complaint?
　　　　　　　　　　　=What's the matter with you? 你哪里不舒服?
Can you describe the symptoms? 你能说一说症状吗?
Where did you hurt yourself? 你伤到哪里了?
How are you feeling? 你感觉怎样?

回答

（1）感冒/发烧

I've got a cold/fever. 我感冒了/发烧了。
I've come down with a cold/fever. 我感冒了/发烧了。

（2）头晕/头疼

I feel dizzy/light-headed. 我头晕。
I have a headache. 我头疼。
My head is killing me. 我头疼死了。

（3）眼睛

My eyelid is swollen. 我眼睑肿了。
My eyes are bloodshot. 我的眼里满是血丝。

（4）鼻子

My nose is bleeding. 我在流鼻血。
My nose is often running. /I have a running nose. 我经常流鼻涕。
I have a stuffy nose. 我鼻塞。

（5）牙齿

I've got a toothache. 我牙疼。
My tooth has been hurting all day. 我这颗牙痛了一天了。

I have a cavity in my tooth. 我的牙齿上有个洞。

（6）胸腔

My chest feels a bit tight. 我觉得胸闷憋气。
I'm having trouble breathing. 我呼吸有些困难。
I can't breathe. 我透不过来气。

（7）胃病

I have a stomachache. 我胃疼。
I'm feeling nauseous. / I always feel like vomiting. 我觉得恶心。/ 我总是感觉想吐。
My appetite has gone completely. =I have no appetite. 我一点胃口也没有。

（8）过敏

I'm allergic to pollen/mango/seafood. 我对花粉/芒果/海鲜过敏。
I have a peanut allergy. I get a rash when I eat just one. 我对花生过敏，我一吃就会起疹子。
My skin is itchy all over. 我浑身都在发痒。

（9）手

My wrist is dislocated. 我的手腕脱臼了。
My hand was scalded/burnt with boiling water. 我的手被开水烫伤了。

（10）腿

I have injured my leg. 我的腿受伤了。
I fractured my right leg. 我摔断了我的右腿。
My ankle is twisted/sprained. 我的脚踝扭伤了。

03 其他问题

（1）得病时间

I have been like this for about two weeks. 我像这样差不多两个星期了。
I have been sick for one week. 我病了一周了。

（2）病史

I have had this before. 我以前得过这个病。
This problem runs in the family. 家族里都得过这个病。

（3）关于药物

Does this drug have any side effects? 这药有副作用吗？

Could you tell me how to take this medicine? 您能告诉我这药怎么服用吗?
How many times a day should I take this medicine? 这药每天吃几次?

(4)复查时间

Do I need to come again? 我还需要再来吗?
When should I come to see you again? 我什么时候再来见您?

(5)病情是否好转

好转:
I am feeling better today. 我今天感觉好多了。
I have completely recovered. =I'm completely over it. =I'm all better. 我已经完全康复了。

没有好转:
There is no sign of recovery. 我一点好转的迹象也没有。
I'm not improving. 我没有好转。

场景对话 Conversation

A: How are you feeling?
B: I feel terrible.
A: I'm sorry to hear that. What's the matter?
B: My head is killing me.
A: Let me see your temperature.
B: Okay.
A: Oh, I think you have a fever.
B: What can I do?
A: Don't worry. I'm going to give you some medicine. You're going to get better soon!
B: That's good.

A: 你感觉怎么样?
B: 我感觉糟透了。
A: 很抱歉听到这个消息。哪里不舒服呢?
B: 我头疼死了。
A: 让我量量你的体温。
B: 好的。
A: 我想你发烧了。
B: 我该怎么办?
A: 别担心,我给你开些药,你很快就会好起来的!
B: 太好了。

Lesson 48　遭遇抢劫
Being Robbed

词汇 Vocabulary

- 相关词汇：

police	英 /pəˈliːs/	美 /pəˈliːs/	警察
ambulance	英 /ˈæmbjələns/	美 /ˈæmbjələns/	救护车
emergency	英 /ɪˈmɜːdʒənsi/	美 /ɪˈmɜːrdʒənsi/	紧急情况
witness	英 /ˈwɪtnəs/	美 /ˈwɪtnəs/	目击者
gun	英 /ɡʌn/	美 /ɡʌn/	枪
knife	英 /naɪf/	美 /naɪf/	刀

- 物品：

handbag	英 /ˈhændbæɡ/	美 /ˈhændbæɡ/	手提包
cellphone	英 /ˈselfəʊn/	美 /ˈselfoʊn/	手机
passport	英 /ˈpɑːspɔːt/	美 /ˈpæspɔːrt/	护照
wallet	英 /ˈwɒlɪt/	美 /ˈwɑːlɪt/	皮夹子
purse	英 /pɜːs/	美 /pɜːrs/	女式钱包
watch	英 /wɒtʃ/	美 /wɑːtʃ/	手表
jewelry	英 /ˈdʒuːəlri/	美 /ˈdʒuːəlri/	珠宝首饰
necklace	英 /ˈnekləs/	美 /ˈnekləs/	项链
bracelet	英 /ˈbreɪslət/	美 /ˈbreɪslət/	手镯
ring	英 /rɪŋ/	美 /rɪŋ/	戒指
earrings	英 /ˈɪərɪŋz/	美 /ˈɪrɪŋz/	耳坠
camera	英 /ˈkæm(ə)rə/	美 /ˈkæm(ə)rə/	相机

实用表达 Useful Expressions

01　遭遇抢劫时

（1）呼救

Somebody, help! 来人啊！
Help! 救命啊！
Please give me a hand! 请帮我一下！
Call the police! 快叫警察！
Call an ambulance! 叫救护车！
Please call a doctor! 快叫医生！

（2）说明情况

I got robbed/mugged. 我被抢劫了。

I got attacked. 我被袭击了。

词汇精讲 Word Study	
rob 英 /rɒb/ 美 /rɑːb/	*v.* 抢劫；掠夺 They planned to rob a bank. 他们计划去抢银行。 I've been robbed! 我被抢劫了！
mug 英 /mʌɡ/ 美 /mʌɡ/	*n.* 1. 马克杯 He gave me a mug as a gift. 他送我一个马克杯作为礼物。 2. 一大杯的量 I drank a mug of coffee. 我喝了一大杯咖啡。 3.（人的）脸 I never want to see his ugly mug again. 我再也不想看到他那张丑恶的面孔。 *v.*（公开）行凶抢劫，打劫 She has been mugged. 她被抢劫了。 I was mugged in broad daylight. 我在光天化日之下被抢劫了。

02 打电话报警

（1）报案

Police: 911 speaking. What's your emergency? 这里是911，请问您有什么紧急事件？

  You: I have been robbed. 我遭到了抢劫。

      I need to report a robbery. 我需要报告一起劫案。

（2）事发地点

Police: Where was your emergency? 在哪里发生的？

  You: I was on the Fifth Avenue and I could see the Empire State Building.
      我当时在第五大道，我能看到帝国大厦。

（3）事发时行为

Police: What were you doing when it happened? 当时您在干什么？

  You: I was just walking on the street. 我只是在街上走着。

      I was just shopping. 我在买东西。

（4）被抢物品

Police: What has been taken? 他抢走了您的什么东西？

You: My <u>handbag/backpack</u>. 我的手提包/背包。

（5）包里物品

Police: What was in your bag? 您的包里有什么东西?
　　You: My <u>cellphone, wallet, camera and my passport</u>. 我的手机、钱包、相机和护照。

（6）携带武器

Police: Were any weapons involved? 有人携带武器吗?
　　You: No, he had no weapon. 没有，他没有武器。
　　　　Yes, he's got a <u>gun/knife</u>. 有，他有一把枪/刀。

（7）关于目击者

Police: Is there a witness that we can contact? 有没有目击者能让我们联系的呢?
　　You: My <u>friend</u> was there with me at that time. 我的朋友当时和我在一起。
　　　　I was alone, but there were many people on the street.
　　　　我一个人，但是当时街上有很多人。

（8）联系方式

Police: Please give me your phone number. We will call you if we receive any information.
　　　　请把您的电话告诉我。如果有消息，我们会打电话通知您的。
　　You: My phone number is <u>12345678</u>. 我的电话号码是 12345678。

场景对话 Conversation

A: 911 speaking. What's your emergency?　　A: 这里是911，请问您有什么紧急事件?
B: I have been robbed.　　　　　　　　　　　B: 我被抢劫了。
A: Where was your emergency?　　　　　　　A: 在哪里发生的?
B: I was on the Fifth Avenue.　　　　　　　　B: 我当时在第五大道。
A: What has been taken?　　　　　　　　　　A: 他抢走了您的什么东西?
B: My handbag.　　　　　　　　　　　　　　B: 我的手提包。
A: Please give me your phone number.　　　　A: 请告诉我您的电话号码。
B: My phone number is 12345678.　　　　　　B: 我的电话号码是 12345678。

Lesson 49 护照遗失
Losing the Passport

词汇 Vocabulary

embassy	英 /ˈembəsi/	美 /ˈembəsi/	大使馆
consulate	英 /ˈkɒnsjələt/	美 /ˈkɑːnsələt/	领事馆
passport	英 /ˈpɑːspɔːt/	美 /ˈpæspɔːrt/	护照
visa	英 /ˈviːzə/	美 /ˈviːzə/	签证
copy	英 /ˈkɒpi/	美 /ˈkɑːpi/	复印件

police station 警察局　　　　　　　proof of identity 身份证明（一般指的就是身份证）
ID card 身份证　　　　　　　　　　police report 警方报告

实用表达 Useful Expressions

到当地警局报警

（1）报失

Police: What's your emergency?
您有什么紧急事件？

You: My passport is missing. /
I lost my passport.
我的护照丢了。

> **Notes:**
> 补办护照的一般步骤：
> （1）到当地警局报警，获取当地警方开具的丢失证明（携带身份证明/护照复印件、签证复印件）；
> （2）到中国大使馆/领事馆申请补办护照或旅行证（携带丢失证明、护照复印件、本人照片）。

（2）丢失时间和地点

Police: When and where did you lose it? 在何时何地丢的？

You: I remember the last place I used it was <u>at the airport yesterday</u>.
我记得最后一次使用护照是昨天在机场。

（3）提供证明材料

Police: Please provide copies of your passport, visa and proof of identity.
请您提供护照和签证的复印件，以及身份证明。

You: Here you are. 给你。

词汇精讲 Word Study

proof
英 /pruːf/
美 /pruːf/

n. 1. 证据，证明
　　Can you provide any proof of identity? 你能提供什么身份证明吗？
　2. 校样，样张
　　I am checking the proofs of the report. 我正在审阅这份报告的校样。
a. （构成复合词）耐……的，能防……的
　　It is a waterproof camera. 这是一个防水的照相机。
　　I need a windproof coat. 我需要一件防风的外套。

> **identity**
> 英 /aɪˈdentəti/
> 美 /aɪˈdentəti/
>
> n. 1. 身份
> We haven't known his identity yet. 我们还不知道他的身份。
> 2. 个性，特性
> As children grow, they establish their own identities.
> 孩子们长大以后会形成自己的个性。
> 3. 同一性，一致性
> The proposal created an identity between two parties.
> 这项提议使两个政党达成了一致。

（4）填写表格

Police: Please complete these forms. 请填写这些表格。
You: Okay. 好的。

（5）领取申报表去大使馆补办

Police: Go to the Chinese Embassy and apply for a replacement. Here is your police report.
您到中国大使馆申请补办护照。这是您的警方报告。
You: Okay. Thank you so much. 好的，非常感谢。

> **词汇精讲 Word Study**
>
> **replacement**
> 英 /rɪˈpleɪsmənt/
> 美 /rɪˈpleɪsmənt/
>
> n. 1. 替换；更换
> I have to pay for the replacement of the damaged TV.
> 我必须支付更换损坏的电视的费用。
> 2. 替代品；替换物
> We need a replacement for our old vacuum cleaner.
> 我们需要换一个新的吸尘器。
> 3. （尤指工作中的）接替者，替代者
> Please stay until we find a replacement.
> 请留下来，直到我们找到替代你的人。

场景对话 Conversation

A: What's your emergency?
B: I lost my passport.
A: Please provide copies of your passport, visa and proof of identity.
B: Here you are.
A: Please complete these forms.
B: Okay.
A: Go to the Chinese Embassy and apply for a replacement. Here is your police report.
B: Okay. Thank you so much.

A：您有什么紧急事件？
B：我的护照丢了。
A：请提供您的护照和签证的复印件，以及身份证明。
B：给你。
A：请填写这些表格。
B：好的。
A：您去中国大使馆申请更换。这是您的警方报告。
B：好的，非常感谢。

Lesson 50　物品遗失
Lost Things

词汇 Vocabulary

- 失物招领处：

  lost and found（美）　　　lost property（英）　　　lost articles（加）

- 物品：

key	英 /kiː/	美 /kiː/	钥匙
glasses	英 /ˈglɑːsɪz/	美 /ˈglæsɪz/	眼镜
sunglasses	英 /ˈsʌnglɑːsɪz/	美 /ˈsʌnglæsɪz/	太阳镜
cellphone	英 /ˈselfəʊn/	美 /ˈselfoʊn/	手机
wallet	英 /ˈwɒlɪt/	美 /ˈwɑːlɪt/	钱包
umbrella	英 /ʌmˈbrelə/	美 /ʌmˈbrelə/	雨伞
mug	英 /mʌg/	美 /mʌg/	马克杯
hat	英 /hæt/	美 /hæt/	帽子
earphones	英 /ˈɪəfəʊnz/	美 /ˈɪrfoʊnz/	耳机
notebook	英 /ˈnəʊtbʊk/	美 /ˈnoʊtbʊk/	本子

  card key 房卡　　　　　　　　　　USB flash drive U 盘

实用表达 Useful Expressions

01　丢东西

I've lost <u>my wallet</u>. 我弄丢了我的钱包。

I can't find my <u>cellphone</u>. 我找不到我的手机了。

I can't remember where I left <u>my keys</u>. 我记不起来把钥匙落在哪儿了。

02　询问他人

Have you seen my <u>glasses</u>？你有没有看到我的眼镜？

Where did you put my <u>notebook</u>？你把我的笔记本放哪儿了？

Could you help me find my <u>earphones</u>？能帮我找找我的耳机吗？

03　询问地点

Did you look on your <u>desk/bed</u>? 你找没找你的桌上 / 床上？

Did you leave them <u>in the car/on the sofa</u>? 你是不是把它们落在车上 / 沙发上了？

Where did you use them last time? 你最后一次用它们是在哪儿？

04 找到了

I've found it/them. 我找到它 / 它们了。
Found it/them! 找到它 / 它们了！

05 失物招领

You: Hello, I've lost my phone and I was wondering if you'd know anything about it. 你好，我把手机弄丢了，不知你是否知道些什么。

Staff: Oh, I see. Let me check the records.
啊，是这样，让我查看一下记录。
Can you describe it?
您能描述一下它吗？

You: It's a black iPhone X.
是个黑色的 iPhone X。

Staff: Oh, someone brought it to us, but you have to fill out this form before you have the phone back.
噢，有人捡到送过来了，但您在领取手机之前必须填写这张表。

You: That's wonderful! Thank you so much!
太好了！非常感谢！

语法点睛 Grammar Notes

- I was wondering if/whether ... 不知您是否……

1. 表示请求
   I was wondering whether I could borrow your car. 请问我能借您的车吗？
   I was wondering if you'd know anything about it. 不知您是否知道些什么。

2. 提出建议
   I was wondering whether you'd like to come with us? 不知您是否愿意和我们一起来。
   I was wondering whether you'd like to go to the party? 不知您是否愿意参加这场聚会。

场景对话 Conversation

A: Hi, how can I help you?
B: I've lost my phone and I was wondering if you'd know anything about it.
A: Oh, I see. Let me check the records.
B: Thank you.
A: Can you describe it?
B: It's a golden iPhone.
A: Yeah, someone brought it to us, but you have to fill out this form before you have the phone back.
B: That's wonderful! Thank you so much!

A：您好，我能帮您什么忙吗？
B：我的手机丢了，不知你是否知道些什么。
A：啊，我明白了。让我查一下记录。
B：谢谢。
A：您能描述一下它吗？
B：是个金色的 iPhone。
A：是的，有人给我们送来了，但您得先填好这张表，然后才能拿回手机。
B：太棒了！非常感谢！

Unit 11　情感 Relationship

Lesson 51　介绍
Introduction

词汇 Vocabulary

introduce	英 /ˌɪntrə'djuːs/	美 /ˌɪntrə'duːs/	(v.) 介绍
introduction	英 /ˌɪntrə'dʌkʃn/	美 /ˌɪntrə'dʌkʃ(ə)n/	(n.) 介绍
chance	英 /tʃɑːns/	美 /tʃæns/	机会
pleasure	英 /'pleʒə(r)/	美 /'pleʒər/	荣幸
crush	英 /krʌʃ/	美 /krʌʃ/	迷恋，着迷
match	英 /mætʃ/	美 /mætʃ/	般配的人（或物）

Mr. Right 理想对象；白马王子

实用表达 Useful Expressions

01 介绍

（1）询问是否认识

Have you met Jack? 你见过杰克吗？
You remember Mary? 你还记得玛丽吗？
You know Jane, right? 你认识简，对吧？

（2）请求介绍

May I introduce Mr. Liu to you? 让我向你介绍一下刘先生。
Allow me to introduce Mr. Liu. 请允许我介绍一下刘先生。
Let me introduce my friend Jack to you. 让我向你介绍我的朋友杰克。

（3）正式介绍

This is Jack and this is Peter. 这是杰克，这是彼得。
This is Peter. He'd like to talk to you. 这是彼得，他想和你说句话。

02 寒暄

（1）很高兴见到你

Nice to meet you. / Nice meeting you. 很高兴见到你。
It's a pleasure to meet you. 很高兴见到你。
I've been looking forward to meeting you! 我一直期待着见到你！
I finally have the chance to meet you in person. 我终于有机会见到你本人了。

句型精讲 Sentence Structure

- chance (for sb.) to do sth. (某人)做某事的机会
  It is a good chance for me to get promoted. 这是我晋升的好机会。
  I have no chance to get my money back. 我没有机会把钱要回来了。

(2) 提起过你

Jack has said good things about you. 杰克说了很多你的好话。
Jack has told me a lot about you. 杰克和我说了很多关于你的事情。
I've heard many great things about you. 我听说过很多关于你的好事。

03 当红娘

He seems to have a crush on you. 他好像喜欢你。
Seems like you two can get along well. 看起来你俩相处得很好。
He is exactly right/perfect for you. 他非常适合你。
You two are a perfect match. 你俩特别配。
He seems like your Mr. Right. 他看起来是那个对的人。
How about I set you two up? 我撮合撮合你俩怎么样?

短语精讲 Phrase Study

- have a crush on sb. 迷恋上某人,一见钟情
  I have a crush on this girl! 我喜欢上了这个女孩!
  I had a real crush on you at university. 我上大学的时候真的喜欢过你。
- be perfect for sb./sth. 正合适
  The flat would be perfect for my life in Shanghai. 这套公寓非常适合我在上海的生活。
  The actor is perfect for this part. 这个演员非常适合这个角色。
- set sb. up (with sb./sth.)
  1. 为(某人)安置职位,使(某人)就职
     After graduation, his father set him up in the company.
     毕业后,他父亲为他在这家公司安排了职位。
  2. 撮合某人
     There's a guy from work I'd really like to set you up with. 我很想撮合你和一个我的同事。
  3. 资助
     A bank loan helped to set him up in business. 他靠一笔银行贷款做起了生意。
  4. 使精力充沛;使健康
     A good breakfast really sets you up for the day.
     一顿好的早餐真的可以让你一天都精力充沛。

Unit 11　情感 Relationship

💬 场景对话 Conversation

A: Hi, are you Jack?
B: Yeah, nice to meet you.
A: Nice to meet you, too. I'm Alice.
B: Oh, Alice! Peter has told me a lot about you.
A: Hope he said only the good things.
B: Yeah, he always says how great you are.
A: Haha, maybe we can have dinner together someday.
B: Sounds great! Call me when you are free.
A: Sure, here's my phone number.
B: Got it! See you then.
A: Bye.

A：嗨，你是杰克吗？
B：是的，很高兴见到你。
A：我也很高兴见到你。我是爱丽丝。
B：噢，爱丽丝！彼得跟我说了很多关于你的事。
A：希望他说的都是好话。
B：是啊，他总是说你有多棒。
A：哈哈，也许哪天我们可以一起吃晚饭。
B：听起来太棒了！有空给我打电话。
A：当然，这是我的电话号码。
B：知道了！到时候见。
A：再见。

Lesson 52 约会
Dating

词汇 Vocabulary

date	英 /deɪt/	美 /deɪt/	约会 / 约会对象
couple	英 /'kʌp(ə)l/	美 /'kʌp(ə)l/	情侣 / 夫妻
boyfriend	英 /'bɔɪfrend/	美 /'bɔɪfrend/	男朋友
girlfriend	英 /'gɜːlfrend/	美 /'gɜːrlfrend/	女朋友

实用表达 Useful Expressions

01 询问是否单身

Are you single? 你单身吗?
Are you dating/seeing anyone now?
你最近在和人约会吗?
Do you have a boyfriend/girlfriend now?
你现在有男朋友 / 女朋友吗?

> **短语精讲** Phrase Study
> - date sb.=see sb. 与某人约会
>   Are you seeing anyone now?
>   你最近在和人约会吗?
>   How long have you been dating Jane?
>   你和简约会多久了?

词汇精讲 Word Study

single
英 /'sɪŋgl/
美 /'sɪŋgl/

a. 1. 单个的；单一的；唯一的
   A single shot rang out. 传来一声响亮的枪声。
2. 单独的；各自的
   The price of a single ticket is 39 pounds. 单程票的价格是 39 英镑。
3. 单身的；未婚的
   Are you single? 你单身吗?
4. （房间）单人的，单人使用的
   I have a reservation for a single room. 我预订了一个单人间。

02 发出邀请

May I ask you out?
我可以邀请你出去吗?
Would you go on a date with me?
你愿意和我约会吗?
Would you like to go out with me?
你愿意和我出去约会吗?
Do you have time for dinner tomorrow night?
你明晚有时间（和我）去吃饭吗?

> **短语精讲** Phrase Study
> - ask sb. out 约某人出去，和某人出去约会
>   =go on a date with sb. =go out with sb.
>   Do you wanna go out with me?
>   你愿意和我出去玩儿吗?
>   Will she say yes if I ask her out?
>   如果我约她出去，她会答应吗?

03 约定时间

I'll pick you up at 7.
我七点接你。

I'll come by whenever you're ready.
你什么时候准备好了我就来。

Can we meet at 7?
我们七点见好吗?

I'll wait for you there. No hurry.
我在那儿等你,不用着急。

短语精讲 Phrase Study

- come by
  1. 弄到,得到
     How did you come by that letter?
     你怎么得到这封信的?
  2. 顺便拜访
     Come by to pick me up at your convenience. 在你方便的时候来接我。

04 结束

I had a really good time tonight.
我今晚很开心。

It was fun. We should go out again later.
很有意思,我们以后再约吧。

Will there be a second date?
还能再约会吗?

短语精讲 Phrase Study

- have a good time 过得愉快,玩得开心
  We had a good time on the holiday.
  我们假期玩得很开心。
  You'll have a good time at the party.
  你会在派对上玩得很开心的。

场景对话 Conversation

A: Are you free this weekend?
B: Yeah. I think so.
A: Would you like to go to watch a movie with me?
B: Sure. I'd love to.
A: I'll pick you up at 6. Is that OK for you?
B: That would be great. Thanks.
A: My pleasure. See you on the weekend then.
B: Alright. Bye.

A:这个周末你有空吗?
B:是的,有空。
A:你愿意和我一起去看电影吗?
B:当然,我很乐意。
A:我6点来接你,这样合适吗?
B:那太好了,谢谢。
A:是我的荣幸。那周末见。
B:好的,再见。

Lesson 53　表白
Confessing Your Love

词汇 Vocabulary

first love 初恋
unrequited love 暗恋
love at first sight 一见钟情
ex-girlfriend 前女友

first kiss 初吻
one-sided love 单恋
ex-boyfriend 前男友

实用表达 Useful Expressions

01 表达喜欢

I really like you.
我真的喜欢你。

I have feelings for you.
我对你有感觉。

You give me butterflies.
你让我心动不已。

I can't stop thinking of you.
我不能停止想你。

I've fallen in love with you.
我爱上你了。

I fell in love with you the first time I saw you.
我对你一见钟情。

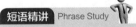 Phrase Study

- have feelings for sb. 对某人有感觉
  I don't have feelings for you.
  我对你没有感觉。
  There is a chance you might still have feelings for your ex.
  你有可能对你的前任仍有感觉。

- give sb. butterflies 让某人意乱情迷 / 心动不已
  You give me butterflies.
  你让我心动不已。
  He always gives me butterflies when he smiles at me.
  他每次对我微笑，我都会心动不已。

- fall in love with sb. 爱上某人
  She started to fall in love with him.
  她开始爱上他了。
  He has fallen in love with Mary.
  他已爱上玛丽。

02 做男女朋友

提问

Will you be my boyfriend/girlfriend?
你愿意做我的男朋友 / 女朋友吗？

Do you want to start a relationship with me?
你想和我开始一段感情吗？

 Grammar Notes

- Will you...? 表示请求，用于询问对方是否愿意做某事
  Will you be my girlfriend? 你愿意做我的女朋友吗？
  Will you marry me? 你愿意嫁给我吗？
  Will you help me? 你愿意帮帮我吗？

短语精讲 Phrase Study

- start a relationship with sb. 和某人开始一段感情
  He didn't want to start a relationship with anyone.
  他不想跟任何人开始一段感情。
  She started a relationship with Peter.
  她和彼得在一起了。

回答

（1）答应

Yeah, we can be boyfriend and girlfriend. 好啊，我们做男女朋友吧。
Yes, let me be your boyfriend/girlfriend. 好，让我成为你的男朋友/女朋友吧。
Sure, I think we'll make a good couple. 当然，我觉得我们很合适。

（2）拒绝

Sorry, I have a boyfriend/girlfriend. 对不起，我有男朋友/女朋友了。
Sorry, I just want to be friends. 对不起，我只想和你做朋友。
Aww, you're adorable. But I'm not ready for a relationship yet.
哇哦，你很好，但是我还没有准备好开始一段感情。

场景对话 Conversation

A: Hi, buddy! What are you looking at?
B: Alice. I think I have a crush on her. She gives me butterflies!
A: Wow! Then try to ask her out, bro! I heard she's still single.
B: I am not sure whether she will say yes or not.
A: Just give it a try.
B: Okay. Wish my luck!

A：嗨，哥们！你在看什么？
B：爱丽丝，我想我喜欢上她了，她让我心动不已！
A：哇！那就试着约她出去，兄弟！我听说她还是单身。
B：我不确定她是否会答应。
A：试试看吧。
B：好的，祝我好运吧！

Lesson 54 分手
Breaking up

词汇 Vocabulary

fight	英 /faɪt/	美 /faɪt/	打架 / 吵架
quarrel	英 /ˈkwɒrəl/	美 /ˈkwɑːrəl/	争吵
give sb. the cold shoulder 冷落某人		cheat on sb. 出轨 / 对某人不忠	
break up=split up 关系破裂			

实用表达 Useful Expressions

01 出现的问题

（1）吵架 / 不理会 / 不认真

We've been fighting a lot recently.
我们最近经常吵架。

I don't think you are serious about our relationship.
我认为你没有认真对待我们之间的关系。

You're being cold lately.
你最近很冷漠。

You're giving me the cold shoulder.
你总是冷落我。

 短语精讲 Phrase Study

- give sb. the cold shoulder
  冷落某人
  Why did you give me the cold shoulder yesterday?
  你昨天为什么不理我？
  Don't give me the cold shoulder.
  不要让我吃闭门羹。

词汇精讲 Word Study

serious
英 /ˈsɪəriəs/
美 /ˈsɪriəs/

a. 1. 不好的，严重的
We are faced with a serious problem. 我们面临着一个严重的问题。
2. 严肃的，需要认真思考的
Be serious for a moment; this is important. 严肃点儿，这件事很重要。

cold
英 /kəʊld/
美 /koʊld/

a. 1. 寒冷的，冷的
It's cold outside. 外面很冷。
2. 冷漠的，不友好的
His cold behavior hurt her deeply. 他冷漠的行为深深地伤害了她。

（2）出轨

Is there someone else? 你是不是有了新欢？
Are you seeing somebody else?
你在和别人约会吗？
You cheated on me. 你背叛了我。

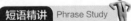 **短语精讲** Phrase Study

- cheat on sb. 出轨；对某人不忠
  How can you cheat on me?
  你怎么可以对我不忠？
  He did cheat on her.
  他的确有外遇了。

02 分手

（1）我们需要谈谈

We need to talk. 我们需要谈谈。

I'd like to talk about us. 我想聊聊我们之间的事。

（2）我们结束了

We're done. 我们结束了。

It's over between us. 我们结束了。

（3）我们分手吧

I think we should break up. 我认为我们应该分手。

I'm gonna split up with you. 我要和你分手。

（4）我们不合适 / 你可以找到更好的

We're not a good match/fit. 我们不合适。

I think you can find someone better.
我觉得你可以找到更好的。

短语精讲 Phrase Study

- break up（with sb.）（与某人）分手
  My girlfriend has broken up with me.
  我的女朋友已跟我分手。
  She wants to break up with you. 她想和你分手。

- split up（with sb.）（与某人）分手，（与某人）离婚
  They have split up.
  他们已经分手 / 离婚了。
  I split up with my boyfriend last year.
  我去年和男友分手了。

场景对话 Conversation

A: Hi, Alice, how's it going?
B: Pretty bad.
A: What happened?
B: John is being cold lately. I don't know what's going on.
A: Maybe you should talk to each other frankly and try to find a solution.
B: You're right. I will call him later.
A: I believe everything is gonna be fine.

A：嗨，爱丽丝，最近怎么样？
B：很糟糕。
A：发生了什么事？
B：约翰最近很冷淡。我不知道这是怎么回事。
A：也许你们应该坦诚地交谈，试着找到一个解决方案。
B：你说得对，我待会儿给他打电话。
A：我相信一切都会好的。

Lesson 55 婚姻
Marriage

词汇 Vocabulary

partner	英 /ˈpɑːtnə(r)/	美 /ˈpɑːrtnər/	配偶
wife	英 /waɪf/	美 /waɪf/	妻子
husband	英 /ˈhʌzbənd/	美 /ˈhʌzbənd/	丈夫
bride	英 /braɪd/	美 /braɪd/	新娘
groom	英 /gruːm/	美 /gruːm/	新郎

best man 伴郎　　　　　　　　maid of honor 伴娘
wedding（ceremony）婚礼　　invitation（letter）请帖
wedding dress 婚纱

实用表达 Useful Expressions

01　求婚

Will you marry me?
你愿意嫁给我吗?

Will you be my wife/husband?
你愿意成为我的妻子/丈夫吗?

Would you like to be my partner in life?
你愿意成为我一生的伴侣吗?

Are you willing to spend the rest of your life with me?
你愿意和我共度余生吗?

> **句型精讲** Sentence Structure
>
> - be willing to do sth. 愿意做某事
>   Are you willing to do that?
>   你愿意那么做吗?
>   I'm willing to do whatever I have to do this time.
>   这次无论什么事情我都愿意做。

词汇精讲 Word Study

marry
英 /ˈmæri/
美 /ˈmæri/

v.（和某人）结婚;嫁;娶
1. marry sb.
   She married a Korean. 她嫁给了一个韩国人。
2. marry + a.
   They married old. 他们年迈的时候结的婚。
3. get married
   I'm gonna get married. 我要结婚了。

02　婚礼

（1）筹划婚礼

When will you have your wedding? 你什么时候举行婚礼?
Who do you want to send invitations to? 你想给谁发请帖?

Who will officiate at the wedding? 谁将主持婚礼？

Where do you want the wedding to be? 你想在哪儿举行婚礼？

Will you be my best man/maid of honor? 你愿意做我的伴郎/伴娘吗？

Have you tried on your wedding dress? 你试穿婚纱了吗？

词汇精讲 Word Study

invitation
英 /ˌɪnvɪ'teɪʃ(ə)n/
美 /ˌɪnvɪ'teɪʃ(ə)n/

n. 1.（口头或书面的）邀请
I can't accept your invitation. 我不能接受你的邀请。
2. 请帖，请柬
Hundreds of invitations are being sent out this week.
本周将寄出数百份请柬。

officiate
英 /ə'fɪʃieɪt/
美 /ə'fɪʃieɪt/

v. 主持（仪式）；履行职务
He officiated at the wedding ceremony. 他主持了婚礼。
She will officiate as manager. 她将担任经理的职务。

（2）婚礼当天（祝福）

We're so happy for you! 我们真为你们开心！

Congratulations on your marriage! 恭喜你们喜结良缘！

I'd like to propose a toast to this couple! 我提议为这对夫妻的幸福干杯！

Wishing you a lifetime of love and happiness! 祝你们一生拥有爱与幸福！

03 离婚

I want a divorce. 我想离婚。

Let's get divorced. 我们离婚吧。

Divorce may be good for both of us.
离婚也许对我们两个人都好。

词汇精讲 Word Study

divorce
英 /dɪ'vɔːs/
美 /dɪ'vɔːrs/

n. 离婚
They have agreed to get a divorce. 他们已同意离婚。

v. 与……离婚
My parents divorced when I was very young. 我很小的时候父母就离婚了。

场景对话 Conversation

A: I have something important to tell you.

B: What happened?

A: Alice and I have decided to get married.

B: Wow, so when will you have your wedding?

A: In next month.

B: Who do you want to send invitations to?

A: Our families and some close friends. And will you be my best man?

B: Of course!

A：我有重要的事要告诉你。

B：发生了什么事？

A：爱丽丝和我已经决定结婚了。

B：哇，那你们什么时候举行婚礼？

A：下个月。

B：你想邀请谁来参加？

A：我们的家人和一些好朋友。你愿意做我的伴郎吗？

B：当然！

Unit 12　节日 Holidays

Lesson 56　圣诞节
Christmas

词汇 Vocabulary

reindeer	英 /ˈreɪndɪə(r)/	美 /ˈreɪndɪr/	驯鹿
sleigh	英 /sleɪ/	美 /sleɪ/	雪橇
mistletoe	英 /ˈmɪsltəʊ/	美 /ˈmɪsltoʊ/	槲寄生
bauble	英 /ˈbɔːb(ə)l/	美 /ˈbɔːb(ə)l/	装饰球
wreath	英 /riːθ/	美 /riːθ/	花环
bell	英 /bel/	美 /bel/	铃铛
turkey	英 /ˈtɜːki/	美 /ˈtɜːrki/	火鸡
ham	英 /hæm/	美 /hæm/	火腿

rib roast 肋排烤肉　　beef wellington 惠灵顿牛肉
Santa Claus 圣诞老人　　Santa hat 圣诞帽
Christmas sweater 圣诞毛衣　　Christmas stocking 圣诞袜
Christmas tree 圣诞树　　candy cane 拐杖糖
Christmas card 圣诞贺卡　　Christmas party 圣诞派对
Christmas fair/market 圣诞集市　　gingerbread cookies 姜饼曲奇
Christmas pudding 圣诞布丁

实用表达 Useful Expressions

01　节日祝福

(Wish you a) Merry Christmas!
Have a joyful Christmas!
Happy Christmas!
圣诞快乐！

02　关于圣诞节的闲聊

A: What are your plans for Christmas?
　　你圣诞节的计划是什么？
B: I'm going to have dinner with my family/girlfriend.
　　我打算和家人/女朋友吃晚饭。

A: Would you like to go to Jack's Christmas party?
　　你想去杰克的圣诞派对吗？

B: Yes, I'd like to. 是的，我想去。
No, I'm gonna stay at home with my family.
不去，我打算和家人待在家里。

A: There's a Christmas fair nearby. Do you wanna come?
附近有一个圣诞集市。你想去吗？

B: Yeah! Sounds great! 好啊！听起来很棒！
I'd love to, but I have to spend that night with my family.
我想去，但是我不得不和家人一起过圣诞夜。

A: Who are you celebrating Christmas with? 你要和谁一起过圣诞节？

B: My family/friends/boyfriend/girlfriend.
我的家人 / 朋友 / 男朋友 / 女朋友。

A: What gifts did you buy? 你买了什么礼物？

B: I bought a sweater for my mom and a pair of shoes for my dad.
我给我妈买了一件毛衣，给我爸买了一双鞋。

A: What's in your Christmas wish list? 你的圣诞心愿是什么？

B: A bike and a guitar. 一辆自行车和一把吉他。

场景对话 Conversation

A: Merry Christmas!
B: Merry Christmas!
A: Oh, what are your plans for Christmas?
B: I'm going to have dinner with my family.
A: Alright. There's a Christmas fair nearby. Do you wanna come?
B: Yeah! Sounds great!
A: Let's go!

A：圣诞快乐！
B：圣诞快乐！
A：噢，你的圣诞节计划是什么？
B：我要和家人一起吃晚饭。
A：好的。附近有个圣诞集市，你想去吗？
B：想啊！听起来太棒了！
A：我们走吧！

Lesson 57　感恩节
Thanksgiving Day

词汇 Vocabulary

gravy　　　　　　英 /'greɪvi/　　　美 /'greɪvi/　　　肉汁
(roasted) turkey （烤）火鸡　　　　pumpkin pie 南瓜派
cranberry sauce 蔓越莓酱　　　　　　pumpkin (pie) spice 南瓜蘸料
mashed potatoes 土豆泥　　　　　　　dinner rolls 餐包
green beans 青豆　　　　　　　　　　Turkey Pardoning 火鸡特赦
Thanksgiving Day Parade 感恩节游行　　NFL Thanksgiving Day Games 感恩节大战

实用表达 Useful Expressions

01　节日祝福

Happy Thanksgiving! 感恩节快乐！
May you have the best Thanksgiving ever! 愿你度过最好的感恩节！
Wish you a happy and blessed Thanksgiving!
愿你度过一个幸福美好的感恩节！

02　关于感恩节的闲聊

A: What are you up to for Thanksgiving Day?
　　你感恩节的时候想做什么？
B: I will be home to have a big dinner with my family. 我会回家和家人吃顿大餐。
　　I am going to watch football games on TV.
　　我会在电视上看橄榄球比赛。

A: Are we going to watch the NFL Thanksgiving Day Games together this year?
　　我们今年一起看感恩节大战吗？
B: Sure thing. /Certainly. 当然啦。
　　I want to but I don't have time. I have a family gathering.
　　我想去，但是我没有时间。我有一个家庭聚会。

A: What do you usually eat at Thanksgiving? 你感恩节的时候经常吃什么？
B: We eat roasted turkey and some vegetable side dishes.
　　我们吃火鸡和一些蔬菜配菜。

场景对话 Conversation

A: Happy Thanksgiving!
B: Happy Thanksgiving to you, too!
A: What are you up to for Thanksgiving Day?
B: I will be home to have dinner with my family. What about you?
A: I am going to watch football games.
B: That's awesome!

A：感恩节快乐!
B：感恩节快乐!
A：感恩节你有什么打算?
B：我要回家和家人一起吃晚饭。你呢?
A：我要去看橄榄球比赛。
B：太棒了!

Lesson 58 万圣节
Halloween

词汇 Vocabulary

单词	英式音标	美式音标	中文
Jack-O'-Lantern	英 /ˌdʒæk ə ˈlæntən/	美 /ˌdʒæk ə ˈlæntərn/	南瓜灯
vampire	英 /ˈvæmpaɪə(r)/	美 /ˈvæmpaɪər/	吸血鬼
werewolf	英 /ˈweəwʊlf/	美 /ˈwerwʊlf/	狼人
mummy	英 /ˈmʌmi/	美 /ˈmʌmi/	木乃伊
pirate	英 /ˈpaɪrət/	美 /ˈpaɪrət/	海盗
cowboy	英 /ˈkaʊbɔɪ/	美 /ˈkaʊbɔɪ/	（男）牛仔
cowgirl	英 /ˈkaʊɡɜːl/	美 /ˈkaʊɡɜːrl/	（女）牛仔
wizard	英 /ˈwɪzəd/	美 /ˈwɪzərd/	男巫师
witch	英 /wɪtʃ/	美 /wɪtʃ/	女巫师
zombie	英 /ˈzɒmbi/	美 /ˈzɑːmbi/	僵尸
prince	英 /prɪns/	美 /prɪns/	王子
princess	英 /ˌprɪnˈses/	美 /ˈprɪnses/	公主
fang	英 /fæŋ/	美 /fæŋ/	尖牙
wig	英 /wɪɡ/	美 /wɪɡ/	假发
mask	英 /mɑːsk/	美 /mæsk/	面具
sword	英 /sɔːd/	美 /sɔːrd/	宝剑
broom	英 /bruːm/	美 /bruːm/	扫帚

trick or treat 不给糖就捣蛋　　Halloween Costume Party 万圣节化装舞会
eye patch 眼罩

实用表达 Useful Expressions

关于万圣节的闲聊

A: What do you do at Halloween? 你万圣节的时候做什么？
B: I normally watch some scary movies with my friends.
我通常和朋友一起看一些恐怖的电影。
I would attend a Halloween costume party. 我会参加万圣节化妆舞会。

A: Would you like to come to a Halloween party? 你想参加万圣节派对吗？
B: Absolutely! That will be fun! 当然啦！那一定很有趣！
No, not really. I'm afraid of those spooky things. 不，我怕那些怪异的东西。

词汇精讲 Word Study

spooky
英 /'spu:ki/
美 /'spu:ki/

a. 怪异吓人的；阴森恐怖的
It's a spooky old house.
这是一座阴森森的老房子。
There is a spooky atmosphere in the house.
这个房子里有一种阴森恐怖的气氛。

A: What costume are you going to wear to the party? 你要穿什么服装去参加派对？
B: I'm not sure. Can you help me choose one costume?
我不确定。你能帮我选一件吗？
I think I will go as <u>a zombie.</u> 我想扮成僵尸。
I decide to dress up as <u>a witch</u>. 我决定扮成女巫。

场景对话 Conversation

A: Would you like to come to a Halloween Party?
B: Absolutely! That will be fun!
A: Then what costume are you going to wear to the party?
B: I think I will go as a zombie. What about you?
A: I decide to dress up as a witch.
B: That's cool! See you tonight.
A: See you.

A：你想参加万圣节派对吗？
B：当然！那会很有趣！
A：那你打算穿什么服装去参加呢？
B：我想我会扮成僵尸去。你呢？
A：我决定扮成一个女巫。
B：那很酷！今晚见。
A：再见。

Lesson 59 情人节
Valentine's Day

词汇 Vocabulary

jewelry	英 /ˈdʒuːəlri/	美 /ˈdʒuːəlri/	珠宝
ring	英 /rɪŋ/	美 /rɪŋ/	戒指
bracelet	英 /ˈbreɪslət/	美 /ˈbreɪslət/	手镯
necklace	英 /ˈnekləs/	美 /ˈnekləs/	项链
handbag	英 /ˈhændbæg/	美 /ˈhændbæg/	手提包
candle	英 /ˈkænd(ə)l/	美 /ˈkænd(ə)l/	蜡烛
perfume	英 /ˈpɜːfjuːm/	美 /pərˈfjuːm/	香水

stuffed animal 毛绒玩具　　　　Teddy bear 泰迪熊
Valentine's Day card 情人节贺卡　　a box of chocolate 一盒巧克力
a bouquet of roses 一束玫瑰花

实用表达 Useful Expressions

01 关于赠送礼物

I would like to buy a box of chocolate for my girlfriend.
我想为我女朋友买一盒巧克力。

Chris sent me a lovely bouquet of roses on Valentine's Day.
克里斯在情人节送给我一束可爱的玫瑰花。

Here are some red roses for you, honey. 亲爱的，这是送你的红玫瑰。
I wrote a poem for my girlfriend. 我为女朋友写了一首诗。
I got you a very cute stuffed animal. 我给你买了一个非常可爱的毛绒玩具。
I found a Valentine's Day card in my locker.
我在储物柜里发现了一张情人节贺卡。

I think candles make a very good gift. 我认为蜡烛是很不错的礼物。
My boyfriend gave me a bottle of perfume for Valentine's Day.
我的男朋友送了我一瓶香水作为情人节礼物。

02 甜言蜜语

I am yours forever. 我永远是你的。

You are so beautiful! 你真美！

You take my breath away. 你美得让我窒息。

Your smile is as bright as the sun as it rises in the morning.
你的微笑和早晨的太阳一样灿烂。

I can't stop thinking about you. 我无法停止想你。

You're the light in my life. 你是我生命中的光。

I love you more than life itself. 我爱你胜过自己的生命。

When I close my eyes, you're all I see. 当我闭上眼睛，我满脑子都是你。

场景对话 Conversation

A: Hi, how can I help you?

B: Hi, I would like to buy something for my girlfriend for Valentine's Day. What do you recommend?

A: Well, we have Teddy bears in different sizes and colors.

B: Perfect! I'll take the big one. Thank you.

A: Very good, sir. That will be 34 dollars.

B: Here you go.

A：嗨，我能为您做些什么吗？

B：嗨，我想给我女朋友买情人节礼物。你有什么推荐的吗？

A：我们有不同大小和颜色的泰迪熊。

B：完美！我要大的那个，谢谢。

A：好的，先生。一共 34 美元。

B：给你。

Lesson 60 其他节日
Other Holidays

词汇 Vocabulary

- 其他常见节日：
  New Year's Day 新年　　　　　　Labor Day 劳动节
  Mother's Day 母亲节　　　　　　Children's Day 儿童节
  Father's Day 父亲节　　　　　　Teacher's Day 教师节

- 常见的中国节日：
  Spring Festival 春节　　　　　　Qingming Festival/Tomb-Sweeping Day 清明节
  The Dragon Boat Festival 端午节　The Mid-Autumn Festival 中秋节
  National Day 国庆节　　　　　　The Double Ninth Festival 重阳节

- 春节相关：
  dumpling　　　　[英]/'dʌmplɪŋ/　　[美]/'dʌmplɪŋ/　　饺子
  spring roll 春卷　　　　　　　　Tangyuan（sweet rice ball）汤圆
  red envelope/packet 红包　　　　CCTV New Year's Gala 春晚
  family reunion dinner/Chinese New Year's Eve dinner 团圆饭/年夜饭

- 端午节相关：
  Zongzi 粽子　　　　　　　　　　dragon boat race 龙舟赛
  five-color silk thread 五彩绳

- 中秋节相关：
  mooncake　　　　[英]/'muːnkeɪk/　　[美]/'muːnkeɪk/　　月饼
  lantern　　　　　[英]/'læntən/　　　[美]/'læntərn/　　灯笼
  hairy crab 大闸蟹　　　　　　　　guess lantern riddles 猜灯谜

实用表达 Useful Expressions

Mother's Day 母亲节

01 节日祝福

Happy Mother's Day, dear mother! Thanks for bringing me up and taking care of me.
母亲节快乐，亲爱的妈妈！感谢您抚养我并照顾我。

Happy Mother's Day! Thank you for everything you've done for us. It's more than we can ever repay you!
母亲节快乐！感谢您为我们所做的一切，我们无以为报！

短语精讲 Phrase Study

- bring sb. up 抚养，养育，长大
  She brought up four children. 她养大了4个孩子。
  His grandmother brought him up. 他的祖母把他养大。
- bring sth. up 提出
  I will bring it up when the time is right. 时机合适的时候我会提这件事。
  She brought up the subject of money. 她提出了钱的话题。

词汇精讲 Word Study

repay
英 /rɪˈpeɪ/
美 /rɪˈpeɪ/

v. 1. 归还；偿还；清偿
He has to repay the debt. 他不得不偿还这笔债务。
2. 报答
I don't know how I can ever repay you. 我不知道怎样才能报答你。

02 关于母亲节的闲聊

A: Have you called your mom today? 你今天给你妈妈打电话了吗？

B: Yeah, I have. I also sent her a Mother's Day message.
打了。我还给她发了母亲节的祝福信息。
I haven't yet. I will call her after work. 我还没打呢，下班之后给她打。

Father's Day 父亲节

01 节日祝福

Happy Father's Day! I'm so proud to be your son/daughter.
父亲节快乐！作为您的儿子/女儿，我感到很自豪。

Dad, you know that I like Batman, and Superman is cool too, but I don't really need them as long as I have you!
爸爸，你知道我喜欢蝙蝠侠，超人也很酷，但是只要我有你，我就不需要他们！

句型精讲 Sentence Structure

- be proud to do sth. 为做某事感到骄傲
  I'm proud to have you as my father.
  有您做我的父亲，我很骄傲。
  I'm very proud to be a part of the team.
  能成为队中的一员，我感到十分荣幸。

02 关于父亲节的闲聊

A: What are you going to get your dad for Father's Day?
父亲节你打算给你爸爸买什么礼物？

B: I am planning to buy a tie and a lighter. 我计划买一条领带和一个打火机。
I am going to buy a pair of shoes. 我打算买一双鞋。

The Spring Festival 春节

A: How do you usually spend the Spring Festival? 你一般怎么过春节？

B: I will go home to attend the family reunion. 我会回家和家人团聚。
I usually watch the New Year's Gala with my family. 我通常和家人一起看春晚。

A: What do you eat for the New Year's Eve? 你们除夕吃什么？

B: The New Year's Eve dinner is usually very large which might include fish and dumplings. 年夜饭通常都非常丰盛，可能会有鱼和饺子。

The Dragon Boat Festival 端午节

A: What do you usually eat during the Dragon Boat Festival? 你们一般端午节吃什么？

B: We usually eat Zongzi. 我们一般吃粽子。

A: How do you usually celebrate the Dragon Boat Festival? 你们通常怎么庆祝端午节？

B: We usually hold dragon boat races and tie five-color silk threads to children's wrists and ankles. 我们通常会举行龙舟赛，在小孩子的手腕和脚踝系上五彩绳。

The Mid-Autumn Festival 中秋节

A: What do you do on the Mid-Autumn Festival? 你们中秋节做什么？

B: We usually have dinner with our family, eat mooncakes, enjoy the moon and guess lantern riddles. 我们通常和家人一起吃晚餐，吃月饼，赏月和猜灯谜。

场景对话 Conversation

A: Hey, what's the next coming holiday?
A：嘿，下一个假期是什么？

B: I think it's Father's Day.
B：我想是父亲节。

A: What are you going to get your dad for Father's Day?
A：父亲节你准备送你爸爸什么礼物？

B: I am planning to buy a tie and a lighter. What about you?
B：我打算买一条领带和一个打火机。你呢？

A: I am going to buy a pair of shoes.
A：我打算去买一双鞋。

B: Good idea!
B：好主意！

Chapter Three

基本问答

导 语

　　本章"基本问答"涵盖了日常生活中最常见的 20 个话题，共分成 4 个单元。第 13 单元和第 14 单元包含了生活日常的 10 个话题，分别是晨间日常、做家务、一日三餐、学习、工作、交通、购物、家庭成员、周末和社交；第 15 单元和第 16 单元包含了兴趣爱好的 10 个话题，分别是宠物、电影、游戏、书籍、音乐、手机应用、运动、拍照、旅游和电视节目。

　　通过问答的形式，本章引出回答问题的一个重要技巧——PDC 原则。

　　PDC 是 Point、Details 和 Conclusion 首字母的缩写，即当我们面对一个提问时，我们首先应该提出观点（Point），然后陈述细节（Details）来丰富我们的回答，最后得出结论（Conclusion）。

　　通过以上三步，我们便能简洁明了又有条理地回答提问。该原则不仅适用于日常生活，在考试中也是非常实用的答题技巧。还等什么？让我们马上开始学习吧！

Unit 13　生活日常（一）Daily Life 1

Lesson 61　晨间日常
Morning Routine

What do you do in the morning?

01 PDC 结构 PDC Structure

表明观点 Point

Well, I'd love to get up early in the morning, since there are lots of things that need doing. 我早上喜欢早起，因为有很多事情需要做。

> **实用替换 Useful Alternatives**
>
> I'd love to get up late in the morning, since I can get more sleep.
> 我早上喜欢晚起，这样我可以睡得更多一些。

陈述细节 Details

1. I usually get up at around 8.
   我通常八点左右起床。

2. I do my bed, and go to the bathroom to brush my teeth and wash my face.
   我整理床铺，去卫生间刷牙洗脸。

   > **实用替换 Useful Alternatives**
   >
   > take a bath/shower 洗澡 / 淋浴
   > shave
   > 刮胡子

3. Then I have some breakfast with my family at home. If I don't have any classes, I'd probably work out or learn English.
   然后我在家和家人一起吃早餐。如果没有课，我可能会锻炼或学英语。

   > **实用替换 Useful Alternatives**
   >
   > drink some water 喝水　　watch TV 看电视
   > stretch my body 伸展身体　listen to music 听音乐
   > check my phone 查看手机　write my daily to-do list 写今日待办清单
   > go to class/work 上课 / 班　read books or newspapers 读书 / 看报

👉 **得出结论 Conclusion**

I just have a busy and organized schedule in the morning.
我的早上就是这么忙碌而又井井有条。

02 表达示例 Example

What do you do in the morning? 你早上做什么？

Well, I'd love to get up early in the morning, since there are lots of things that need doing. I usually get up at around 8. I do my bed, and go to the bathroom to brush my teeth and wash my face. Then I have some breakfast with my family at home. If I don't have any classes, I'd probably work out or learn English. I just have a busy and organized schedule in the morning.

我早上喜欢早起，因为有很多事情需要做。我通常八点左右起床，整理床铺，去卫生间刷牙洗脸。然后我在家和家人一起吃早餐。如果没有课，我可能会锻炼或学英语。我的早上就是这么忙碌而又井井有条。

Lesson 62 做家务
Doing Housework

Do you usually do housework?

肯定回答 Positive Attitude

01 PDC 结构 PDC Structure

表明观点 Point

When it comes to housework, I usually find it fun.
说到家务，我通常觉得是有意思的。

陈述细节 Details

1. Because to me, it's like a hobby. 因为对我来说，它就像是一个爱好。
2. Also, it really gets me moving. So, while cleaning up my place, I can exercise my body.
   它还可以让我动起来，所以打扫卫生的时候，我可以锻炼身体。

实用替换 Useful Alternatives

其他常见的家务类型：

sweep	英 /swiːp/	美 /swiːp/	扫地
vacuum	英 /ˈvækjuːm/	美 /ˈvækjuːm/	用吸尘器清扫
dust	英 /dʌst/	美 /dʌst/	擦灰尘

mop floors 拖地
do laundry 洗衣服
clean bathrooms 清洁浴室
water plants 给植物浇水
feed pets 喂宠物
wash dishes 洗碗
wash windows 擦窗户
prepare meals 准备食物
take out the trash 倒垃圾

3. I don't know why, but whenever I feel down or depressed, I feel like cleaning up my house really cheers me up.
   我不知道为什么，但是每当我感到沮丧失意，我觉得打扫房间真的能让我开心起来。

得出结论 Conclusion

Doing housework just makes my life better in every way.
做家务让我的生活在各个方面都变得更好。

02 表达示例 Example

Do you usually do housework? 你经常做家务吗?

> When it comes to housework, I usually find it fun. Because to me, it's like a hobby. Also, it really gets me moving. So, while cleaning up my place, I can exercise my body. I don't know why, but whenever I feel down or depressed, I feel like cleaning up my house really cheers me up. Doing housework just makes my life better in every way.
>
> 说到家务,我通常觉得是有意思的。因为对我来说,它就像是一个爱好。它还可以让我动起来,所以打扫卫生的时候,我可以锻炼身体。我不知道为什么,但是每当我感到沮丧失意,我觉得打扫房间真的能让我开心起来。做家务让我的生活在各个方面都变得更好。

否定回答 Negative Attitude

01 PDC 结构 PDC Structure

➤ 表明观点 Point

I really don't like doing housework. 我真的不喜欢做家务。

➤ 陈述细节 Details

1. I feel like I can use my time to do a lot of more meaningful things.
   我觉得我可以利用这些时间去做很多更有意义的事情。
2. I get pretty lazy when I see all the dishes and stuff I have to clean up.
   我看见要洗的餐具就懒得动。
3. My friends tell me I should hire a cleaning person or a maid, but I don't have the money for that.
   我的朋友告诉我,我应该雇一个清洁人员或保洁阿姨,但我没有这个钱。

➤ 得出结论 Conclusion

At the end of the day, I just really don't want to think about housework.
到头来,我就真的不想去思考家务这件事情。

02 表达示例 Example

Do you usually do housework? 你经常做家务吗?

I really don't like doing housework. I feel like I can use my time to do a lot of more meaningful things. I get pretty lazy when I see all the dishes and stuff I have to clean up. My friends tell me I should hire a cleaning person or a maid, but I don't have the money for that. At the end of the day, I just really don't want to think about housework.

我真的不喜欢做家务。我觉得我可以利用这些时间去做很多更有意义的事情。我看见要洗的餐具就懒得动。我的朋友告诉我，我应该雇一个清洁人员或保洁阿姨，但我没有这个钱。到头来，我就真的不想去思考家务这件事情。

Lesson 63　一日三餐
Meals

> **What do you typically eat in a day?**

01 PDC 结构 PDC Structure

👉 表明观点 Point

I usually have two meals a day. 我通常一天吃两顿。

👉 陈述细节 Details

1. I rarely eat breakfast because I don't have enough time.
   我几乎不吃早餐，因为时间不够。

实用替换 Useful Alternatives

For breakfast, I usually have two slices of toast, a cup of milk and some fruit.
早餐我一般吃两片吐司，喝一杯牛奶，以及吃一些水果。

常见的早餐食物：

milk	英 /mɪlk/	美 /mɪlk/	牛奶	juice	英 /dʒuːs/	美 /dʒuːs/	果汁
bread	英 /bred/	美 /bred/	面包	fruit	英 /fruːt/	美 /fruːt/	水果
toast	英 /təʊst/	美 /toʊst/	吐司	salad	英 /ˈsæləd/	美 /ˈsæləd/	沙拉
cake	英 /keɪk/	美 /keɪk/	蛋糕	porridge	英 /ˈpɒrɪdʒ/	美 /ˈpɔːrɪdʒ/	粥
yogurt	英 /ˈjɒgət/	美 /ˈjoʊgərt/	酸奶	dumpling	英 /ˈdʌmplɪŋ/	美 /ˈdʌmplɪŋ/	饺子
coffee	英 /ˈkɒfi/	美 /ˈkɔːfi/	咖啡	steamed bun/Mantou 馒头			
noodles	英 /ˈnuːd(ə)lz/	美 /ˈnuːd(ə)lz/	面条	steamed stuffed bun/Baozi 包子			
cereal	英 /ˈsɪəriəl/	美 /ˈsɪriəl/	麦片粥	soybean milk 豆浆			
egg	英 /eg/	美 /eg/	鸡蛋	(Chinese) fried dough sticks 油条			

2. Lunch and dinner, however, are a completely different story. I love eating lunch with my coworkers, when I can go out to get some pizza or hamburgers.
   但是午餐和晚餐就完全是另一回事儿了。我喜欢和同事吃午餐，我会出去吃披萨或汉堡。

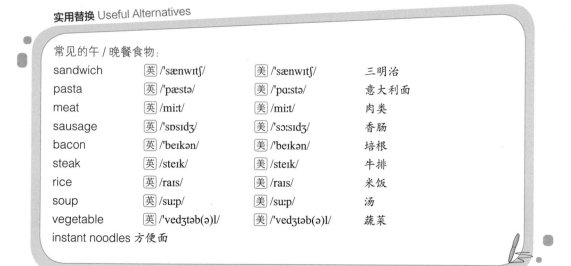

实用替换 Useful Alternatives

常见的午/晚餐食物：

sandwich	英 /'sænwɪtʃ/	美 /'sænwɪtʃ/	三明治
pasta	英 /'pæstə/	美 /'pɑːstə/	意大利面
meat	英 /miːt/	美 /miːt/	肉类
sausage	英 /'sɒsɪdʒ/	美 /'sɔːsɪdʒ/	香肠
bacon	英 /'beɪkən/	美 /'beɪkən/	培根
steak	英 /steɪk/	美 /steɪk/	牛排
rice	英 /raɪs/	美 /raɪs/	米饭
soup	英 /suːp/	美 /suːp/	汤
vegetable	英 /'vedʒtəb(ə)l/	美 /'vedʒtəb(ə)l/	蔬菜

instant noodles 方便面

3. For dinner I go all out. I love having dinner with my friends or my family. I feel that after a long day of work, I deserve a big dinner.

我晚餐吃得很丰盛。我喜欢和朋友或者家人一起吃。我觉得在一天漫长的工作后，一顿大餐是我应得的。

👉 得出结论 Conclusion

That's what I usually eat in a day. 这就是我一天通常吃的东西。

02 表达示例 Example

What do you typically eat in a day? 你一天通常吃什么？

I usually have two meals a day. I rarely eat breakfast because I don't have enough time. Lunch and dinner, however, are a completely different story. I love eating lunch with my coworkers, when I can go out to get some pizza or hamburgers. For dinner I go all out. I love having dinner with my friends or my family. I feel that after a long day of work, I deserve a big dinner. That's what I usually eat in a day.

我通常一天吃两顿。我几乎不吃早餐，因为时间不够。但是午餐和晚餐就完全是另一回事儿了。我喜欢和同事吃午餐，我会出去吃披萨或汉堡。我晚餐吃得很丰盛。我喜欢和朋友或者家人一起吃。我觉得在一天漫长的工作后，一顿大餐是我应得的。这就是我一天通常吃的东西。

Lesson 64　学习
Studying

> Do you like studying?

肯定回答 Positive Attitude

01　PDC 结构 PDC Structure

👉 提出观点 Point

I love studying. 我爱学习。

👉 陈述细节 Details

1. Studying allows me to gain more knowledge and that's something you can never get enough of. 学习让我获得更多知识，这是永远都不嫌多的。

2. Today, in the society, having more knowledge means having more competitive abilities. This means you can have a better chance of finding a great job.
在今天的社会中，掌握更多的知识意味着拥有更强的竞争能力，这意味着你找到好工作的概率更大。

3. I feel more confident and more relaxed when I have knowledge.
掌握知识让我更加自信从容。

实用替换 Useful Alternatives

get into a great school
进入好学校
get promoted 获得升职
earn more money
赚更多的钱

👉 得出结论 Conclusion

That is why I like studying. 这就是我喜欢学习的原因。

02　表达示例 Example

Do you like studying? 你喜欢学习吗？

　　I love studying. Studying allows me to gain more knowledge and that's something you can never get enough of. Today, in the society, having more knowledge means having more competitive abilities. This means you can have a better chance of finding a great job. I feel more confident and more relaxed when I have knowledge. That is why I like studying.

　　我爱学习。学习让我获得更多知识，这是永远都不嫌多的。在今天的社会中，掌握更多的知识意味着拥有更强的竞争能力，这意味着你找到好工作的概率更大。掌握知识让我更加自信从容。这就是我喜欢学习的原因。

否定回答 Negative Attitude

01 PDC 结构 PDC Structure

▶ 提出观点 Point

I hate studying. 我讨厌学习。

▶ 陈述细节 Details

1. There are always a lot of things going on in my life and studying takes too much time. I feel like if I want to enjoy life, I need to use time to do other things.
   我的生活中总是有很多事情发生,而学习花费太多时间。我觉得要享受生活的话,我需要把时间花在其他事情上。

2. In addition, the energy and concentration it takes to study are also too much.
   而且学习需要花费的精力和专注力也很多。

3. If these reasons aren't enough, I just don't have an interest in it.
   如果这些原因还不够的话,那我就只是对此不感兴趣。

▶ 得出结论 Conclusion

To sum up, I don't want to put my time and effort into studying.
总之,我不想在学习上面花费时间和精力。

02 表达示例 Example

Do you like studying? 你喜欢学习吗?

> I hate studying. There are always a lot of things going on in my life and studying takes too much time. I feel like if I want to enjoy life, I need to use time to do other things. In addition, the energy and concentration it takes to study are also too much. If these reasons aren't enough, I just don't have an interest in it. To sum up, I don't want to put my time and effort into studying.
>
> 我讨厌学习。我的生活中总是有很多事情发生,而学习花费太多时间。我觉得要享受生活的话,我需要把时间花在其他事情上。而且学习需要花费的精力和专注力也很多。如果这些原因还不够的话,那我就只是对此不感兴趣。总之,我不想在学习上面花费时间和精力。

Lesson 65 工作 Working

> **How do you like your job?**

肯定回答 Positive Attitude

01 PDC 结构 PDC Structure

☞ 表明观点 Point

I really like working as a teacher. 我真的喜欢当老师。

☞ 陈述细节 Details

1. This job is full of challenges, but it's also very stable.
   这份工作虽然充满挑战,但同时它也很稳定。

2. I find working as a teacher gives my life lots of meaning. It's really interesting to feel how it fulfills me and gives me a sense of responsibility.
   我发现当老师赋予了我的生命很多意义,而且这份工作给我带来满足感,还让我有一种责任感,这真的很有趣。

3. The money is also pretty good. It doesn't make me rich, but it makes sure I don't have to worry about money every day for my family.
   报酬也很不错,它并不能使我变得富有,但能保证我不必每天担心养家糊口的问题。

实用替换 Useful Alternatives

其他常见的职业名称:

单词	英式音标	美式音标	中文
salesperson	/ˈseɪlzpɜːsn/	/ˈseɪlzpɜːrsn/	售货员
clerk	/klɑːk/	/klɜːrk/	店员
engineer	/ˌendʒɪˈnɪə(r)/	/ˌendʒɪˈnɪr/	工程师
pilot	/ˈpaɪlət/	/ˈpaɪlət/	飞行员
secretary	/ˈsekrət(ə)ri/	/ˈsekrəteri/	秘书
editor	/ˈedɪtə(r)/	/ˈedɪtər/	编辑
artist	/ˈɑːtɪst/	/ˈɑːrtɪst/	艺术家
painter	/ˈpeɪntə(r)/	/ˈpeɪntər/	画家
photographer	/fəˈtɒgrəfə(r)/	/fəˈtɑːgrəfər/	摄影师
model	/ˈmɒd(ə)l/	/ˈmɑːd(ə)l/	模特
director	/dəˈrektə(r)/	/dəˈrektər/	导演
singer	/ˈsɪŋə(r)/	/ˈsɪŋər/	歌手
actor	/ˈæktə(r)/	/ˈæktər/	男演员
actress	/ˈæktrəs/	/ˈæktrəs/	女演员

sales manager 销售经理   product manager 产品经理
project manager 项目经理

👉 得出结论 Conclusion

Being a teacher is the best. 当老师是最好的。

02 表达示例 Example

How do you like your job? 你怎么看待你的工作？

> I really like working as a teacher. This job is full of challenges, but it's also very stable. I find working as a teacher gives me lots of meaning. It's really interesting to feel how it fulfills me and gives me a sense of responsibility. The money is also pretty good. It doesn't make me rich, but it makes sure I don't have to worry about money every day for my family. Being a teacher is the best.
>
> 我真的喜欢当老师。这份工作虽然充满挑战，但同时它也很稳定。我发现当老师赋予了我的生命很多意义，而且这份工作给我带来满足感，还让我有一种责任感，这真的很有趣。报酬也很不错，它并不能使我变得富有，但能保证我不必每天担心养家糊口的问题。当老师是最好的。

否定回答 Negative Attitude

01 PDC 结构 PDC Structure

👉 表明观点 Point

I don't like my job. 我不喜欢我的工作。

👉 陈述细节 Details

1. It's so stressful that I'm suffering from insomnia recently.
   这份工作的压力真的很大，以至于我最近都失眠了。

   实用替换 Useful Alternatives
   loss of appetite 食欲不振
   get fat 发胖

2. Moreover, it involves a lot of repetitive tasks which make me feel bored, and I am losing my passion for it.
   而且它包含大量重复性的任务，这些使我感到无聊，我正在丧失工作热情。

3. What's worse is that the salary is too low to even support myself.
   更糟糕的是，工资太低了，以至于都不能养活我自己。

👉 得出结论 Conclusion

I just want to find a new job as soon as possible. 我只想赶紧找一份新的工作。

02 表达示例 Example

How do you like your job? 你怎么看待你的工作?

I don't like my job. It's so stressful that I'm suffering from insomnia recently. Moreover, it involves a lot of repetitive tasks which make me feel bored, and I am losing my passion for it. What's worse is that the salary is too low to even support myself. I just want to find a new job as soon as possible.

我不喜欢我的工作。这份工作的压力真的很大,以至于我最近都失眠了。而且它包含大量重复性的任务,这些使我感到无聊,我正在丧失工作热情。更糟糕的是,工资太低了,以至于都不能养活我自己。我只想赶紧找一份新的工作。

Unit 14　生活日常（二） Daily Life 2

Lesson 66　交通
Transportation

> How do you get to school/work?

01　PDC 结构 PDC Structure

表明观点 Point

I usually take the subway. 我通常坐地铁。

实用替换 Useful Alternatives

其他常见的交通方式：
on foot=walk　　　　[英]/wɔːk/　　　　[美]/wɔːk/　　　　走路
by car=drive　　　　[英]/draɪv/　　　　[美]/draɪv/　　　　开车
by plane/air=take a flight=fly　　　[英]/flaɪ/　　　[美]/flaɪ/　　　坐飞机
by bus=take a bus 坐公交车
by subway=take the subway 坐地铁
by taxi=take a taxi 坐出租车
by train=take a train 坐火车
by bike/bicycle=ride a bike/bicycle=cycle 骑自行车
by high-speed rail=take the high-speed rail 坐高铁
by boat/water=take a boat 坐船

陈述细节 Details

1. The subway is really convenient for me. I can get to the subway station just by walking for five minutes.
   地铁对我来说真的很方便，我走路五分钟就可以到达地铁站。

2. It costs about two dollars every time I take it, so it's really cheap.
   坐一次地铁大概花两美元，真的很便宜。

3. Also, I feel like it's safer to take the subway. I never heard about the subway having an accident. This puts my mind at ease.
   而且我觉得坐地铁更安全。我从没听说过地铁出事故，这让我很安心。

得出结论 Conclusion

Taking the subway is safe, convenient, and a money saver. I can't think of another way I want to get to places.
坐地铁不仅安全方便，而且省钱，这是我能想到的最好的交通方式了。

02 表达示例 Example

How do you get to school/work? 你怎么去上学 / 上班？

I usually take the subway. The subway is really convenient for me. I can get to the subway station just by walking for five minutes. It costs about two dollars every time I take it, so it's really cheap. Also, I feel like it's safer to take the subway. I never heard about the subway having an accident. This puts my mind at ease. Taking the subway is safe, convenient, and a money saver. I can't think of another way I want to get to places.

我通常坐地铁。地铁对我来说真的很方便，我走路五分钟就可以到达地铁站。坐一次地铁大概花两美元，真的很便宜。而且我觉得坐地铁更安全。我从没听说过地铁出事故，这让我很安心。坐地铁不仅安全方便，而且省钱，这是我能想到的最好的交通方式了。

Lesson 67 购物 Shopping

> **Do you like shopping?**

肯定回答 Positive Attitude

01 PDC 结构 PDC Structure

表明观点 Point

I love shopping. 我喜欢购物。

陈述细节 Details

1. Shopping fulfills me in ways I can't explain. Just the feeling of going out and buying stuff makes me excited.
   说不上来为什么，购物让我很满足，那种出门买东西的感觉就让我感到兴奋。

2. Whenever I have a lot of stress or I am just really tired from work, I go shopping. Shopping cures all problems.
   每当我压力很大或者工作真的很累的时候，我就去购物。购物解决所有的问题。

3. I think buying new clothes or getting things you want in life is a great way to make you have a higher standard of living.
   我认为买新衣服或是想要的东西能很好地提高生活水平。

实用替换 Useful Alternatives

其他常见的商品类型：

shoes	英 /ʃuːz/	美 /ʃuːz/	鞋子
cosmetics	英 /kɒzˈmetɪks/	美 /kɑːzˈmetɪks/	化妆品
jewelry	英 /ˈdʒuːəlri/	美 /ˈdʒuːəlri/	珠宝
book	英 /bʊk/	美 /bʊk/	书籍
stationery	英 /ˈsteɪʃənri/	美 /ˈsteɪʃəneri/	文具
electronic product 电子产品			

得出结论 Conclusion

That's why I love shopping. 这就是我喜欢购物的原因。

02 表达示例 Example

Do you like shopping? 你喜欢购物吗？

I love shopping. Shopping fulfills me in ways I can't explain. Just the feeling of going out and buying stuff makes me excited. Whenever I have a lot of stress or I am just really tired from work, I go shopping. Shopping cures all problems. I think buying new clothes or getting things you want in life is a great way to make you have a higher standard of living. That's why I love shopping.

我喜欢购物。说不上来为什么，购物让我很满足，那种出门买东西的感觉就让我感到兴奋。每当我压力很大或者工作真的很累的时候，我就去购物。购物解决所有的问题。我认为买新衣服或是想要的东西能很好地提高生活水平。这就是我喜欢购物的原因。

否定回答 Negative Attitude

01 PDC 结构 PDC Structure

表明观点 Point

I can't stand the idea of shopping. 我受不了购物。

陈述细节 Details

1. Shopping is a complete waste of time. I have to get up, go to a mall and walk around to find something I want to buy.
   购物完全是浪费时间。我得起床、去商场、走来走去找我要买的东西。

实用替换 Useful Alternatives

其他常见的购物场所：

supermarket	英 /ˈsuːpəmɑːkɪt/	美 /ˈsuːpərmɑːrkɪt/	超市
drugstore	英 /ˈdrʌgstɔː(r)/	美 /ˈdrʌgstɔːr/	药店
bakery	英 /ˈbeɪkəri/	美 /ˈbeɪkəri/	面包店
florist's	英 /ˈflɒrɪsts/	美 /ˈflɔːrɪsts/	花店
greengrocer's	英 /ˈgriːnɡrəʊsə(r)z/	美 /ˈgriːnɡroʊsərz/	蔬菜水果店

shopping mall/center 购物中心　　　department store 百货商场
outlet（store）奥特莱斯店（经销店，折扣店）
convenience store 便利店　　　grocery store 杂货店
book store 书店　　　hardware store 五金店

2. I don't feel the need to get myself new clothes; to me it's just a waste of money.
   我没有买新衣服的需求。对于我来说，这只是在浪费钱。
3. To top it all off, shopping makes me exhausted. I can't think of anything more tiring than shopping.
   更糟糕的是，购物让我筋疲力尽。购物是让我觉得最累的事情。

👉 得出结论 Conclusion

I hate shopping. 我讨厌购物。

02 表达示例 Example

Do you like shopping? 你喜欢购物吗？

> I can't stand the idea of shopping. Shopping is a complete waste of time. I have to get up, go to a mall and walk around to find something I want to buy. I don't feel the need to get myself new clothes; to me it's just a waste of money. To top it all off, shopping makes me exhausted. I can't think of anything more tiring than shopping. I hate shopping.
>
> 我受不了购物。购物完全是浪费时间。我得起床、去商场、走来走去找我要买的东西。我没有买新衣服的需求。对于我来说，这只是在浪费钱。更糟糕的是，购物让我筋疲力尽。购物是让我觉得最累的事情。我讨厌购物。

Lesson 68　家庭成员
Family Members

> Can you say something about your family?

01 PDC 结构 PDC Structure

👉 表明观点 Point

I have a big family of five, my parents, my wife, my daughter, and me.
我的大家庭有五口人，我父母、妻子、女儿，还有我。

实用替换 Useful Alternatives

描述家庭大小：

There are five people in my family.
我家里有五口人。

I have a（big/small）family of six.
我的（大/小）家庭有六口人。

I come from a big/small family.
我来自一个大/小家庭。

My family is（quite/very）big/small.
我的家庭（相当/非常）大/小。

家庭成员的名称：

英文	英式音标	美式音标	中文
parent	英 /ˈpeərənt/	美 /ˈperənt/	父亲；母亲
father	英 /ˈfɑːðə(r)/	美 /ˈfɑːðər/	
=dad	英 /dæd/	美 /dæd/	父亲
mother	英 /ˈmʌðə(r)/	美 /ˈmʌðər/	
=mom	英 /mɒm/	美 /mɑːm/	
=mum	英 /mʌm/	美 /mʌm/	母亲
son	英 /sʌn/	美 /sʌn/	儿子
daughter	英 /ˈdɔːtə(r)/	美 /ˈdɔːtər/	女儿
husband	英 /ˈhʌzbənd/	美 /ˈhʌzbənd/	丈夫
wife	英 /waɪf/	美 /waɪf/	妻子
grandparent	英 /ˈgrænpeərənt/	美 /ˈgrænperənt/	（外）祖父母
grandfather	英 /ˈgrænfɑːðə(r)/	美 /ˈgrænfɑːðər/	（外）祖父
grandmother	英 /ˈgrænmʌðə(r)/	美 /ˈgrænmʌðər/	（外）祖母
sibling	英 /ˈsɪblɪŋ/	美 /ˈsɪblɪŋ/	兄弟姐妹
brother	英 /ˈbrʌðə(r)/	美 /ˈbrʌðər/	兄弟
sister	英 /ˈsɪstə(r)/	美 /ˈsɪstər/	姐妹

older/younger brother 哥哥 / 弟弟
older/younger sister 姐姐 / 妹妹

niece	英 /niːs/	美 /niːs/	侄女；外甥女
nephew	英 /ˈnefjuː/	美 /ˈnefjuː/	侄子；外甥
uncle	英 /ˈʌŋk(ə)l/	美 /ˈʌŋk(ə)l/	

和父母同辈的男性亲戚（舅/叔/伯伯/姑父/姨父）

| aunt | 英 /ɑːnt/ | 美 /ænt/ | |

和父母同辈的女性亲戚（姑/姨/伯母/婶母/舅母）

| cousin | 英 /ˈkʌz(ə)n/ | 美 /ˈkʌz(ə)n/ | 表/堂兄弟姐妹 |

step-father, step-mother 继父，继母
half-brother, half-sister 同母异父（或同父异母）的兄弟，姐妹
father-in-law, mother-in-law, son-in-law, daughter-in-law 岳父，岳母，女婿，儿媳

陈述细节 Details

1. My parents were workers before. Now they have retired and live on a pension.
   我的父母之前都是工人。现在他们都已经退休，靠养老金生活。

2. My wife is a freelance journalist. Now she is responsible for writing news stories for several websites. My daughter is 11 years old and she is in elementary school.
   我妻子是一名自由新闻工作者。她现在负责给几家网站撰写新闻报道。我的女儿11岁了，在读小学。

3. As for me, I am a bank clerk. My work is tough sometimes, but I work hard so that I may get promoted and support my family better.
   至于我，我是一名银行职员。我的工作有时很辛苦，但是我努力工作，这样才能升职养家。

> **实用替换 Useful Alternatives**
>
> My mom is a high school teacher and my father is a policeman.
> 我妈妈是一名高中教师，我爸爸是一名警察。

得出结论 Conclusion

I have a happy family and I love all of them.
我拥有一个幸福的家庭，我爱他们。

02 表达示例 Example

Can you say something about your family? 能讲讲你的家庭吗？

I have a big family of five, my parents, my wife, my daughter, and me. My parents were workers before. Now they have retired and live on a pension. My wife is a freelance journalist. Now she is responsible for writing news stories for several websites. My daughter is 11 years old and she is in elementary school. As for me, I am a bank clerk. My work is tough sometimes, but I work hard so that I may get promoted and support my family better. I have a happy family and I love all of them.

我的大家庭有五口人，我父母、妻子、女儿，还有我。我的父母之前都是工人。现在他们都已经退休，靠养老金生活。我妻子是一名自由新闻工作者。她现在负责给几家网站撰写新闻报道。我的女儿11岁了，在读小学。至于我，我是一名银行职员。我的工作有时很辛苦，但是我努力工作，这样才能升职养家。我拥有一个幸福的家庭，我爱他们。

Lesson 69 周末
Weekends

> How do you usually spend your weekends?

01 PDC 结构 PDC Structure

表明观点 Point

I usually spend my weekends going hiking. 我周末通常去徒步旅行。

实用替换 Useful Alternatives

其他常见的周末活动：

- work overtime 加班
- go for a picnic 野餐
- do housework 做家务
- play sports 做运动
- watch movies 看电影
- go to a concert 去听音乐会
- go camping 去野营
- wander around 闲逛
- hang out with friends 和朋友出去
- date sb. 和某人约会
- visit parents 去看望父母
- go shopping 去购物

陈述细节 Details

1. Work usually gives me a lot of stress and hiking just melts it all away. It is also a great way to keep in shape.
   工作通常会给我带来很大的压力，而徒步旅行可以消除这一切。而且这也是保持健康的好方法。

2. Sometimes I go with my friends or coworkers. It helps me connect with them and allows us to have a better relationship.
   有时我和朋友或者同事一起去徒步旅行，它帮助我和他们建立联系，让我们的关系更亲密。

3. I think it's really important to have a hobby. For me, hiking is the hobby I want to do every weekend for the rest of my life.
   我认为拥有业余爱好非常重要。对我来说，徒步旅行就是我一生中每个周末都想做的事情。

得出结论 Conclusion

In a word, I really enjoy going hiking on the weekends.
总之，我真的享受周末去远足。

02 表达示例 Example

How do you usually spend your weekends? 你通常怎么度过周末?

I usually spend my weekends going hiking. Work usually gives me a lot of stress and hiking just melts it all away. It is also a great way to keep in shape. Sometimes I go with my friends or coworkers. It helps me connect with them and allows us to have a better relationship. I think it's really important to have a hobby. For me, hiking is the hobby I want to do every weekend for the rest of my life. In a word, I really enjoy going hiking on the weekends.

我周末通常去徒步旅行。工作通常会给我带来很大的压力,而徒步旅行可以消除这一切。而且这也是保持健康的好方法。有时我和朋友或者同事一起去徒步旅行,它帮助我和他们建立联系,让我们的关系更亲密。我认为拥有业余爱好非常重要。对我来说,徒步旅行就是我一生中每个周末都想做的事情。总之,我真的享受周末去徒步旅行。

Lesson 70 社交 Socializing

> Do you like socializing?

肯定回答 Positive Attitude

01 PDC 结构 PDC Structure

表明观点 Point

I love socializing. 我喜欢社交。

陈述细节 Details

1. No matter what your job is or what you do, having more friends and being able to help more people are just smart.
   不管你的工作是什么，有更多的朋友、能够帮助更多的人都是一种聪明的选择。

2. No one is good at everything, so when you meet new people, there are always things you can learn from them.
   没有人擅长所有的事情，所以当你结识新的人，他们身上永远都有你可以学习的地方。

3. Nothing beats the new and fresh feeling of meeting someone for the first time and getting to know each other.
   第一次和别人见面并彼此了解是让我感到最新鲜的事情了。

得出结论 Conclusion

Socializing is something everyone must do. 社交是每个人都必须做的事情。

02 表达示例 Example

Do you like socializing? 你喜欢社交吗？

I love socializing. No matter what your job is or what you do, having more friends and being able to help more people are just smart. No one is good at everything, so when you meet new people, there are always things you can learn from them. Nothing beats the new and fresh feeling of meeting someone for the first time and getting to know each other. Socializing is something everyone must do.

我喜欢社交。不管你的工作是什么，有更多的朋友、能够帮助更多的人都是一种聪明的选择。没有人擅长所有的事情，所以当你结识新的人，他们身上永远都有你可以学习的地方。第一次和别人见面并彼此了解是让我感到最新鲜的事情了。社交是每个人都必须做的事情。

否定回答 Negative Attitude

01 PDC 结构 PDC Structure

表明观点 Point

I hate socializing. 我讨厌社交。

陈述细节 Details

1. I have a few close friends but making a lot of friends who never really talk to each other is just a waste of time.
   我有几个亲密的朋友，但结交很多从未真正互相交谈的朋友只是在浪费时间。

2. Socializing also costs a lot of money. You have to spend money going to events and then buy people dinner or drinks. It just seems too complicated.
   社交还会花费很多金钱。你必须花钱参加活动，然后请人吃饭喝酒，这都太复杂了。

3. Finally, I don't understand why I have to spend my energy on people who don't really matter to me.
   最后，我不明白我为什么要把精力花在对我来说不重要的人身上。

得出结论 Conclusion

Socializing is just not for me. 社交不适合我。

> **实用替换 Useful Alternatives**
>
> 其他常见的社交活动：
> go dating　　　　去约会
> go for a drink　　去喝一杯
> go to the disco　　去蹦迪
> go to parties　　参加聚会
> go to weddings　　参加婚礼
> attend family reunions
> 参加家庭聚会
> hang out with friends
> 和朋友出去闲逛

02 表达示例 Example

Do you like socializing? 你喜欢社交吗？

> I hate socializing. I have a few close friends but making a lot of friends who never really talk to each other is just a waste of time. Socializing also costs a lot of money. You have to spend money going to events and then buy people dinner or drinks. It just seems too complicated. Finally, I don't understand why I have to spend my energy on people who don't really matter to me. Socializing is just not for me.
>
> 我讨厌社交。我有几个亲密的朋友，但结交很多从未真正互相交谈的朋友只是在浪费时间。社交还会花费很多金钱。你必须花钱参加活动，然后请人吃饭喝酒，这都太复杂了。最后，我不明白我为什么要把精力花在对我来说不重要的人身上。社交不适合我。

Unit 15 兴趣爱好（一） Hobbies 1

Lesson 71 养宠物
Having Pets

> Do you like pets?

肯定回答 Positive Attitude

01 PDC 结构 PDC Structure

▸ 表明观点 Point

I love pets. It doesn't matter if it's a cat or a dog.
我喜欢宠物，是猫还是狗都没关系。

实用替换 Useful Alternatives

常见的宠物类型：

cat	英 /kæt/	美 /kæt/	猫
dog	英 /dɒg/	美 /dɔːg/	狗
fish	英 /fɪʃ/	美 /fɪʃ/	鱼
bird	英 /bɜːd/	美 /bɜːrd/	鸟
rabbit	英 /ˈræbɪt/	美 /ˈræbɪt/	兔子
hamster	英 /ˈhæmstə(r)/	美 /ˈhæmstər/	仓鼠
guinea pig	英 /ˈgɪni pɪg/	美 /ˈgɪni pɪg/	豚鼠
turtle	英 /ˈtɜːt(ə)l/	美 /ˈtɜːrt(ə)l/	乌龟
horse	英 /hɔːs/	美 /hɔːrs/	马
poultry	英 /ˈpəʊltri/	美 /ˈpoʊltri/	家禽

▸ 陈述细节 Details

1. Pets can spend time with me when I feel lonely. They never get bored of me. Whenever I want to play, they will always be there to play.
   当我感到孤独时，宠物可以陪伴我。它们从不嫌我烦。每当我想玩的时候，它们总是会陪我玩耍。

2. Pets are just so cute to have around. They can improve my mood.
   宠物太可爱了，有它们在身边，我的心情就能变好。

3. They also give me lots of love which can enrich my life.
   它们还给我很多的爱，丰富了我的生活。

得出结论 Conclusion

I just can't think of a reason not to have pets. 我觉得没有理由不养宠物。

02 表达示例 Example

Do you like pets? 你喜欢宠物吗？

> I love pets. It doesn't matter if it's a cat or a dog. Pets can spend time with me when I feel lonely. They never get bored of me. Whenever I want to play, they will always be there to play. Pets are just so cute to have around. They can improve my mood. They also give me lots of love which can enrich my life. I just can't think of a reason not to have pets.
>
> 我喜欢宠物，是猫还是狗都没关系。当我感到孤独时，宠物可以陪伴我。它们从不嫌我烦。每当我想玩的时候，它们总是会陪我玩耍。宠物太可爱了，有它们在身边，我的心情就能变好。它们还给我很多的爱，丰富了我的生活。我觉得没有理由不养宠物。

否定回答 Negative Attitude

01 PDC 结构 PDC Structure

表明观点 Point

I don't like pets. 我不喜欢宠物。

陈述细节 Details

1. I know pets are cute, but I also need to take the cost into consideration. The daily expenses such as food, toys and other supplies are large already, let alone what if they get sick.
   我知道宠物很可爱，但也需要把花销考虑进去。包括食物、玩具和其他用品在内的日常开支已经很大了，更不用说如果它们生病了。

2. I feel like taking care of them requires a lot of time and energy. I would much rather use the time and energy on myself to make my life better.
   我觉得照顾它们需要花费很多时间和精力。我更愿意把这些时间和精力花在自己身上，过上更好的生活。

3. Pets also have a short lifespan, except for turtles. When they pass away, I would be really sad.

宠物的寿命也很短，乌龟除外。它们去世的时候，我会很难过。

得出结论 Conclusion

To sum everything up, I really don't want to have pets. 总之，我真的不想养宠物。

02 表达示例 Example

Do you like pets? 你喜欢宠物吗？

I don't like pets. I know pets are cute, but I also need to take the cost into consideration. The daily expenses such as food, toys and other supplies are large already, let alone what if they get sick. I feel like taking care of them requires a lot of time and energy. I would much rather use the time and energy on myself to make my life better. Pets also have a short lifespan, except for turtles. When they pass away, I would be really sad. To sum everything up, I really don't want to have pets.

我不喜欢宠物。我知道宠物很可爱，但也需要把花销考虑进去。包括食物、玩具和其他用品在内的日常开支已经很大了，更不用说如果它们生病了。我觉得照顾它们需要花费很多时间和精力。我更愿意把这些时间和精力花在自己身上，过上更好的生活。宠物的寿命也很短，乌龟除外。它们去世的时候，我会很难过。总之，我真的不想养宠物。

Lesson 72　看电影
Watching Movies

> Do you like watching movies?

肯定回答 Positive Attitude

01 PDC 结构 PDC Structure

表明观点 Point

I love movies, especially comedies and sci-fi movies.
我爱电影，特别是喜剧片和科幻片。

实用替换 Useful Alternatives

其他常见的电影类型：

action	英 /ˈækʃ(ə)n/	美 /ˈækʃ(ə)n/	动作片
romance	英 /rəʊˈmæns/	美 /ˈroʊmæns/	爱情片
horror	英 /ˈhɒrə(r)/	美 /ˈhɔːrər/	恐怖片
crime	英 /kraɪm/	美 /kraɪm/	犯罪片
adventure	英 /ədˈventʃə(r)/	美 /ədˈventʃər/	探险片
documentary	英 /ˌdɒkjuˈment(ə)ri/	美 /ˌdɑːkjuˈment(ə)ri/	纪录片
superhero	英 /ˈsuːpəhɪərəʊ/	美 /ˈsuːpərhɪroʊ/	超级英雄电影
fantasy	英 /ˈfæntəsi/	美 /ˈfæntəsi/	奇幻片
suspense	英 /səˈspens/	美 /səˈspens/	悬疑片
literary	英 /ˈlɪtərəri/	美 /ˈlɪtəreri/	文艺片

陈述细节 Details

1. Watching movies is just a great way to relax. 看电影是一种很好的放松方式。
2. What's better is that you can learn so much while having a great time.
   更棒的是，你可以在娱乐的同时学到很多东西。
3. My work keeps me pretty busy, but I also want to experience something different from my life. Movies really help me out with this. From watching movies, I can pretend to be someone else.
   我工作很忙，但我也想体验和我的生活不一样的东西。电影真的帮我解决了这个问题，通过看电影，我可以假装自己是另外一个人。

▸ 得出结论 Conclusion

Watching movies is just the best. 看电影就是最棒的事情。

02 表达示例 Example

Do you like watching movies? 你喜欢看电影吗?

> I love movies, especially comedies and sci-fi movies. Watching movies is just a great way to relax. What's better is that you can learn so much while having a great time. My work keeps me pretty busy, but I also want to experience something different from my life. Movies really help me out with this. From watching movies, I can pretend to be someone else. Watching movies is just the best.
>
> 我爱电影,特别是喜剧片和科幻片。看电影是一种很好的放松方式。更棒的是,你可以在娱乐的同时学到很多东西。我工作很忙,但我也想体验和我的生活不一样的东西。电影真的帮我解决了这个问题,通过看电影,我可以假装自己是另外一个人。看电影就是最棒的事情。

否定回答 Negative Attitude

01 PDC 结构 PDC Structure

▸ 表明观点 Point

I don't really like watching movies. 我不太喜欢看电影。

▸ 陈述细节 Details

1. The tickets are really expensive. I could use that money to do a lot of other things.
   电影票真的很贵,我可以用这些钱去做很多别的事情。

2. Movies are all fake. Spending money on fake things is just not for me. I prefer living in my real life. I know a lot of people think movies are really interesting, but I just find it really hard to get into it.
   电影都是假的。我不想把钱花在虚假的事情上,我更喜欢生活在现实世界中。我知道很多人觉得电影真的很有趣,但我真的很难对电影提起兴趣。

3. Moreover, watching movies takes way too long.
   而且,看电影花费的时间太长了。

☞ **得出结论 Conclusion**

I just don't enjoy watching movies. 我就是不喜欢看电影。

02 表达示例 Example

Do you like watching movies? 你喜欢看电影吗?

> I don't really like watching movies. The tickets are really expensive. I could use that money to do a lot of other things. Movies are all fake. Spending money on fake things is just not for me. I prefer living in my real life. I know a lot of people think movies are really interesting, but I just find it really hard to get into it. Moreover, watching movies takes way too long. I just don't enjoy watching movies.
>
> 我不太喜欢看电影。电影票真的很贵,我可以用这些钱去做很多别的事情。电影都是假的。我不想把钱花在虚假的事情上,我更喜欢生活在现实世界中。我知道很多人觉得电影真的很有趣,但我真的很难对电影提起兴趣。而且,看电影花费的时间太长了。我就是不喜欢看电影。

Lesson 73　玩游戏
Playing Video Games

> **Do you like playing video games?**

肯定回答 Positive Attitude

01 PDC 结构 PDC Structure

▶ 表明观点 Point

I like playing video games. 我喜欢玩电子游戏。

▶ 陈述细节 Details

1. It helps me relax when I feel stressed out. 当我感到焦虑不安时，它可以帮助我放松。
2. I can meet a lot of people I can't meet in real life. In games, everything is less complicated. I don't have to worry about what people look like or what they do. The friendship is just simpler. 我可以遇到很多我在现实生活中无法遇到的人。在游戏中，一切都没有那么复杂。我不必担心人们的长相或是职业。游戏中的友谊更简单。
3. Also, it's a lot easier to feel good about yourself in games. Even though it's not the real world, there are a lot of things you can achieve. 而且，在游戏中让自己感觉良好要容易得多。即使不是现实世界，你在游戏中也可以实现很多目标。

▶ 得出结论 Conclusion

It's been a lifestyle for me. 对于我而言，这已经成为一种生活方式。

02 表达示例 Example

Do you like playing video games? 你喜欢玩电子游戏吗？

I like playing video games. It helps me relax when I feel stressed out. I can meet a lot of people I can't meet in real life. In games, everything is less complicated. I don't have to worry about what people look like or what they do. The friendship is just simpler. Also, it's a lot easier to feel good about yourself in games. Even though it's not the real world, there are a lot of things you can achieve. It's been a lifestyle for me.

我喜欢玩电子游戏。当我感到焦虑不安时，它可以帮助我放松。我可以遇到很多我在现实生活中无法遇到的人。在游戏中，一切都没有那么复杂，我不必担心人们的长相或是职业，游戏中的友谊更简单。而且，在游戏中让自己感觉良好要容易得多。即使不是现实世界，你在游戏中也可以实现很多目标。对于我而言，这已经成为一种生活方式。

否定回答 Negative Attitude

01 PDC 结构 PDC Structure

▶ 表明观点 Point

I don't play video games. 我不打电子游戏。

▶ 陈述细节 Details

1. It's really worthless to spend all day on games. I'm inclined to keep my spare time for my hobbies or to play with my friends.
   花一整天在游戏上真是不值得。我倾向于把空闲时间花在爱好上，或者和朋友一起玩。
2. Playing games also costs a lot of money if you want to upgrade quickly. For me I would buy some real goods rather than virtual game items.
   如果想要快速升级，玩游戏也要花很多钱。对我来说，我宁愿买些真实的商品，而不是虚拟的游戏装备。
3. Moreover, many will stay up late to play games, which is very harmful to health.
   并且，许多人会熬夜打游戏，这对健康非常有害。

▶ 得出结论 Conclusion

Playing video games is the last thing I want to do. 打游戏是我最不想做的一件事情。

02 表达示例 Example

Do you like playing video games? 你喜欢玩电子游戏吗？

> I don't play video games. It's really worthless to spend all day on games. I'm inclined to keep my spare time for my hobbies or to play with my friends. Playing games also costs a lot of money if you want to upgrade quickly. For me I would buy some real goods rather than virtual game items. Moreover, many will stay up late to play games, which is very harmful to health. Playing video games is the last thing I want to do.
>
> 我不打电子游戏。花一整天在游戏上真是不值得。我倾向于把空闲时间花在爱好上，或者和朋友一起玩。如果想要快速升级，玩游戏也要花很多钱。对我来说，我宁愿买些真实的商品，而不是虚拟的游戏装备。并且，许多人会熬夜打游戏，这对健康非常有害。打游戏是我最不想做的一件事情。

Lesson 74 读书 Reading Books

> Do you like reading books?

肯定回答 Positive Attitude

01 PDC 结构 PDC Structure

表明观点 Point

Reading books is all I do. I like reading novels and biographies.
读书是我的全部。我喜欢读小说和传记。

实用替换 Useful Alternatives

其他常见的书籍类型：

magazine	英 /ˌmæɡəˈziːn/	美 /ˈmæɡəziːn/	杂志
textbook	英 /ˈtekstbʊk/	美 /ˈtekstbʊk/	教科书
autobiography	英 /ˌɔːtəbaɪˈɒɡrəfi/	美 /ˌɔːtəbaɪˈɑːɡrəfi/	自传
comic	英 /ˈkɒmɪk/	美 /ˈkɑːmɪk/	漫画
classic	英 /ˈklæsɪk/	美 /ˈklæsɪk/	经典著作
encyclopedia	英 /ɪnˌsaɪkləˈpiːdiə/	美 /ɪnˌsaɪkləˈpiːdiə/	百科全书

children's book 儿童图书　　popular science book 科普读物
reference book 参考书　　history book 历史书

陈述细节 Details

1. There is just so much knowledge in books. It really lets me be a better person.
   书里有很多知识，让我变成更好的人。

2. Sometimes it's great to become immersed in another world and experience someone else's life by using my imagination.
   有时候，通过我的想象力融入另一个世界并体验他人的人生，这种感觉真是太好了。

3. Besides, I enjoy relaxing while reading and having a quiet time.
   此外，我喜欢在阅读时放松身心并享受安静的时光。

⊙ 得出结论 Conclusion

I can't think of a better thing to do than reading books.
读书就是我能想到的最好的事情。

02 表达示例 Example

Do you like reading books? 你喜欢读书吗?

> Reading books is all I do. I like reading novels and biographies. There is just so much knowledge in books. It really lets me be a better person. Sometimes it's great to become immersed in another world and experience someone else's life by using my imagination. Besides, I enjoy relaxing while reading and having a quiet time. I can't think of a better thing to do than reading books.
>
> 读书是我的全部。我喜欢读小说和传记。书里有很多知识,让我变成更好的人。有时候,通过我的想象力融入另一个世界并体验他人的人生,这种感觉真是太好了。此外,我喜欢在阅读时放松身心并享受安静的时光。读书就是我能想到的最好的事情。

否定回答 Negative Attitude

01 PDC 结构 PDC Structure

⊙ 表明观点 Point

I don't really read books very often. 我不经常读书。

⊙ 陈述细节 Details

1. I feel like it's kind of time-consuming. I can find better things to do with my time.
   我觉得这很耗时,我可以利用这些时间做更好的事情。
2. Books are not cheap to buy either. 而且书也并不便宜。
3. Finally, it's hard for me to really concentrate on the books and my mind wanders a lot while reading.
   最后,我很难把注意力集中在书本上,读书的时候我经常走神。

⊙ 得出结论 Conclusion

I just don't really like reading books. 我真的不太喜欢读书。

02 表达示例 Example

Do you like reading books? 你喜欢读书吗?

I don't really read books very often. I feel like it's kind of time-consuming. I can find better things to do with my time. Books are not cheap to buy either. Finally, it's hard for me to really concentrate on the books and my mind wanders a lot while reading. I just don't really like reading books.

我不经常读书。我觉得这很耗时,我可以利用这些时间做更好的事情。而且书也并不便宜。最后,我很难把注意力集中在书本上,读书的时候我经常走神。我真的不太喜欢读书。

Lesson 75 听音乐
Listening to Music

> What kind of music do you like to listen to?

01 PDC 结构 PDC Structure

表明观点 Point

I usually listen to pop music. 我通常听流行音乐。

实用替换 Useful Alternatives

其他常见的音乐类型:

单词	英式音标	美式音标	中文
jazz	英 /dʒæz/	美 /dʒæz/	爵士
hip-hop	英 /ˈhɪp hɒp/	美 /ˈhɪp hɑːp/	嘻哈
classical	英 /ˈklæsɪk(ə)l/	美 /ˈklæsɪk(ə)l/	古典音乐
rock'n'roll	英 /ˈrɒkənrəʊl/	美 /ˈrɑːkənroʊl/	
=rock	英 /rɒk/	美 /rɑːk/	摇滚乐
rap	英 /ræp/	美 /ræp/	说唱音乐
blues	英 /bluːz/	美 /bluːz/	布鲁斯音乐，蓝调
R&B	英 /ˌɑː(r)ənˈbiː/	美 /ˌɑːrənˈbiː/	节奏布鲁斯
country	英 /ˈkʌntri/	美 /ˈkʌntri/	乡村音乐

陈述细节 Details

1. It's really fun and enjoyable to listen to, and at the same time it helps me relax.
   听流行音乐真的很有趣，而且很令人愉快，同时也可以帮助我放松。

2. Those pop songs get me thinking about the good times I used to share with my friends and family.
   那些流行歌曲让我想起了过去与朋友和家人共度的美好时光。

3. Some songs have really great lyrics and engaging rhythms, which allow me to immerse myself into the music. They can always evoke various emotions such as happiness, sadness or even anger.
   有些歌曲的歌词非常好，节奏也非常引人入胜，让我沉浸其中。它们总能唤起我的各种情绪，比如开心、悲伤、甚至是愤怒。

得出结论 Conclusion

Pop music is just my favorite music genre. 流行乐是我最喜欢的音乐类型。

02 表达示例 Example

What kind of music do you like to listen to? 你喜欢听什么类型的音乐?

I usually listen to pop music. It's really fun and enjoyable to listen to, and at the same time it helps me relax. Those pop songs get me thinking about the good times I used to share with my friends and family. Some songs have really great lyrics and engaging rhythms, which allow me to immerse myself into the music. They can always evoke various emotions such as happiness, sadness or even anger. Pop music is just my favorite music genre.

我通常听流行音乐。听流行音乐真的很有趣，而且很愉快，同时也可以帮助我放松。那些流行歌曲让我想起了过去与朋友和家人共度的美好时光。有些歌曲的歌词非常好，节奏也非常引人入胜，让我沉浸其中。它们总能唤起我的各种情绪，比如开心、悲伤，甚至是愤怒。流行乐是我最喜欢的音乐类型。

Unit 16　兴趣爱好（二）Hobbies 2

Lesson 76　玩手机
Using Apps on Mobile Phones

> **Do you often use apps on mobile phones?**

肯定回答 Positive Attitude

01　PDC 结构 PDC Structure

表明观点 Point

I love apps on my mobile phone. 我喜欢我手机上的应用。

陈述细节 Details

1. They make my life so convenient. No matter where I go or what I do, there will always be an app to make my life easier.
   它们使我的生活如此便利。无论我去哪里或做什么，总会有一款应用使我的生活更轻松。
2. Entertainment is very important in life, and apps make that easier for people to get. 娱乐在生活中是很重要的，而应用程序让人们更容易得到娱乐。
3. Finally, I can share what I am doing with all my friends and family members. Apps really help people stay in touch with each other. 最后，我可以与所有朋友和家人分享我正在做什么。应用程序确实可以帮助人们彼此保持联系。

得出结论 Conclusion

I can't stop using my apps. 我刷手机刷到停不下来。

02　表达示例 Example

Do you often use apps on mobile phones? 你经常使用手机上的应用吗？

I love apps on my mobile phone. They make my life so convenient. No matter where I go or what I do, there will always be an app to make my life easier. Entertainment is very important in life, and apps make that easier for people to get. Finally, I can share what I am doing with all my friends and family members. Apps really help people stay in touch with each other. I can't stop using my apps.

我喜欢我手机上的应用。它们使我的生活如此便利。无论我去哪里或做什么，总会有一款应用使我的生活更轻松。娱乐在生活中是很重要的，而应用程序让人们更容易得到娱乐。最后，我可以与所有朋友和家人分享我正在做什么。应用程序确实可以帮助人们彼此保持联系。我刷手机刷到停不下来。

否定回答 Negative Attitude

01 PDC 结构 PDC Structure

▶ 表明观点 Point

I don't really use apps on my mobile phone very often.
我不经常使用手机上的应用软件。

▶ 陈述细节 Details

1. Apps are very addictive to use and I worry about it affecting my life. I want to concentrate on things that really matter to me.
   应用程序非常容易上瘾，我担心它会影响我的生活。我想全神贯注地做对我来说真正重要的事情。

2. According to some studies, too much screen time can hurt my eyes. Continuous exposure to blue light might cause vision problems.
   一些研究表明，看屏幕的时间太长会伤害到我的眼睛。持续暴露在蓝光下可能会导致视力问题。

3. Apps also waste too much of my time doing trivial things.
   应用程序还让我浪费太多时间在无关紧要的事情上。

▶ 得出结论 Conclusion

I rarely play with the apps on my phone. 我很少玩手机上的应用程序。

02 表达示例 Example

Do you often use apps on mobile phones? 你经常使用手机上的应用吗？

> I don't really use apps on my mobile phone very often. Apps are very addictive to use and I worry about it affecting my life. I want to concentrate on things that really matter to me. According to some studies, too much screen time can hurt my eyes. Continuous exposure to blue light might cause vision problems. Apps also waste too much of my time doing trivial things. I rarely play with the apps on my phone.
>
> 我不经常使用手机上的应用软件。应用程序非常容易上瘾，我担心它会影响我的生活。我想全神贯注地做对我来说真正重要的事情。一些研究表明，看屏幕的时间太长会伤害到我的眼睛。持续暴露在蓝光下可能会导致视力问题。应用程序还让我浪费太多时间在无关紧要的事情上。我很少玩手机上的应用程序。

Lesson 77 运动
Playing Sports

> Do you like playing sports?

肯定回答 Positive Attitude

01 PDC 结构 PDC Structure

表明观点 Point

I love sports. I often play basketball and tennis with my friends.
我爱运动。我经常和朋友一起打篮球和网球。

实用替换 Useful Alternatives

play
- baseball 打棒球
- table tennis 打乒乓球
- badminton 打羽毛球
- volleyball 打排球

go
- swimming 游泳
- jogging 慢跑
- climbing 爬山
- hiking 徒步旅行

do
- boxing 打拳击
- Pilates 做普拉提
- yoga 做瑜伽
- judo 练柔道

陈述细节 Details

1. It really helps me to stay in shape. 运动的确帮助我保持健康。
2. Playing sports is also a wonderful way to meet new friends and deepen relationships. 运动也是结识新朋友并增进彼此关系的绝佳方式。
3. Furthermore, it can help relieve my daily stress and anxiety. After the game is finished, I can relax and chat with my friends, which is really awesome.
而且，运动可以帮助我缓解日常压力和焦虑。运动结束后，我可以放松地与朋友聊天，这真是太棒了。

得出结论 Conclusion

It's just a great way to spend my spare time. 运动是我休闲娱乐的好方式。

02 表达示例 Example

Do you like playing sports? 你喜欢做运动吗?

> I love sports. I often play basketball and tennis with my friends. It really helps me to stay in shape. Playing sports is also a wonderful way to meet new friends and deepen relationships. Furthermore, it can help relieve my daily stress and anxiety. After the game is finished, I can relax and chat with my friends, which is really awesome. It's just a great way to spend my spare time.
>
> 我爱运动。我经常和朋友一起打篮球和网球。运动的确帮助我保持健康。运动也是结识新朋友并增进彼此关系的绝佳方式。而且,运动可以帮助我缓解日常压力和焦虑。运动结束后,我可以放松地与朋友聊天,这真是太棒了。运动是我休闲娱乐的好方式。

否定回答 Negative Attitude

01 PDC 结构 PDC Structure

▶ 表明观点 Point

I don't do sports. 我不运动。

▶ 陈述细节 Details

1. My work has occupied most of my time, so I never get the time to play sports.
   工作已经占据了我大部分的时间,所以我没有时间去运动。

2. Even when I can, I worry that I will get hurt and that will cause problems for my daily life.
   即使我有时间运动,我也担心自己会受伤,这会给我的日常生活带来麻烦。

3. Finally, I usually feel worn out after work, so when my friends ask me to go out to play sports, I just can't find the energy to do it.
   最后,工作之后我通常感到筋疲力尽,所以当朋友叫我出去运动的时候,我已经没有精力去做了。

▶ 得出结论 Conclusion

Sports are just not the thing for me. 运动不适合我。

02　表达示例 Example

Do you like playing sports? 你喜欢做运动吗?

I don't do sports. My work has occupied most of my time, so I never get the time to play sports. Even when I can, I worry that I will get hurt and that will cause problems for my daily life. Finally, I usually feel worn out after work, so when my friends ask me to go out to play sports, I just can't find the energy to do it. Sports are just not the thing for me.

我不运动。工作已经占据了我大部分的时间,所以我没有时间去运动。即使我有时间运动,我也担心自己会受伤,这会给我的日常生活带来麻烦。最后,工作之后我通常感到筋疲力尽,所以当朋友叫我出去运动的时候,我已经没有精力去做了。运动不适合我。

Lesson 78 拍照
Taking Photos

> Do you like to take photos?

肯定回答 Positive Attitude

01 PDC 结构 PDC Structure

表明观点 Point

Taking photos is my favorite hobby. 拍照是我最喜欢的爱好。

陈述细节 Details

1. A picture can tell a thousand words. When I look at the old pictures I have, I get really excited about all the memories that come flooding back. 一张照片胜过千言万语。当我看着旧照片时，所有的记忆一下子涌上来，这让我感到非常兴奋。

2. Photographs are also a great way to communicate nowadays. Through posting them on the social media, I can share my life with my family, friends and other users. 照片如今也是交流的一种好方法。通过在社交媒体上发布照片，我可以与家人、朋友以及其他用户分享我的生活。

3. Finally, I find it very creative. I can express my ideas or emotions through my pictures, which is really fantastic! 最后，我觉得摄影非常具有创造性。我可以通过照片表达自己的想法或情绪，这简直是太棒了！

得出结论 Conclusion

I love taking pictures. 我爱拍照。

02 表达示例 Example

Do you like to take photos? 你喜欢拍照吗？

Taking photos is my favorite hobby. A picture can tell a thousand words. When I look at the old pictures I have, I get really excited about all the memories that come flooding back. Photographs are also a great way to communicate nowadays. Through posting them on the social media, I can share my life with my family, friends and other users. Finally, I find it very creative. I can express my ideas or emotions through my pictures, which is really fantastic! I love taking pictures.

拍照是我最喜欢的爱好。一张照片胜过千言万语。当我看着旧照片时，所有的记忆

> 一下子涌上来，这让我感到非常兴奋。照片如今也是交流的一种好方法。通过在社交媒体上发布照片，我可以与家人、朋友以及其他用户分享我的生活。最后，我觉得摄影非常具有创造性。我可以通过照片表达自己的想法或情绪，这简直是太棒了！我爱拍照。

否定回答 Negative Attitude

01 PDC 结构 PDC Structure

➤ 表明观点 Point

I don't really take pictures. 我不怎么拍照。

➤ 陈述细节 Details

1. Whenever I try to take a picture of someone, they tell me that I make them look really bad. 每当我试图给别人拍照时，他们都说我把他们拍得很难看。

2. When I try to practice on myself, it's even worse. I look so terrible in pictures that I don't want to look at them anymore. 当我尝试练习给自己拍照时，情况甚至更糟。我在照片里看起来非常糟糕，以至于我都不想再看了。

3. I get so shy and awkward when someone is taking pictures of me. I am even unsure of what to do with my hands.
当有人为我拍照时，我会感到非常害羞和尴尬。我甚至都不确定两只手要怎么放。

➤ 得出结论 Conclusion

Taking pictures is just not suitable for me. 我不适合拍照。

02 表达示例 Example

Do you like to take photos? 你喜欢拍照吗？

> I don't really take pictures. Whenever I try to take a picture of someone, they tell me that I make them look really bad. When I try to practice on myself, it's even worse. I look so terrible in pictures that I don't want to look at them anymore. I get so shy and awkward when someone is taking pictures of me. I am even unsure of what to do with my hands. Taking pictures is just not suitable for me.
>
> 我不怎么拍照。每当我试图给别人拍照时，他们都说我把他们拍得很难看。当我尝试练习给自己拍照时，情况甚至更糟。我在照片里看起来非常糟糕，以至于我都不想再看了。当有人为我拍照时，我会感到非常害羞和尴尬。我甚至都不确定两只手要怎么放。我不适合拍照。

Lesson 79 旅游
Traveling

> Do you like traveling?

肯定回答 Positive Attitude

01 PDC 结构 PDC Structure

表明观点 Point

I love traveling. 我喜欢旅游。

陈述细节 Details

1. It doesn't matter who I travel with. It's always relaxing.
   和谁一起去不重要,旅行总是可以让我放松。
2. I get the chance to look at all the different scenery and breathe in all the different cultures.
   我有机会欣赏不同的风景,感受不同的文化气息。
3. No matter where I go, I can find new and interesting people to talk to.
   无论走到哪里,我总能和新认识的有趣的人聊天。

得出结论 Conclusion

Traveling is just the best hobby to have. 旅游是最棒的爱好。

02 表达示例 Example

Do you like traveling? 你喜欢旅游吗?

> I love traveling. It doesn't matter who I travel with. It's always relaxing. I get the chance to look at all the different scenery and breathe in all the different cultures. No matter where I go, I can find new and interesting people to talk to. Traveling is just the best hobby to have.
>
> 我喜欢旅游。和谁一起去不重要,旅行总是可以让我放松。我有机会欣赏不同的风景,感受不同的文化气息。无论走到哪里,我总能和新认识的有趣的人聊天。旅游是最棒的爱好。

否定回答 Negative Attitude

01 PDC 结构 PDC Structure

▶ 表明观点 Point

I hate traveling. 我讨厌旅游。

▶ 陈述细节 Details

1. No matter what I do in my life, I find it really difficult to relax when I am far away from home. So, when I go out to take a vacation, I get really tired.
   无论我做什么，只要我离开家，我就很难放松自己。所以当我外出度假时，我真的觉得很累。

2. Besides, I have to spend a lot of time making travel plans, getting to hotels and waiting in long lines at tourist attractions. It's just so time-consuming.
   此外，我必须花费大量时间制定旅行计划、去旅馆、在旅游景点排长队等，太花时间了。

3. I don't want to blow my money on hotels, transportation and admission tickets, too.
   我也不想把我的钱花在酒店、交通和门票上。

▶ 得出结论 Conclusion

Traveling is just not right for me. 旅游不适合我。

02 表达示例 Example

Do you like traveling? 你喜欢旅游吗？

I hate traveling. No matter what I do in my life, I find it really difficult to relax when I am far away from home. So, when I go out to take a vacation, I get really tired. Besides, I have to spend a lot of time making travel plans, getting to hotels and waiting in long lines at tourist attractions. It's just so time-consuming. I don't want to blow my money on hotels, transportation and admission tickets, too. Traveling is just not right for me.

我讨厌旅游。无论我做什么，只要我离开家，我就很难放松自己。所以当我外出度假时，我真的觉得很累。此外，我必须花费大量时间制定旅行计划、去旅馆、在旅游景点排长队等，太花时间了。我也不想把我的钱花在酒店、交通和门票上。旅游不适合我。

Lesson 80　看电视节目
Watching TV Shows

> **What kind of TV shows do you usually watch?**

01 PDC 结构 PDC Structure

表明观点 Point

I like to watch talk shows. 我喜欢看脱口秀。

实用替换 Useful Alternatives

其他常见的电视节目类型：

	英	美	
documentary	/ˌdɒkjuˈment(ə)ri/	/ˌdɑːkjuˈment(ə)ri/	纪录片
sports	/spɔːts/	/spɔːrts/	体育节目
news	/njuːz/	/njuːz/	新闻
cartoon	/kɑːˈtuːn/	/kɑːrˈtuːn/	动画片
sitcom	/ˈsɪtkɒm/	/ˈsɪtkɑːm/	情景喜剧

TV series 电视连续剧　　　　　soap opera 肥皂剧
reality show 真人秀　　　　　 cooking show 烹饪节目
talent show 选秀节目

陈述细节 Details

1. I find it the best way to unwind after a long and hard day. After work, I usually spend most of my free time sitting in front of screen, eating some snacks and talking with my family, which is just the best.
经过漫长而辛苦的一天，我发现这是放松身心的最佳方式。下班后，我通常将大部分空闲时间都花在银幕前，吃些零食并与家人聊天，这就是最好的事情。

2. Besides, I can learn a lot of knowledge on different issues from talk shows, which opens my mind.
此外，我还可以从脱口秀节目中学习到很多有关不同议题的知识，这使我大开眼界。

3. Sometimes I can even see my favorite celebrities there.
有时候我甚至可以看到自己最喜欢的明星。

得出结论 Conclusion

I can't think of anything better than to sit on my couch and watch my favorite talk shows.

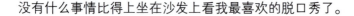

没有什么事情比得上坐在沙发上看我最喜欢的脱口秀了。

02 表达示例 Example

What kind of TV shows do you usually watch? 你通常看什么电视节目？

I like to watch talk shows. I find it the best way to unwind after a long and hard day. After work, I usually spend most of my free time sitting in front of screen, eating some snacks and talking with my family, which is just the best. Besides, I can learn a lot of knowledge on different issues from talk shows, which opens my mind. Sometimes I can even see my favorite celebrities there. I can't think of anything better than to sit on my couch and watch my favorite talk shows.

我喜欢看脱口秀。经过漫长而辛苦的一天，我发现这是放松身心的最佳方式。下班后，我通常将大部分空闲时间都花在银幕前，吃些零食并与家人聊天，这就是最好的事情。此外，我还可以从脱口秀节目中学习到很多有关不同议题的知识，这使我大开眼界。有时候我甚至可以看到自己最喜欢的明星。没有什么事情比得上坐在沙发上看我最喜欢的脱口秀了。

学会描述

导 语

  本章"学会描述"涵盖了人物、地点、事件和物品四个大方面,通过对这四大话题的讨论,我们能够掌握用于描述的 5W1H 原则。

  5W1H 原则中的 5W 指的是 what(是什么)、who(是谁)、where(在哪里)、when(什么时候)和 why(为什么),而 1H 指的是 how(感受如何/如何使用等)。

  不管我们要对人物、地点、事件还是物品进行描述,都可以从以上六个方面着手,让我们不仅有话可说,还可以描述得清晰具体且有条理。而且该方法不止在英语口语中适用,在我们的日常生活和工作中也能有广泛应用。那么就让我们开始本章的学习吧!

Unit 17　描述人物 Describe a Person

Lesson 81　谁是你最好的朋友？
Who is your best friend?

本单元我们将以描述"你最好的朋友"为例，用 5 小节的内容来学习如何通过 5W1H 原则来描述一个人，即这个人是谁（who），你们是如何认识的（when，where，how），她／他的长相和性格是什么样的（what），为什么她／他是你最好的朋友（why）。

这一部分需要描述你最好的朋友是谁，其中可能包括这个人的姓名、和你的关系、年龄、家乡、爱好、教育情况以及职业等基本信息。

01　姓名以及和你的关系

I have many close friends, but I think that Alice is my bestie.
我有很多好朋友，但我觉得爱丽丝是我闺蜜。

实用替换 Useful Alternatives

和你的关系：
（1）家人
mother	英 /ˈmʌðə(r)/	美 /ˈmʌðər/	妈妈
father	英 /ˈfɑːðə(r)/	美 /ˈfɑːðər/	爸爸
grandma	英 /ˈɡrænmɑː/	美 /ˈɡrænmɑː/	奶奶
grandpa	英 /ˈɡrænpɑː/	美 /ˈɡrænpɑː/	爷爷

（2）朋友
friend	英 /frend/	美 /frend/	朋友
bro	英 /brəʊ/	美 /broʊ/	哥们儿
sis	英 /sɪs/	美 /sɪs/	姐们儿
buddy	英 /ˈbʌdi/	美 /ˈbʌdi/	老铁
bestie	英 /ˈbesti/	美 /ˈbesti/	闺蜜
homie	英 /ˈhəʊmi/	美 /ˈhoʊmi/	像家人一样的挚友
BFF（best friend forever）一辈子的朋友			

（3）师生
teacher	英 /ˈtiːtʃə(r)/	美 /ˈtiːtʃər/	老师
tutor	英 /ˈtjuːtə(r)/	美 /ˈtuːtər/	家庭教师
supervisor	英 /ˈsuːpəvaɪzə(r)/	美 /ˈsuːpərvaɪzər/	导师
student	英 /ˈstjuːd(ə)nt/	美 /ˈstuːd(ə)nt/	学生

（4）同学
classmate	英 /ˈklɑːsmeɪt/	美 /ˈklæsmeɪt/	同学
alumnus	英 /əˈlʌmnəs/	美 /əˈlʌmnəs/	校友

（5）工作关系
colleague	英 /ˈkɒliːɡ/	美 /ˈkɑːliːɡ/	同事
co-worker	英 /ˈkəʊ wɜːkə(r)/	美 /ˈkoʊ wɜːrkər/	合作者

boss	英 /bɒs/	美 /bɔːs/	老板
superior	英 /suːˈpɪəriə(r)/	美 /suːˈpɪriər/	上司
partner	英 /ˈpɑːtnə(r)/	美 /ˈpɑːrtnər/	搭档
client	英 /ˈklaɪənt/	美 /ˈklaɪənt/	客户
customer	英 /ˈkʌstəmə(r)/	美 /ˈkʌstəmər/	顾客
consumer	英 /kənˈsjuːmə(r)/	美 /kənˈsuːmər/	消费者

（6）崇拜的对象

idol	英 /ˈaɪdl/	美 /ˈaɪdl/	偶像
hero	英 /ˈhɪərəʊ/	美 /ˈhɪroʊ/	英雄
role model 榜样			

（7）陌生人

stranger	英 /ˈstreɪndʒə(r)/	美 /ˈstreɪndʒər/	陌生人

a person I came across 偶然遇到的一个人

02 年龄

She is 25 years old, one year older than me. 她 25 岁，比我大一岁。

实用替换 Useful Alternatives

描述年龄：
She/He is 25 years old,
她 / 他 25 岁，
She/He was born in 1999,
她 / 他出生于 1999 年，
She/He was born on October 20, 1999,
她 / 他出生于 1999 年 10 月 20 日，

one year older than me.
比我大一岁。
and we are the same age.
我们同岁。
two years younger than me.
比我小两岁。

03 家乡

She comes from America. 她来自美国。

实用替换 Useful Alternatives

描述家乡：
She/He is from England. 她 / 他来自英国。
She/He comes from Yunnan Province. 她 / 他来自云南省。
She/He was born and raised in Shanghai. 她 / 他在上海出生、长大。

04 职业

She is currently an English teacher and works at an online education company.
她现在在一家在线教育公司做英语老师。

实用替换 Useful Alternatives

描述工作：

She/He is an English teacher (at a local high school) .
她 / 他是（当地一所高中的）英语老师。

She/He works as a programmer (at an Internet company) .
她 / 他是（一家互联网公司的）程序员。

She/He works for/at a law firm/Facebook.
她 / 他在一家律所 / 脸书工作。

She/He works in the marketing department (for an Italy company) .
她 / 他在（一家意大利公司的）市场部工作。

She/He has been working as an accountant for five years.
她 / 他已经当会计五年了。

✓ 表达示例 Example

Who is your best friend? 谁是你最好的朋友？

I have many close friends, but I think that Alice is my bestie. She is 25 years old, one year older than me, and she comes from America. She is currently an English teacher and works at an online education company.

我有很多好朋友，但我觉得爱丽丝是我的闺蜜。她 25 岁，比我大一岁，来自美国，现在在一家在线教育公司做英语老师。

Lesson 82　你们是怎么认识的?
How did you meet?

这一部分需要描述你和最好的朋友是在什么场合认识的、什么时候认识的、认识多久了、如何认识的以及相处如何。

01 认识的场合和时间

Alice and I met at work in 2018. 爱丽丝和我是 2018 年在工作中认识的。

实用替换 Useful Alternatives

at a mutual friend's birthday party 在一个共同朋友的生日派对上
in an activity 在一次活动中　　　　in a class 在一次课上
in the dormitory 在宿舍里　　　　　in a bar 在酒吧里
on campus 在校园中　　　　　　　 on the plane 在飞机上
on the Internet 在网上

02 认识的状况

We were both new to the office at the time. 那时我们都新到办公室上班。

实用替换 Useful Alternatives

We were both new to the place/school.
我们都新到这个地方 / 这个学校上学。
We were both in elementary/middle/high school/college.
我们都在上小学 / 初中 / 高中 / 大学。
We were both in London/Beijing/Hangzhou.
我们都在伦敦 / 北京 / 杭州。

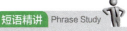 **短语精讲** Phrase Study

- new (to sth.) 初来乍到的；初学乍练的
He is new to the town.
他刚刚来到这座小镇。
Are you new here?
你是新来的吗？

03 认识的方式和相处方式

She was introduced by my boss. 她是经我老板介绍认识的。

实用替换 Useful Alternatives

不同类型的介绍人：
my friend(s) 我的朋友　　　　　my parent(s) 我的父母
my colleague(s) 我的同事　　　 my superior 我的上司
my classmate(s) 我的同学　　　 my roommate(s) 我的室友

词汇精讲 Word Study

introduce
英 /ˌɪntrəˈdjuːs/
美 /ˌɪntrəˈduːs/

v. 1. 介绍；引见
Can I introduce myself? 让我来自我介绍一下吧。

2. 主持（节目）；介绍（讲演者或演员）
I'd like to introduce our next guest.
让我来介绍我们的下一位嘉宾。

3. 使初次了解；使尝试
He introduced the pleasure of swimming to me.
他最先让我体会到了游泳的乐趣。

4. 推行；采用；引进
The company has introduced many advanced technologies.
该公司引进了许多先进技术。

We got along well because we had a lot in common, such as we're both fanatical about foods, sports and so forth.
我们相处融洽，因为我们有很多共同点，比如我们都很喜欢美食和运动等。

实用替换 Useful Alternatives

相处如何：
We were not close because we were very different people.
我们并不亲近，因为我们是非常不同的人。
We never really got on because we just didn't like each other.
我们从未和睦相处，因为我们都不喜欢对方。

短语精讲 Phrase Study

- have sth. in common（with sb.）（想法、兴趣等方面）（与某人）相同
  Tony and I have nothing in common. 托尼和我毫无共同之处。
  We have much in common. 我们有很多共同之处。

- get on/along with sb. 与某人和睦相处，关系良好
  They've never got on with each other. 他们从未和睦相处过。
  It's really important to get along with your colleagues. 和同事搞好关系真的很重要。

- be fanatical about sth. 对……着迷
  She's fanatical about yoga. 她对瑜伽着了迷。
  I am fanatical about basketball. 我非常喜欢篮球。

04 认识时间的长短

We have been friends for six years since then.
自那时起，我们已经是六年的朋友了。

实用替换 Useful Alternatives

We've been friends for seven years. 我们已经是七年的朋友了。
We've been friends since 2013. 自 2013 年以来我们一直是朋友。
We've known each other almost our whole lives/for about ten years.
我们快认识对方一辈子了 / 大约十年了。
We met each other seven years ago. 我们七年前认识的。

✓ 表达示例 Example

How did you meet? 你们怎么遇见的?

Alice and I met at work in 2018. We were both new to the office at the time. She was introduced by my boss and we got along well because we had a lot in common, such as we're both fanatical about foods, sports and so forth. We have been friends for six years since then.

爱丽丝和我是 2018 年在工作中认识的。那时我们都新到办公室上班。她是经我老板介绍认识的。我们相处融洽，因为我们有很多共同点，比如都很喜欢美食和运动等。自那时起，我们已经是六年的朋友了。

Lesson 83　她 / 他长什么样?
What does she/he look like?

这一部分需要描述人物的长相，其中可能包括总体印象、身高、体型、发型、眼睛、鼻子、嘴巴和脸型等要素。

01　总体印象

Alice is really beautiful. 爱丽丝真的很美。

实用替换 Useful Alternatives

attractive	英 /əˈtræktɪv/	美 /əˈtræktɪv/	吸引人的
good-looking	英 /ˌɡʊd ˈlʊkɪŋ/	美 /ˌɡʊd ˈlʊkɪŋ/	好看的
gorgeous	英 /ˈɡɔːdʒəs/	美 /ˈɡɔːrdʒəs/	
=stunning	英 /ˈstʌnɪŋ/	美 /ˈstʌnɪŋ/	非常美丽的
lovely	英 /ˈlʌvli/	美 /ˈlʌvli/	
=cute	英 /kjuːt/	美 /kjuːt/	
=adorable	英 /əˈdɔːrəb(ə)l/	美 /əˈdɔːrəb(ə)l/	可爱的
pretty	英 /ˈprɪti/	美 /ˈprɪti/	漂亮的
handsome	英 /ˈhænsəm/	美 /ˈhænsəm/	帅气的

02　身高、体型及发型

She is quite short and athletic with blonde hair.
爱丽丝个头很矮，身材健美，一头金发。

实用替换 Useful Alternatives

（1）身高
（quite/very）tall/short（相当）高 / 矮　of medium/average height 中等身材
around 160 cm/1.6 m（tall）大约一米六

（2）体型

slender	英 /ˈslendə(r)/	美 /ˈslendər/	
=slim	英 /slɪm/	美 /slɪm/	纤细的；苗条的
skinny	英 /ˈskɪni/	美 /ˈskɪni/	干瘦的；皮包骨的
underweight	英 /ˌʌndəˈweɪt/	美 /ˌʌndərˈweɪt/	体重不足的
lean	英 /liːn/	美 /liːn/	清瘦的；瘦且健康的
fat	英 /fæt/	美 /fæt/	肥胖的
plump	英 /plʌmp/	美 /plʌmp/	丰腴的

Unit 17　描述人物 Describe a Person

chubby	英 /ˈtʃʌbi/	美 /ˈtʃʌbi/	
	胖乎乎的；圆胖的（一般为褒义，多用于小孩）		
overweight	英 /ˌəʊvəˈweɪt/	美 /ˌoʊvərˈweɪt/	超重的
fit	英 /fɪt/	美 /fɪt/	健康的
athletic	英 /æθˈletɪk/	美 /æθˈletɪk/	健美的
well-built	英 /ˌwel ˈbɪlt/	美 /ˌwel ˈbɪlt/	强壮的
curvy	英 /ˈkɜːvi/	美 /ˈkɜːrvi/	有曲线的

（3）发型

a. 头发颜色

dark	英 /dɑːk/	美 /dɑːrk/	深发（肤）色的
fair	英 /feə(r)/	美 /fer/	浅发（肤）色的
black	英 /blæk/	美 /blæk/	黑色的
white	英 /waɪt/	美 /waɪt/	白色的
grey/gray	英 /greɪ/	美 /greɪ/	灰色的
brown	英 /braʊn/	美 /braʊn/	棕色的
caramel	英 /ˈkærəmel/	美 /ˈkærəml/	焦糖色的
red	英 /red/	美 /red/	红色的
blonde	英 /blɒnd/	美 /blɑːnd/	金色的

b. 头发长度

long	英 /lɒŋ/	美 /lɔːŋ/	长的
short	英 /ʃɔːt/	美 /ʃɔːrt/	短的

medium-length 中等长度的
shoulder-length 齐肩长度的

c. 其他特征

straight	英 /streɪt/	美 /streɪt/	直的
wavy	英 /ˈweɪvi/	美 /ˈweɪvi/	波浪的
curly	英 /ˈkɜːli/	美 /ˈkɜːrli/	卷的
thick	英 /θɪk/	美 /θɪk/	头发厚的
thin	英 /θɪn/	美 /θɪn/	头发薄的
bald	英 /bɔːld/	美 /bɔːld/	头发秃的

03 眼睛、鼻子和嘴唇

she has a pair of big blue eyes, a straight nose and thin lips.
她有一双蓝色的大眼睛、直挺的鼻子和薄唇。

实用替换 Useful Alternatives

（1）眼睛

a. 眼睛的颜色

brown	英 /braʊn/	美 /braʊn/	棕色的
black	英 /blæk/	美 /blæk/	黑色的
grey/gray	英 /greɪ/	美 /greɪ/	灰色的
blue	英 /bluː/	美 /bluː/	蓝色的
green	英 /griːn/	美 /griːn/	绿色的
hazel	英 /ˈheɪz(ə)l/	美 /ˈheɪz(ə)l/	淡绿褐色的
amber	英 /ˈæmbə(r)/	美 /ˈæmbər/	琥珀色的

b. 其他特征

big	英 /bɪg/	美 /bɪg/	大的
small	英 /smɔːl/	美 /smɔːl/	小的
monolids	英 /ˈmɒnəʊlɪdz/	美 /ˈmɑːnoʊlɪdz/	单眼皮
almond eyes	英 /ˈɑːmənd aɪz/	美 /ˈɑːmənd aɪz/	杏仁眼
upturned eyes	英 /ˌʌpˈtɜːnd aɪz/	美 /ˌʌpˈtɜːrnd aɪz/	上挑眼
downturned eyes	英 /ˈdaʊntɜːnd aɪz/	美 /ˈdaʊntɜːrnd aɪz/	下垂眼

double eyelids 双眼皮　　　　　　wear glasses 戴眼镜

（2）鼻子

big/small nose 大/小鼻子　　　　　turned-up nose 翘鼻子
straight nose 直挺的鼻子　　　　　button nose 小而圆的鼻子

crooked nose	英 /ˈkrʊkɪd nəʊz/	美 /ˈkrʊkɪd nəʊz/	歪鼻子
hooked nose	英 /hʊkt nəʊz/	美 /hʊkt nəʊz/	鹰钩鼻

（3）嘴唇

thin lips 薄嘴唇　　　　　　　　　thick lips 厚嘴唇
full lips 丰满的嘴唇

pouty lips	英 /ˈpaʊti lɪps/	美 /ˈpaʊti lɪps/	翘唇

04 脸型

You might also love her high cheekbones. 你或许还会喜欢她高高的颧骨。

实用替换 Useful Alternatives

round face 圆脸　　　　　　　　　square face 方脸
oval face 鹅蛋脸　　　　　　　　　heart-shaped face 瓜子脸
broad forehead 宽额头　　　　　　narrow forehead 窄额头

05 总结

Anyway, she looks like a goddess. 总之，她看起来像个女神。

实用替换 Useful Alternatives

angel	英 /ˈeɪndʒl/	美 /ˈeɪndʒl/	天使
supermodel	英 /ˈsuːpəmɒdl/ 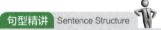	美 /ˈsuːpərmɑːdl/	超模
prince	英 /prɪns/	美 /prɪns/	王子
princess	英 /ˌprɪnˈses/	美 /ˈprɪnses/	公主
movie star 电影明星			

句型精讲 Sentence Structure

- sb. look(s) like a/an + *n*. 某人看起来像一个……
  You look like a programmer. 你看起来像个程序员。
  She looks like an angel. 她看起来像个天使。

✓ 表达示例 Example

What does she/he look like? 她 / 他长什么样子？

Alice is really beautiful. She is quite short and athletic with blonde hair and she has a pair of big blue eyes, a straight nose and thin lips. You might also love her high cheekbones. Anyway, she looks like a goddess.

爱丽丝真的很美。她个头很矮，身材健美，一头金发。她有一双蓝色的大眼睛、直挺的鼻子和薄唇。你或许还会喜欢她高高的颧骨。总之，她看起来像个女神。

Lesson 84 她 / 他是什么样的人?
What is she/he like?

这一部分需要描述这个人的性格,其中包括这个人是内向还是外向、人品如何、与他人的相处等方面。

01 总体印象

Alice also has a great character. 爱丽丝的性格也很好。

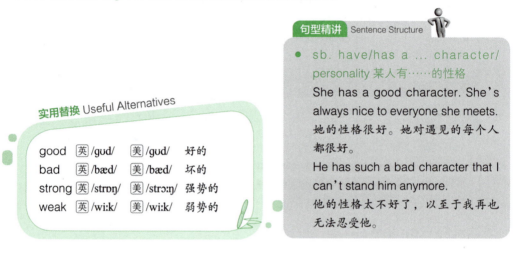

句型精讲 Sentence Structure

- sb. have/has a ... character/personality 某人有……的性格

She has a good character. She's always nice to everyone she meets.
她的性格很好。她对遇见的每个人都很好。

He has such a bad character that I can't stand him anymore.
他的性格太不好了,以至于我再也无法忍受他。

实用替换 Useful Alternatives

good	英 /gʊd/	美 /gʊd/	好的
bad	英 /bæd/	美 /bæd/	坏的
strong	英 /strɒŋ/	美 /strɔːŋ/	强势的
weak	英 /wiːk/	美 /wiːk/	弱势的

02 内向 / 外向

She's a little bit shy, but when you get to know her better, you'll find that she's a pretty humorous girl.
她有些害羞,但是当你更加了解她以后,你会发现她是一个很幽默的人。

实用替换 Useful Alternatives

extroverted	英 /ˈekstrəvɜːtɪd/	美 /ˈekstrəvɜːrtɪd/	
=outgoing	英 /ˈaʊtɡəʊɪŋ/	美 /ˈaʊtɡoʊɪŋ/	外向的
talkative	英 /ˈtɔːkətɪv/	美 /ˈtɔːkətɪv/	
=chatty	英 /ˈtʃæti/	美 /ˈtʃæti/	健谈的
sociable	英 /ˈsəʊʃəb(ə)l/	美 /ˈsoʊʃəb(ə)l/	好交际的
funny	英 /ˈfʌni/	美 /ˈfʌni/	有趣的
introverted	英 /ˈɪntrəvɜːtɪd/	美 /ˈɪntrəvɜːrtɪd/	内向的
quiet	英 /ˈkwaɪət/	美 /ˈkwaɪət/	安静的
reserved	英 /rɪˈzɜːvd/	美 /rɪˈzɜːrvd/	矜持的
serious	英 /ˈsɪəriəs/	美 /ˈsɪriəs/	严肃的
boring	英 /ˈbɔːrɪŋ/	美 /ˈbɔːrɪŋ/	无趣的

03 人品好坏

She is very **sincere and reliable** as well. 她还非常真诚且可靠。

实用替换 Useful Alternatives

honest	英 /ˈɒnɪst/	美 /ˈɑːnɪst/	
=truthful	英 /ˈtruːθfl/	美 /ˈtruːθfl/	诚实的
frank	英 /fræŋk/	美 /fræŋk/	坦率的
trustworthy	英 /ˈtrʌstwɜːði/	美 /ˈtrʌstwɜːrði/	值得信任的
loyal	英 /ˈlɔɪəl/	美 /ˈlɔɪəl/	
=faithful	英 /ˈfeɪθf(ə)l/	美 /ˈfeɪθf(ə)l/	忠诚的
dishonest	英 /dɪsˈɒnɪst/	美 /dɪsˈɑːnɪst/	
=untruthful	英 /ʌnˈtruːθfl/	美 /ʌnˈtruːθfl/	不诚实的
insincere	英 /ˌɪnsɪnˈsɪə(r)/	美 /ˌɪnsɪnˈsɪr/	虚情假意的
secretive	英 /ˈsiːkrətɪv/	美 /ˈsiːkrətɪv/	不外露的；有城府的
untrustworthy	英 /ʌnˈtrʌstwɜːði/	美 /ʌnˈtrʌstwɜːrði/	不值得信任的
unreliable	英 /ˌʌnrɪˈlaɪəb(ə)l/	美 /ˌʌnrɪˈlaɪəb(ə)l/	不可靠的
disloyal	英 /dɪsˈlɔɪəl/	美 /dɪsˈlɔɪəl/	
=unfaithful	英 /ʌnˈfeɪθf(ə)l/	美 /ʌnˈfeɪθf(ə)l/	不忠诚的

You can trust her at any time. 你任何时候都可以信任她。

实用替换 Useful Alternatives

You can't trust her/him 100%. 你不能百分之百信任她/他。
You can never trust her/him. 你永远不能信任她/他。
You can't trust a word she/he says. 她/他说的话你一个字也不能信。

04 和他人的相处

You'll also feel very **comfortable** around her, because she's really **thoughtful**. 在她身边你也会感到很舒服，因为她真的很体贴周到。

实用替换 Useful Alternatives

（1）在某人身边的感觉

happy	英 /ˈhæpi/	美 /ˈhæpi/	开心的
relaxed	英 /rɪˈlækst/	美 /rɪˈlækst/	放松的

uncomfortable	英 /ʌnˈkʌmftəb(ə)l/	美 /ʌnˈkʌmftəb(ə)l/	不舒服的
nervous	英 /ˈnɜːvəs/	美 /ˈnɜːrvəs/	紧张的
bored	英 /bɔːd/	美 /bɔːrd/	无聊的
embarrassed	英 /ɪmˈbærəst/	美 /ɪmˈbærəst/	尴尬的
at ease 舒适,自在			

（2）给他人的感觉

considerate	英 /kənˈsɪdərət/	美 /kənˈsɪdərət/	体贴的
caring	英 /ˈkeərɪŋ/	美 /ˈkerɪŋ/	关心他人的
inconsiderate	英 /ˌɪnkənˈsɪdərət/	美 /ˌɪnkənˈsɪdərət/	不体谅他人的
thoughtless	英 /ˈθɔːtləs/	美 /ˈθɔːtləs/	欠考虑的
cold-hearted	英 /ˌkəʊld ˈhɑːtɪd/	美 /ˌkoʊld ˈhɑːrtɪd/	冷酷无情的

✓ 表达示例 Example

What is she/he like? 她/他什么性格？

Alice also has a great character. She's a little bit shy, but when you get to know her better, you'll find that she's a pretty humorous girl. She is very sincere and reliable as well. You can trust her at any time. You'll also feel very comfortable around her, because she's really thoughtful.

爱丽丝的性格也很好。她有些害羞，但是当你更加了解她以后，你会发现她是一个很幽默的人。她还非常真诚且可靠，你任何时候都可以信任她。在她身边你也会感到很舒服，因为她真的很体贴周到。

Lesson 85 为什么她/他是你最好的朋友?
Why is she/he your best friend?

这一部分需要描述为什么这个人和你成为最好的朋友，可能是因为这个人一直陪伴着你、支持你，以及你们的相处很愉快等。

01 总体概括

She is my best friend, because she always supports me no matter what I do and keeps me company when I feel lonely.

她是我最好的朋友，因为无论我做什么她都会支持我，在我孤单的时候她都会陪着我。

实用替换 Useful Alternatives

respect me 尊重我
accept me 接纳我
trust me 信任我
be there with me 陪伴我
share secrets with me 和我分享秘密
bring me up 把我养大
set an example to me 为我树立了榜样
have a lot in common with me 和我有许多共同之处

encourage me 鼓励我
empathize with me 和我产生共鸣
care about me 关心我
laugh with me 和我一起笑
take good care of me 很好地照顾我
teach me a lot 教会了我很多东西

02 陪伴我

She has been there for me through thick and thin. 她一直和我同甘共苦。

短语精讲 Phrase Study

- through thick and thin 不顾艰难险阻；赴汤蹈火；同甘共苦
  Over the years, we went through thick and thin.
  我们同甘共苦许多年。
  They stuck together through thick and thin.
  即使遇到问题或困难，他们也互相支持。

03 支持我

When I want to do something that I like, she always supports me unconditionally.
当我想做自己喜欢的事情时，她总是无条件地支持我。

词汇精讲 Word Study

unconditionally
英 /ʌnkən'dɪʃənəli/
美 /ʌnkən'dɪʃənəli/

ad. 无条件地
I support you unconditionally. 我无条件支持你。
They surrendered unconditionally. 他们无条件投降了。

04 相处愉快

Moreover, I feel happy and relaxed when we are together. We've made many memories together and I hope we will make more in the future.

而且我们在一起的时候,我感到开心和放松。我们一起留下了很多回忆,我希望我们以后能留下更多。

短语精讲 Phrase Study

- make/create memories 留下回忆
I want to create great memories with you. 我想和你一起留下美好的回忆。
We all want to make happy memories for ourselves, which will keep us smiling for decades.
我们都想为自己留下快乐的回忆,这在未来几十年里都能让我们感到开心。

✓ 表达示例 Example

Why is she/he your best friend? 她 / 他为什么是你最好的朋友?

She is my best friend, because she always supports me no matter what I do and keeps me company when I feel lonely. She has been there for me through thick and thin. When I want to do something that I like, she always supports me unconditionally. Moreover, I feel happy and relaxed when we are together. We've made many memories together and I hope we will make more in the future.

她是我最好的朋友,因为无论我做什么她都会支持我,在我孤单的时候她都会陪着我。她一直和我同甘共苦。当我想做自己喜欢的事情时,她总是无条件地支持我。而且我们在一起的时候,我感到开心和放松。我们一起留下了很多回忆,我希望我们以后能留下更多。

▶ 描述人物汇总

Do you have a best friend? 你有最好的朋友吗?

Yes, I have many close friends, but I think that Alice is my bestie. She is 25 years old, one year older than me, and she comes from America. She is currently an English teacher and works at an online education company.

Alice and I met at work in 2018. We were both new to the office at the time. She was introduced by my boss and we got along well because we had a lot in common, such as we're both fanatical about foods, sports and so forth. We have been friends for six years since then.

Alice is really beautiful. She is quite short and athletic with blonde hair and she has a pair of big blue eyes, a straight nose and thin lips. You might also love her high cheekbones. Anyway, she looks like a goddess.

Alice also has a great character. She's a little bit shy, but when you get to know her better, you'll find that she's a pretty humorous girl. She is very sincere and reliable as well. You can trust her at any time. You'll also feel very comfortable around her, because she's really thoughtful.

She is my best friend, because she always supports me no matter what I do and keeps me company when I feel lonely. She has been there for me through thick and thin. When I want to do something that I like, she always supports me unconditionally. Moreover, I feel happy and relaxed when we are together. We've made many memories together and I hope we will make more in the future.

有，我有很多好朋友，但我觉得爱丽丝是我的闺蜜。她25岁，比我大一岁，来自美国，现在在一家在线教育公司做英语老师。

爱丽丝和我是2018年在工作中认识的。那时我们都新到办公室上班。她是经我老板介绍认识的。我们相处融洽，因为我们有很多共同点，比如都很喜欢美食和运动等。现在我们已经是六年的朋友了。

爱丽丝真的很美。她个头很矮，身材健美，一头金发。她有一双蓝色的大眼睛、直挺的鼻子和薄唇。你或许还会喜欢她高高的颧骨。总之，她看起来像个女神。

爱丽丝的性格也很好。她有些害羞，但是当你更加了解她以后，你会发现她是一个很幽默的人。她还非常真诚且可靠，你任何时候都可以信任她。在她身边你也会感到很舒服，因为她真的很体贴周到。

她是我最好的朋友，因为无论我做什么她都会支持我，在我孤单的时候她都会陪着我。她一直和我同甘共苦。当我想做自己喜欢的事情时，她总是无条件地支持我。而且我们在一起的时候我感到开心和放松。我们一起留下了很多回忆，我希望我们以后能留下更多。

Unit 18　描述地点 Describe a Place

Lesson 86　你最近去过哪个城市？
Which city have you been to recently?

本单元我们将以描述"你最近去过的城市"为例，用 5 小节的内容来学习如何通过 5W1H 原则来描述一个地方，即这个城市在哪儿（where）、是什么样的（what），什么时候去的这个城市（when）、和谁一起去的（who），在那里做了什么（what），这个城市给你的感觉（how），以及你为什么喜欢或者不喜欢这个城市（why）。

这一部分需要描述是哪个城市，以及这个城市的基本信息，包括面积、城市类型、地理位置、人口和城市地位等。

01　城市名称

The city I've been to most recently is Beijing. 我最近去过的城市是北京。

实用替换 Useful Alternatives

常见的国家及首都名称：

英文	英音	美音	中文
Asia	英 /'eɪʒə/	美 /'eɪʒə/	亚洲
China	英 /'tʃaɪnə/	美 /'tʃaɪnə/	中国
——Beijing 北京			
Japan	英 /dʒə'pæn/	美 /dʒə'pæn/	日本
——Tokyo	英 /'təʊkiəʊ/	美 /'toʊkioʊ/	东京
South Korea 韩国			
——Seoul	英 /səʊl/	美 /soʊl/	首尔
North Korea 朝鲜			
——Pyongyang	英 /ˌpjɒŋ'jæŋ/	美 /ˌpjʌŋ'jɑːŋ/	平壤
Russia	英 /'rʌʃə/	美 /'rʌʃə/	俄罗斯
——Moscow	英 /'mɒskəʊ/	美 /'mɑːskaʊ/	莫斯科
Thailand	英 /'taɪlænd/	美 /'taɪlænd/	泰国
——Bangkok	英 /'bæŋkɒk/	美 /'bæŋ,kɑːk/	曼谷
Oceania	英 /ˌəʊsi'ɑːniə/	美 /ˌoʊʃi'ɑːniə/	大洋洲
Australia	英 /ɒ'streɪliə/	美 /ɔː'streɪliə/	澳大利亚
——Canberra	英 /'kænbərə/	美 /'kænbərə/	堪培拉
New Zealand 新西兰			
——Wellington	英 /'welɪŋtən/	美 /'welɪŋtən/	惠灵顿
Europe	英 /'jʊərəp/	美 /'jʊrəp/	欧洲
the United Kingdom 英国			
——London	英 /'lʌndən/	美 /'lʌndən/	伦敦

Germany	英 /ˈdʒɜːməni/	美 /ˈdʒɜːrməni/	德国
——Berlin	英 /bɜːˈlɪn/	美 /bɜːrˈlɪn/	柏林
France	英 /frɑːns/	美 /fræns/	法国
——Paris	英 /ˈpærɪs/	美 /ˈpærɪs/	巴黎
Italy	英 /ˈɪtəli/	美 /ˈɪtəli/	意大利
——Rome	英 /rəʊm/	美 /roʊm/	罗马

North/South America 北 / 南美洲

the United States of America 美国			
——Washington	英 /ˈwɒʃɪŋtən/	美 /ˈwɑːʃɪŋtən/	华盛顿
Canada	英 /ˈkænədə/	美 /ˈkænədə/	加拿大
——Ottawa	英 /ˈɒtəwə/	美 /ˈɑːtəwə/	渥太华
Mexico	英 /ˈmeksɪkəʊ/	美 /ˈmeksɪkoʊ/	墨西哥
——Mexican City 墨西哥城			
Brazil	英 /brəˈzɪl/	美 /brəˈzɪl/	巴西
——Brasilia	英 /brəˈzɪliə/	美 /brəˈzɪliə/	巴西利亚

Africa 英 /ˈæfrɪkə/ 美 /ˈæfrɪkə/ 非洲

Egypt	英 /ˈiːdʒɪpt/	美 /ˈiːdʒɪpt/	埃及
——Cairo	英 /ˈkaɪərəʊ/	美 /ˈkaɪəroʊ/	开罗
Nigeria	英 /naɪˈdʒɪəriə/	美 /naɪˈdʒɪriə/	尼日利亚
——Abuja	英 /aːˈbuːdʒɑː/	美 /aːˈbuːdʒɑː/	阿布贾

02 城市类型及地理位置

As you might know, it's a metropolis located in the North China.
就像你可能知道的那样，北京是一座大都市，坐落于中国华北。

实用替换 Useful Alternatives

（1）城市类型

capital	英 /ˈkæpɪt(ə)l/	美 /ˈkæpɪt(ə)l/	首都；首府
municipality	英 /mjuːˌnɪsɪˈpæləti/	美 /mjuːˌnɪsɪˈpæləti/	自治市 / 区
metropolis	英 /məˈtrɒpəlɪs/	美 /məˈtrɑːpəlɪs/	大都市

large/small city 大 / 小城市　　small town/village 小城镇 / 村庄
world heritage city 世界遗产城市　　inland city 内陆城市
coastal city 沿海城市　　first-tier city 一线城市
second-tier city 二线城市　　third-tier city 三线城市

（2）地理位置
主要的方位词：

north	英 /nɔːθ/	美 /nɔːrθ/	北
south	英 /saʊθ/	美 /saʊθ/	南
west	英 /west/	美 /west/	西
east	英 /iːst/	美 /iːst/	东
north-west	英 /ˌnɔːθ 'west/	美 /ˌnɔːrθ 'west/	西北
north-east	英 /ˌnɔːθ 'iːst/	美 /ˌnɔːrθ 'iːst/	东北
south-west	英 /ˌsaʊθ 'west/	美 /ˌsaʊθ 'west/	西南
south-east	英 /ˌsaʊθ 'iːst/	美 /ˌsaʊθ 'iːst/	东南

主要方位词对应的形容词：

northern	英 /'nɔːðən/	美 /'nɔːrðərn/	北方的
southern	英 /'sʌðən/	美 /'sʌðərn/	南方的
western	英 /'westən/	美 /'westərn/	西方的
eastern	英 /'iːstən/	美 /'iːstərn/	东方的
north-western	英 /ˌnɔːθ 'westən/	美 /ˌnɔːrθ 'westərn/	西北方的
north-eastern	英 /ˌnɔːθ 'iːstən/	美 /ˌnɔːrθ 'iːstərn/	东北方的
south-western	英 /ˌsaʊθ 'westən/	美 /ˌsaʊθ 'westərn/	西南方的
south-eastern	英 /ˌsaʊθ 'iːstən/	美 /ˌsaʊθ 'iːstərn/	东南方的

中国各地区名称：

North China 华北　　　　　　North-east China 东北
East China 华东　　　　　　　South Central China 中南
South-west China 西南　　　　North-west China 西北

表示方位的短语：

be located + 介词　　　　　be situated + 介词
A be（located/situated）in the northern part of B A 位于 B 的北部（A 在 B 的范围内）
A be（located/situated）in the north of B A 位于 B 的北部（A 在 B 的范围内）
A be（located/situated）on the north of B A 位于 B 的北边（A 和 B 相邻）
A be（located/situated）to the north of B A 位于 B 的北方（A 和 B 有一定距离）

03 人口

It has a massive population of over 21 million. 北京有超过 2100 万的人口。

实用替换 Useful Alternatives

small population 人口少　　　　　huge/large/massive population 人口多
urban population 城市人口
（urban　　　英 /'ɜːbən/　　　美 /'ɜːrbən/　　　城市的）

> rural population 农村人口
> (rural　　　　　[英]/ˈruərəl/　　　　[美]/ˈrurəl/　　　　农村的)
> indigenous population 原住民人口
> (indigenous　　[英]/ɪnˈdɪdʒənəs/　　[美]/ɪnˈdɪdʒənəs/　　本地的，当地的)
> migrant population 外来人口
> (migrant　　　　[英]/ˈmaɪɡrənt/　　　[美]/ˈmaɪɡrənt/　　　迁移的，流动的)

04 地位

As the capital of China, Beijing is also the center for politics, economics and culture.
作为中国的首都，北京也是政治、经济和文化中心。

实用替换 Useful Alternatives

- be the center for diplomacy/education/science and technology/finance
  是外交 / 教育 / 科技 / 金融中心
- be the largest/second largest city in China
  是中国最大 / 第二大的城市
- be among the top 10 most livable cities in the world/China
  是全世界 / 中国十大宜居城市之一
- be the most/second populous city in America
  是美国人口最多 / 第二多的城市
- be one of China's most popular tourist destinations
  是中国最受欢迎的旅游目的地之一
- be one of the fast-growing cities in the world
  是世界上发展最快的城市之一

✓ 表达示例 Example

Which city have you been to recently? 你最近去过哪个城市？

The city I've been to most recently is Beijing. As you might know, it's a metropolis located in the North China with a massive population of over 21 million. As the capital of China, Beijing is also the center for politics, economics and culture.

我最近去过的城市是北京。就像你可能知道的那样，北京是一座大都市，坐落于中国华北，有超过 2100 万人口。作为中国的首都，北京也是政治、经济和文化中心。

Lesson 87　什么时候去的、和谁一起去的?
When did you go there and who did you go with?

这一部分需要描述什么时候去的这个城市、去了多久、和谁一起去，以及住在什么地方。

01　时间

I went there in August and stayed for a couple of days.
我八月份去的北京，在那边待了几天。

实用替换 Useful Alternatives

（1）时间点
- last year 去年
- in 2020　2020 年
- in the spring 在春天
- in + 月份（January/February/...）在几月（一月/二月/……）
- at + 节日（the Spring Festival/Christmas/...）在什么节日（春节/圣诞节/……）
- two years ago 两年前
- on the weekend 在周末

（2）时间段
- for a few days 几天
- for the entire month of January 整个一月
- for ten years 十年
- for one's whole life 一生
- for a week 一周
- for the whole spring 整个春天
- for a long time 很长时间

02　人物

I visited there with my friends for travel. 我和朋友一起去北京旅游。

实用替换 Useful Alternatives

（1）同伴的类型
- alone/by myself/on my own 独自
- with my husband/wife/children 和丈夫/妻子/孩子
- with my boyfriend/girlfriend 和男/女朋友
- with my colleague(s) 和同事
- with my parent(s) 和父母
- with my classmate(s) 和同学

（2）旅行的目的
- for work/business 为了工作/出差
- for relaxation 为了放松
- for visiting my friends/relatives/parents 为了拜访我的朋友/亲戚/父母
- for study 为了学习
- for a date 为了约会

03 地点

We stayed in a hotel close to the city center.
我们住在一个靠近市中心的酒店里。

实用替换 Useful Alternatives

（1）住宿地点类型
    in a relative's house 在亲戚家　　in my friend's house 在朋友家
    in the dormitory 在宿舍　　　　in a rented house 在出租屋
    in my parents' house 在父母家

（2）地理位置
    in the city center 在市中心　　　　close to a subway station 靠近地铁站
    near tourist attractions 靠近旅游景点　in the suburbs 在郊区
    on the outskirts of the city 在市郊　　in a village 在村子里
    in the middle of nowhere 在偏远的地方

✓ 表达示例 Example

When did you go there and who did you go with? 什么时候去的、和谁一起去的？

I went there in August and stayed for a couple of days. I visited there with my friends for travel and we stayed in a hotel close to the city center.

我八月份去的北京，在那边待了几天。我和朋友一起去那里旅游。我们住在一个靠近市中心的酒店里。

Lesson 88 你的第一印象是什么?
What's your first impression?

这一部分需要描述这个城市给你留下的第一印象,可能包括该城市的人口密度、空气质量、交通设施等。

01 总体感受

I felt shocked when I arrived in Beijing. 到达北京时,我感到震惊。

实用替换 Useful Alternatives

surprised	英 /sə'praɪzd/	美 /sər'praɪzd/	惊讶的
astonished	英 /ə'stɒnɪʃt/	美 /ə'stɑːnɪʃt/	
=amazed	英 /ə'meɪzd/	美 /ə'meɪzd/	十分惊讶的
impressed	英 /ɪm'prest/	美 /ɪm'prest/	印象深刻的
excited	英 /ɪk'saɪtɪd/	美 /ɪk'saɪtɪd/	兴奋的
disappointed	英 /ˌdɪsə'pɔɪntɪd/	美 /ˌdɪsə'pɔɪntɪd/	失望的
overwhelmed	英 /ˌəʊvə'welmd/	美 /ˌoʊvər'welmd/	不知所措的

02 人口密度

I had never seen so many people before. 我以前从未见过这么多人。

实用替换 Useful Alternatives

There were loads of tourists. 游客很多。
There were a few tourists. 有零星几位游客。
It's crowded everywhere. 到处都挤满了人。
It's a heavily/densely/sparsely/thinly populated city/area.
这是一个人口密集 / 稀疏的城市 / 地区。

03 空气质量

The air quality was not that great. 空气质量也不是很好。

实用替换 Useful Alternatives

I liked the fresh air there. 我喜欢那里新鲜的空气。
I didn't really like the smog. 我不太喜欢雾霾。
The air I breathed there was really bad. 那里的空气非常糟糕。

04 交通设施

Luckily, the public transportation there was really efficient and convenient since the lines have covered nearly all the major locations in Beijing.

幸运的是，那里的公共交通真的非常高效便捷，因为线路几乎覆盖了北京的所有主要地点。

实用替换 Useful Alternatives

单词	英	美	中文
cheap	/tʃiːp/	/tʃiːp/	便宜的
comfortable	/ˈkʌmftəb(ə)l/	/ˈkʌmftəbl/	舒服的
well-organized	/wel' ɔːgənaɪzd/	/wel' ɔːrgənaɪzd/	有序的
inconvenient	/ˌɪnkənˈviːniənt/	/ˌɪnkənˈviːniənt/	不便利的
expensive	/ɪkˈspensɪv/	/ɪkˈspensɪv/	昂贵的
uncomfortable	/ʌnˈkʌmftəb(ə)l/	/ʌnˈkʌmftəb(ə)l/	不舒服的
inefficient	/ˌɪnɪˈfɪʃ(ə)nt/	/ˌɪnɪˈfɪʃ(ə)nt/	效率低的
chaotic	/keɪˈɒtɪk/	/keɪˈɑːtɪk/	混乱的

短语精讲 Phrase Study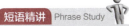

- **public transport/transportation 公共交通**
  Hong Kong's public transport is able to satisfy all the needs of tourists.
  香港的公共交通能够满足游客的各种需求。
  I go to work by public transport.
  我乘坐公共交通上班。

✓ **表达示例 Example**

What's your first impression? 你的第一印象是什么？

I felt shocked when I arrived in Beijing. I had never seen so many people before and the air quality was not that great. Luckily, the public transportation there was really efficient and convenient since the lines have covered nearly all the major locations in Beijing.

到达北京时，我感到震惊。我以前从未见过这么多人，而且空气质量也不是很好。幸运的是，那里的公共交通真的非常高效便捷，因为线路几乎覆盖了北京的所有主要地点。

Lesson 89 你在那里都做了什么？
What did you do there?

这一部分需要描述在这个地方都做了什么事情，可能包括吃、玩、购物、工作、学习、拜访亲戚等。

01 玩

We spent a lot of time visiting famous sites like the Forbidden City which was amazing.

我们花了很多时间参观著名的景点，例如紫禁城，真是令人惊叹。

实用替换 Useful Alternatives

（1）中国著名的景点名称
- the Great Wall of China 长城
- Tian'anmen Square 天安门广场
- the Terracotta Army 兵马俑
- the Summer Palace 颐和园
- the West Lake 西湖
- the Bund/Waitan 外滩
- the Classical Gardens of Suzhou 苏州园林
- the Potala Palace 布达拉宫
- Chengdu Research Base of Giant Panda Breeding 成都大熊猫繁育研究基地

（2）形容景点的常见表达

单词	英式音标	美式音标	释义
beautiful	/ˈbjuːtɪf(ə)l/	/ˈbjuːtɪf(ə)l/	美丽的
=lovely	/ˈlʌvli/	/ˈlʌvli/	
breathtaking	/ˈbreθteɪkɪŋ/	/ˈbreθteɪkɪŋ/	令人惊叹的
picturesque	/ˌpɪktʃəˈresk/	/ˌpɪktʃəˈresk/	如画一般的
marvelous	/ˈmɑːvələs/	/ˈmɑːrvələs/	壮丽的
=splendid	/ˈsplendɪd/	/ˈsplendɪd/	
peaceful	/ˈpiːsf(ə)l/	/ˈpiːsf(ə)l/	宁静的
=tranquil	/ˈtræŋkwɪl/	/ˈtræŋkwɪl/	

- beyond/below expectation 超出/低于预期
- the best place to spend a vacation 度假的最佳场所
- the most interesting place I've visited 我去过的最有趣的地方

02 吃

We also tasted many local dishes such as Peking Duck and instant-boiled mutton. They were all fantastic!

我们还品尝了许多当地的美食，例如北京烤鸭和涮羊肉，都很好吃！

实用替换 Useful Alternatives

（1）经典的中国菜名称
- hotpot 〔英〕/ˈhɒtpɒt/ 〔美〕/ˈhɑːtpɑːt/ 火锅
- Peking Duck 北京烤鸭
- Instant-boiled mutton 涮羊肉
- Kung Pao Chicken 宫保鸡丁
- Mapo Tofu 麻婆豆腐
- Sweet and Sour Ribs 糖醋排骨
- Twice-cooked Pork 回锅肉
- Yangzhou Fried Rice 扬州炒饭

（2）表达食物味道的常见形容词

a. 好吃的
- tasty 〔英〕/ˈteɪsti/ 〔美〕/ˈteɪsti/
- =yummy 〔英〕/ˈjʌmi/ 〔美〕/ˈjʌmi/
- =delicious 〔英〕/dɪˈlɪʃəs/ 〔美〕/dɪˈlɪʃəs/
- =flavorful 〔英〕/ˈfleɪvəfʊl/ 〔美〕/ˈfleɪvərfʊl/
- =palatable 〔英〕/ˈpælətəb(ə)l/ 〔美〕/ˈpælətəb(ə)l/ 美味的，可口的，好吃的

b. 非常好吃的
- fantastic 〔英〕/fænˈtæstɪk/ 〔美〕/fænˈtæstɪk/
- =amazing 〔英〕/əˈmeɪzɪŋ/ 〔美〕/əˈmeɪzɪŋ/
- =incredible 〔英〕/ɪnˈkredəb(ə)l/ 〔美〕/ɪnˈkredəb(ə)l/ 极好的，令人惊叹的，极棒的

c. 好吃极了的
- lip-smacking 好吃到吧唧嘴的
- mouth-watering 好吃到让人看到就想流口水的
- finger-licking good 好吃到舔手指的

d. 难吃的
- stale 〔英〕/steɪl/ 〔美〕/steɪl/ 不新鲜的
- greasy 〔英〕/ˈɡriːsi/ 〔美〕/ˈɡriːsi/ 油腻的
- tasteless 〔英〕/ˈteɪstləs/ 〔美〕/ˈteɪstləs/
- =flavorless 〔英〕/ˈfleɪvələs/ 〔美〕/ˈfleɪvərləs/
- =insipid 〔英〕/ɪnˈsɪpɪd/ 〔美〕/ɪnˈsɪpɪd/ 无味的
- awful 〔英〕/ˈɔːf(ə)l/ 〔美〕/ˈɔːf(ə)l/ 难吃的
- terrible 〔英〕/ˈterəb(ə)l/ 〔美〕/ˈterəb(ə)l/ 糟糕的
- disgusting 〔英〕/dɪsˈɡʌstɪŋ/ 〔美〕/dɪsˈɡʌstɪŋ/
- =nasty 〔英〕/ˈnɑːsti/ 〔美〕/ˈnæsti/ 令人恶心的
- inedible 〔英〕/ɪnˈedəb(ə)l/ 〔美〕/ɪnˈedəb(ə)l/ 不能食用的

03 购物

Besides, we bought a bunch of local specialties and souvenirs before we left.
除此之外，在离开那里之前，我们买了一堆当地的特产和纪念品。

实用替换 Useful Alternatives

常见的产品类型：

souvenir	英 /ˌsuːvəˈnɪə(r)/	美 /ˌsuːvəˈnɪr/	纪念品
clothes	英 /kləʊðz/	美 /kloʊðz/	衣服
shoes	英 /ˈʃuːz/	美 /ˈʃuːz/	鞋子
hat	英 /hæt/	美 /hæt/	帽子
jewelry	英 /ˈdʒuːəlri/	美 /ˈdʒuːəlri/	珠宝
cosmetics	英 /kɒzˈmetɪks/	美 /kɑːzˈmetɪks/	化妆品

local specialty 当地特产　　luxury goods 奢侈品

specialty foods 特色食品

短语精讲 Phrase Study

- a bunch of 大量；大批

I have a whole bunch of stuff to do this morning. 我今天上午有一大堆活儿。
There's a whole bunch of places I want to visit. 我有一堆想要去参观的地方。

词汇精讲 Word Study

specialty
英 /ˈspeʃəlti/
美 /ˈspeʃəlti/

n. 1. 特产，名产；特色菜
What's your specialty? 贵餐厅的特色菜是什么？
2. 专业，专长
My specialty is physics. 我的专业是物理学。

04 总结

We really enjoyed ourselves in Beijing. 我们在北京玩得很开心。

短语精讲 Phrase Study

- enjoy oneself 玩得痛快；得到乐趣

We enjoyed ourselves at the party. 我们在聚会上玩得很开心。
Come on, enjoy yourself. Let yourself go! 来吧，尽情地玩，玩个痛快吧！

✓ 表达示例 Example

What did you do there? 你在那里都做了什么？

Unit 18　描述地点 Describe a Place

We spent a lot of time visiting famous sites like the Forbidden City which was amazing. We also tasted many local dishes such as Peking Duck and instant-boiled mutton. They were all fantastic! Besides, we bought a bunch of local specialties and souvenirs before we left. We really enjoyed ourselves in Beijing.

我们花了很多时间参观著名的景点，例如紫禁城，真是令人惊叹。我们还品尝了许多当地的美食，例如北京烤鸭和涮羊肉，都很好吃！除此之外，在离开那里之前，我们买了一堆当地的特产和纪念品。我们在北京玩得很开心。

Lesson 90 你喜欢去过的这个城市吗?
Do you like this city you have visited?

这一部分需要描述你为什么喜欢/不喜欢这个地方，可能包括这个地方的文化、生活节奏和当地人等。

01 总体概括

Overall, I love Beijing. 总的来说，我是爱北京的。

实用替换 Useful Alternatives

I like Beijing (very much). 我（非常）喜欢北京。
I don't (really) like Beijing. 我不（太）喜欢北京。
I don't like Beijing at all. 我一点儿也不喜欢北京。

词汇精讲 Word Study

overall
英 /ˌəʊvərˈɔːl/
美 /ˌoʊvərˈɔːl/

a. 全面的，总体的，全部的
I believe the overall situation is good. 我认为整体情况是好的。

ad. 1. 全部，总计
They planned to invest one million dollars overall in a new project.
他们计划在一个新项目上投资100万美元。

2. 一般来说；大致上；总体上
Overall, he is a great student. 总的来说，他是一名好学生。

02 文化

It got such a rich culture that I was so fascinated by.
它拥有如此丰富的文化，令我着迷。

实用替换 Useful Alternatives

This city is developing so quickly while preserving ancient cultural heritage.
这座城市正在迅速发展，同时还保留着古代的文化遗产。

短语精讲 Phrase Study

- be fascinated by sth. 入迷的；极感兴趣的
  They were absolutely fascinated by the game. 他们被比赛深深吸引。
  I was fascinated by her voice. 她的声音让我入迷。

03 生活节奏

I also like the fast-paced life in Beijing because there's always something interesting going on around you.

我也喜欢北京的快节奏生活，总有一些有趣的事情在发生。

实用替换 Useful Alternatives

It's a quiet place and I really enjoy the slow pace of life here.
这是个安静的地方，我真的很享受这里慢节奏的生活。

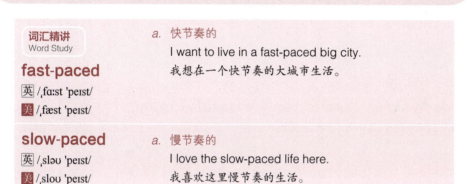

词汇精讲 Word Study

fast-paced
英 /ˌfɑːst ˈpeɪst/
美 /ˌfæst ˈpeɪst/

a. 快节奏的
I want to live in a fast-paced big city.
我想在一个快节奏的大城市生活。

slow-paced
英 /ˌsləʊ ˈpeɪst/
美 /ˌsloʊ ˈpeɪst/

a. 慢节奏的
I love the slow-paced life here.
我喜欢这里慢节奏的生活。

04 当地人

Finally, the people there were nice and easy to make friends with.
最后，那里的人都很好，很容易交朋友。

实用替换 Useful Alternatives

friendly	英 /ˈfrendli/	美 /ˈfrendli/	友好的
hospitable	英 /hɒˈspɪtəb(ə)l/	美 /ˈhɑːspɪtəb(ə)l/	
=welcoming	英 /ˈwelkəmɪŋ/	美 /ˈwelkəmɪŋ/	好客的
warm	英 /wɔːm/	美 /wɔːrm/	友善的
helpful	英 /ˈhelpf(ə)l/	美 /ˈhelpf(ə)l/	愿意帮忙的
naive	英 /naɪˈiːv/	美 /naɪˈiːv/	天真的
unfriendly	英 /ʌnˈfrendli/	美 /ʌnˈfrendli/	不友好的
xenophobic	英 /ˌzenəˈfəʊbɪk/	美 /ˌzinəˈfoʊbɪk/	排外的
cold	英 /kəʊld/	美 /koʊld/	冷漠的
unhelpful	英 /ʌnˈhelpfl/	美 /ʌnˈhelpfl/	不愿帮忙的
sophisticated	英 /səˈfɪstɪkeɪtɪd/	美 /səˈfɪstɪkeɪtɪd/	精于世故的

表达示例 Example

Do you like this city you have visited? 你喜欢去过的这个城市吗？

> Overall, I love Beijing. It got such a rich culture that I was so fascinated by. I also like the fast-paced life in Beijing because there's always something interesting going on around you. Finally, the people there were nice and easy to make friends with. I'll definitely visit it again in the future.
>
> 总的来说，我爱北京。它拥有如此丰富的文化，令我着迷。我还喜欢北京的快节奏生活，总有一些有趣的事情在发生。最后，那里的人都很好，很容易交朋友。我将来肯定会再来一次的。

描述地点汇总

Which city have you been to recently and what was it like?
你最近去过哪个城市？那里怎么样？

> The city I've been to most recently is Beijing. As you might know, it's a metropolis located in the North China with a massive population of over 21 million. As the capital of China, Beijing is also the center for politics, economics and culture.
>
> I went there in August and stayed for a couple of days. I visited there with my friends for travel and we stayed in a hotel close to the city center.
>
> I felt shocked when I arrived in Beijing. I had never seen so many people before and the air quality was not that great. Luckily, the public transportation there was really efficient and convenient since the lines have covered nearly all the major locations in Beijing.
>
> We spent a lot of time visiting famous sites like the Forbidden City which was amazing. We also tasted many local dishes such as Peking Duck and instant-boiled mutton. They were all fantastic! Besides, we bought a bunch of local specialties and souvenirs before we left. We really enjoyed ourselves in Beijing.
>
> Overall, I love Beijing. It got such a rich culture that I was so fascinated by. I also like the fast-paced life in Beijing because there's always something interesting going on around you. Finally, the people there were nice and easy to make friends with. I'll definitely visit it again in the future.
>
> 我最近去过的城市是北京。就像你可能知道的那样，北京是一座大都市，坐落于

中国华北，有超过2100万人口。作为中国的首都，北京也是政治、经济和文化中心。

我八月份去的北京，在那边待了几天。我和朋友一起去那里旅游。我们住在一个靠近市中心的酒店里。

到达北京时，我感到很震惊。我以前从未见过这么多人，而且空气质量也不是很好。幸运的是，那里的公共交通真的非常高效便捷，因为线路几乎覆盖了北京的所有主要地点。

我们花了很多时间参观著名的景点，例如紫禁城，真是令人惊叹。我们还品尝了许多当地的美食，例如北京烤鸭和涮羊肉，都很好吃！除此之外，在离开那里之前，我们买了一堆当地的特产和纪念品。我们在北京玩得很开心。

总的来说，我爱北京。它拥有如此丰富的文化，令我着迷。我还喜欢北京的快节奏生活，总有一些有趣的事情在发生。最后，那里的人都很好，很容易交朋友。我将来肯定会再来一次的。

Unit 19 描述事件 Describe an Event

Lesson 91 什么事让你印象深刻?
What event made a lasting impression on you?

本单元我们将以描述"你印象深刻的一件事"为例,用5小节的内容来学习如何通过5W1H原则来描述一个事件,即是什么事件(what)、什么时候发生的(when)、在哪里发生的(where)、和谁一起做的(who)、过程是什么感受(how)、为什么这件事令你印象深刻(why)、你从中学到了什么(what)。

这一部分需要描述是什么事件、什么时候发生的,以及在哪里发生的。

01 事件

I have many memories of important events in my life, but the one that stands out the most is I learnt to ride a bike.
我记得人生中的许多重要事件,但是印象最深刻的是我学骑自行车。

实用替换 Useful Alternatives

fly for the first time 第一次坐飞机
live on my own 独居
watch a show/game 观看一场节目 / 比赛
fall in love with sb. 爱上某人
break my leg 摔断腿
lose my wallet 丢钱包
make a huge mistake 犯大错误
have a big fight/quarrel with my friend(s) 和朋友大吵一架

adopt a cat/dog 收养一只猫 / 狗
win the competition 在比赛中获胜
meet my idol in person 见到偶像本人
have an accident 出意外事故
lose my pet 丢失宠物
drop my phone 摔掉手机

短语精讲 Phrase Study

- sb. have/has memories of... 某人有……的记忆
  Somebody has memories of being a baby. That's magical!
  有人有自己婴儿时期的记忆,这太神奇了!
  I have vivid memories of my grandma. 我依然清楚地记得我的祖母。
- stand out 突出;显眼
  She can always stand out in a crowd. 她总能在人群中脱颖而出。
  Make sure your ideas stand out in the interview. 确保你的想法在面试中脱颖而出。

02 时间

I was only six at that time. I planned to cycle to school with my friends.
当时我只有六岁。我计划和朋友一起骑车去上学。

实用替换 Useful Alternatives

look for a (new) job 找一份（新）工作
go shopping 购物
visit my parent(s)/friend(s)/relative(s) 去拜访父母 / 朋友 / 亲戚
hang out 出去玩

apply for a new project 申请一个新项目
go on a trip 去旅行

03 地点

So I started to learn it at the park near our apartment every afternoon.
所以我开始每天下午在我们公寓附近的一个公园里学习骑自行车。

实用替换 Useful Alternatives

at home 在家
at the shopping mall 在商场
in the company 在公司
in the supermarket 在超市
in the hospital 在医院
on the street 在街上
near the apartment 公寓附近

at school 在学校
at the airport 在飞机场
in the restaurant 在餐厅
in the stadium 在体育场
in the car 在车里
on the subway 在地铁上

✓ 表达示例 Example

What event made a lasting impression on you? 什么事让你印象深刻？

I have many memories of important events in my life, but the one that stands out the most is I learnt to ride a bike. I was only six at that time. I planned to cycle to school with my friends, so I started to learn it at the park near our apartment every afternoon.

我记得人生中的许多重要事件，但是印象最深刻的是我学骑自行车。当时我只有六岁，计划和朋友一起骑车去上学。所以我开始每天下午在公寓附近的一个公园里学习骑自行车。

Lesson 92 你和谁一起?
Who were you with?

这一部分需要描述是和谁一起做的这件事情,其中包括这个人的性格、你们的相处过程,以及过程中这个人带给你的感受等。

01 人物

It was my dad who taught me how to ride a bike. 是我爸爸教我骑自行车的。

实用替换 Useful Alternatives

my parents 我的父母	my siblings 我的兄弟姐妹
my (best) friend 我(最好)的朋友	my teacher 我的老师
my boyfriend/girlfriend 我的男/女朋友	one of my exes 我的一个前任
my colleague 我的同事	my boss 我的老板
my dog/cat 我的狗/猫	a stranger 一个陌生人
an old man/woman 一个老人/老太太	a nice guy 一个好心人

02 性格

He was really patient and caring. 他非常有耐心且体贴。

实用替换 Useful Alternatives

warm	英 /wɔːm/	美 /wɔːrm/	友善的
sweet	英 /swiːt/	美 /swiːt/	善良的
cooperative	英 /kəʊˈɒpərətɪv/	美 /koʊˈɑːpərətɪv/	配合的
tolerant	英 /ˈtɒlərənt/	美 /ˈtɑːlərənt/	宽容的
open-minded	英 /ˌəʊpən ˈmaɪndɪd/	美 /ˌoʊpən ˈmaɪndɪd/	思想开明的
generous	英 /ˈdʒenərəs/	美 /ˈdʒenərəs/	慷慨大方的
humble	英 /ˈhʌmb(ə)l/	美 /ˈhʌmb(ə)l/	谦虚的
cold	英 /kəʊld/	美 /koʊld/	冷漠的
mean	英 /miːn/	美 /miːn/	不友好的
uncooperative	英 /ˌʌnkəʊˈɒpərətɪv/	美 /ˌʌnkoʊˈɑːpərətɪv/	不愿配合的
intolerant	英 /ɪnˈtɒlərənt/	美 /ɪnˈtɑːlərənt/	不宽容的
narrow-minded	英 /ˌnærəʊ ˈmaɪndɪd/	美 /ˌnæroʊ ˈmaɪndɪd/	思想狭隘的
miserly	英 /ˈmaɪzəli/	美 /ˈmaɪzərli/	吝啬的
arrogant	英 /ˈærəgənt/	美 /ˈærəgənt/	傲慢的

03 相处的过程

At first, he explained to me the theory how to keep my balance on the bike. Then he held the bike by the seat post as I rode along the road.

一开始，他向我解释如何在自行车上保持平衡，然后我沿路骑车时他会扶住座管。

实用替换 Useful Alternatives

At first, he taught me how to float in the water. Then he let me practice exhaling underwater and kicking my legs.
一开始，他教我如何在水中漂浮，然后他让我练习在水下呼气和踢腿。
At first, the coach told me how to back my car into a parking lot. Then he taught me how to drive uphill and switch lanes.
一开始，教练告诉我如何倒车入库，然后他教我如何上坡和变换车道。

短语精讲 Phrase Study

- keep one's balance 保持平衡
  I struggled to keep my balance on my new skates.
  我穿着新溜冰鞋，努力保持平衡。
  She had to hold onto the railings to keep her balance.
  她不得不扶住栏杆来保持平衡。

04 给你的感觉

I felt secure to be with him. 在他身边我感到很安心。

实用替换 Useful Alternatives

comfortable	英 /ˈkʌmftəb(ə)l/	美 /ˈkʌmftəb(ə)l/	舒服的
happy	英 /ˈhæpi/	美 /ˈhæpi/	开心的
relaxed	英 /rɪˈlækst/	美 /rɪˈlækst/	放松的
uncomfortable	英 /ʌnˈkʌmftəb(ə)l/	美 /ʌnˈkʌmftəb(ə)l/	不舒服的
nervous	英 /ˈnɜːvəs/	美 /ˈnɜːrvəs/	紧张的
bored	英 /bɔːd/	美 /bɔːrd/	无聊的
embarrassed	英 /ɪmˈbærəst/	美 /ɪmˈbærəst/	尴尬的

at ease 舒适，自在

05 总结

It will always be one of my **fondest** memories with my dad.
这将永远是我与爸爸最美好的回忆之一。

实用替换 Useful Alternatives

	英	美	
wonderful	/ˈwʌndəf(ə)l/	/ˈwʌndəf(ə)l/	美好的；愉快的
precious	/ˈpreʃəs/	/ˈpreʃəs/	珍贵的
glorious	/ˈɡlɔːriəs/	/ˈɡlɔːriəs/	荣耀的
painful	/ˈpeɪnf(ə)l/	/ˈpeɪnf(ə)l/	令人痛苦的
unpleasant	/ʌnˈplez(ə)nt/	/ʌnˈplez(ə)nt/	令人不快的
sad	/sæd/	/sæd/	悲伤的

词汇精讲 Word Study

fond
英 /fɒnd/
美 /fɑːnd/

a.（回忆）美好的
I have very fond memories of my childhood.
我对童年时光有着美好的回忆。
We said a fond farewell to each other.
我们彼此友好地道别。

✓ 表达示例 Example

Who were you with? 你和谁一起？

It was my dad who taught me how to ride a bike. He was really patient and caring. At first, he explained to me the theory how to keep my balance on the bike. Then he held the bike by the seat post as I rode along the road. I felt secure to be with him. It will always be one of my fondest memories with my dad.

是我爸爸教我骑自行车的。他非常有耐心且体贴。一开始，他向我解释如何在自行车上保持平衡，然后我沿路骑车时他会扶住座管。在他身边我感到很安心。这将永远是我与爸爸最美好的回忆之一。

Lesson 93 过程中你的感受如何?
How did you feel during the event?

这一部分需要描述在整个事件中你的感受，其中包括一开始、中间和结尾的感受。

01 总体概括

In general, my learning to ride a bike can be divided into three stages.
总的来说，我学骑自行车的过程可以分为三个阶段。

> **短语精讲** Phrase Study
>
> - **in general** 总的说来；从总体上看
>   In general, Alexander is a friendly and sincere man.
>   总的来说，亚历山大是一个友好而真诚的人。
>   In general, we need more hospitals. 总的来说，我们需要更多的医院。
> - **divide sth. into sth.** 分割；分成
>   The physical benefits of exercise can be divided into three factors.
>   锻炼对身体的好处可以分成三个方面。
>   She divided all the students into several discussion groups.
>   她把所有的学生分成几个讨论小组。

02 开始

In the beginning, I was frightened and nervous because I didn't know how to keep my balance on the bike.
一开始，我感到害怕和紧张，因为我不知道如何在自行车上保持平衡。

实用替换 Useful Alternatives

表达自己的感受：

单词	英式音标	美式音标	中文
satisfied	英 /'sætɪsfaɪd/	美 /'sætɪsfaɪd/	满意的
pleased	英 /pli:zd/	美 /pli:zd/	高兴的
impressed	英 /ɪm'prest/	美 /ɪm'prest/	印象深刻的
amazed	英 /ə'meɪzd/	美 /ə'meɪzd/	大为惊奇的
touched	英 /tʌtʃt/	美 /tʌtʃt/	感动的
excited	英 /ɪk'saɪtɪd/	美 /ɪk'saɪtɪd/	兴奋的
annoyed	英 /ə'nɔɪd/	美 /ə'nɔɪd/	恼怒的
anxious	英 /'æŋkʃəs/	美 /'æŋkʃəs/	焦虑的
disgusted	英 /dɪs'gʌstɪd/	美 /dɪs'gʌstɪd/	厌恶的
guilty	英 /'gɪlti/	美 /'gɪlti/	感到内疚的
sympathetic	英 /ˌsɪmpə'θetɪk/	美 /ˌsɪmpə'θetɪk/	同情的
broken-hearted	英 /ˌbrəʊkən 'hɑ:tɪd/	美 /ˌbroʊkən 'hɑ:rtɪd/	心碎的

词汇精讲 Word Study

frightened
英 /ˈfraɪtnd/
美 /ˈfraɪtnd/

a. 受惊的；害怕的
Don't be frightened. 别害怕。
I'm frightened of walking home alone in the dark.
我害怕在黑夜中单独走路回家。

03 中间

As I became more skilled in doing it, I found it really interesting and exciting.
随着我变得更加熟练，我发现骑自行车真的很有趣和令人兴奋。

实用替换 Useful Alternatives

表达事物带给自己的感受：

satisfying	英 /ˈsætɪsfaɪɪŋ/	美 /ˈsætɪsfaɪɪŋ/	令人满意的
pleasing	英 /ˈpliːzɪŋ/	美 /ˈpliːzɪŋ/	令人高兴的
impressive	英 /ɪmˈpresɪv/	美 /ɪmˈpresɪv/	令人印象深刻的
amazing	英 /əˈmeɪzɪŋ/	美 /əˈmeɪzɪŋ/	令人惊叹的
touching	英 /ˈtʌtʃɪŋ/	美 /ˈtʌtʃɪŋ/	感人的
encouraging	英 /ɪnˈkʌrɪdʒɪŋ/	美 /ɪnˈkɜːrɪdʒɪŋ/	鼓舞人心的
annoying	英 /əˈnɔɪɪŋ/	美 /əˈnɔɪɪŋ/	令人讨厌的
disgusting	英 /dɪsˈɡʌstɪŋ/	美 /dɪsˈɡʌstɪŋ/	令人厌恶的
boring	英 /ˈbɔːrɪŋ/	美 /ˈbɔːrɪŋ/	无聊的
tricky	英 /ˈtrɪki/	美 /ˈtrɪki/	难办的；难对付的
heartbreaking	英 /ˈhɑːtbreɪkɪŋ/	美 /ˈhɑːrtbreɪkɪŋ/	令人心碎的
disappointing	英 /ˌdɪsəˈpɔɪntɪŋ/	美 /ˌdɪsəˈpɔɪntɪŋ/	令人失望的

短语精讲 Phrase Study

- **be skilled in/at sth.** 熟练做某事
  She is highly skilled at dealing with difficult customers.
  应付难缠的顾客她很有一手。
  He is very skilled in cooking. 他做饭很熟练。

04 结尾

When I finally could cycle to school by myself, I gained a great sense of achievement.
当我终于可以独自骑车去学校时，我获得了巨大的成就感。

实用替换 Useful Alternatives

sense of responsibility 责任感
sense of security 安全感
sense of occasion 仪式感
sense of belonging 归属感
sense of urgency 紧迫感

✓ 表达示例 Example

How did you feel during the event? 过程中你的感受如何？

In general, my learning to ride a bike can be divided into three stages. In the beginning, I was frightened and nervous because I didn't know how to keep my balance on the bike. As I became more skilled in doing it, I found it really interesting and exciting. When I finally could cycle to school by myself, I gained a great sense of achievement.

总的来说，我学骑自行车的过程可以分为三个阶段。一开始，我感到害怕和紧张，因为我不知道如何在自行车上保持平衡。随着我变得更加熟练，我发现骑自行车真的很有趣且令人兴奋。当我终于可以独自骑车去学校时，我获得了巨大的成就感。

Lesson 94　为什么这件事特别？
Why is this event special?

这一部分需要描述这一事件特别的原因，可能与事件发生的时间和地点、事件发生的过程，以及与参与其中的人有关。

01　总体陈述

I treasure this memory over other important events.
和其他重要的事件比起来，我更珍惜这份回忆。

> **词汇精讲 Word Study**
>
> **treasure**
> 英 /ˈtreʒə(r)/
> 美 /ˈtreʒər/
>
> v. 珍视；珍爱；珍重；珍藏
> I treasure his friendship. 我珍视他的友谊。
> I will always treasure those memories of my childhood.
> 我会永远珍藏我童年的回忆。

02　事件发生的时间和地点

It's part of my precious recollections of my hometown and childhood.
这是我关于家乡和童年珍贵回忆的一部分。

> **实用替换 Useful Alternatives**
>
> my high school/university/... 我的高中 / 大学 /……
> my father/mother/... 我父亲 / 母亲 /……
> my time in Beijing/Shanghai/... 我在北京 / 上海 /……的时光
> my first/last work 我的第一份 / 上一份工作
> my trip to London/Paris/... 我去伦敦 / 巴黎 /……的旅行

> **词汇精讲 Word Study**
>
> **recollection**
> 英 /ˌrekəˈlekʃ(ə)n/
> 美 /ˌrekəˈlekʃ(ə)n/
>
> n. 1. 记忆力
> His powers of recollection are extraordinary.
> 他的记忆力惊人。
> 2. 往事；回忆
> I have a vivid recollection of the time we spent together.
> 我依然清晰地记得我们当时共度的时光。

03　事件的过程

Although I got many bruises and scratches, I never gave up even when it was hard.
尽管我多了很多瘀青和划伤，但即使困难我也没有放弃。

实用替换 Useful Alternatives

（1）描述遇到的挫折

I ran into many difficulties 我遇到了很多困难
I was confronted by strong opposition 我遭到了强烈的反对
it was my first time to do it 这是我第一次做这件事
I fell behind at first 一开始我落后了

（2）描述取得的收获

I became independent enough 我变得足够独立
it made me more mature 这件事让我更成熟了
it changed/ruined my life 这件事改变了/毁了我的生活
it made me a rich/famous person 这件事让我富有/成名
my dream came true 我的梦想成真了
I solved the problem finally 我最后把问题解决了
I made it eventually 我最后成功了

词汇精讲 Word Study

bruise
英 /bruːz/
美 /bruːz/

n. 1. 青肿，挫伤
Her face is covered in bruises. 她的脸上满是瘀伤。
2. （水果等的）伤痕，擦痕
Many apples have bruises on them. 许多苹果上有碰伤。

scratch
英 /skrætʃ/
美 /skrætʃ/

n. 1. （皮肤或物体表面上的）划痕，划伤
There is a scratch on the chair. 椅子上面有一道划痕。
2. 抓，搔，刮
She gave her arm a good scratch. 她好好地挠了挠手臂。

短语精讲 Phrase Study

- give up 放弃
He never gives up easily. 他决不轻易认输。
I give up—tell me the answer. 我放弃了，把答案告诉我吧。

04 事件中的人

And I really had a good time with my <u>dad</u>.
而且我真的和父亲度过了一段美好的时光。

 短语精讲 Phrase Study

- have a good time 过得愉快，玩得开心
  We had a good time on the holiday. 我们假期玩得很开心。
  You'll have a good time at the party. 你会在派对上玩得很开心的。

✔ 表达示例 Example

Why is this event special? 为什么这件事很特别？

I treasure this memory over other important events because it's part of my precious recollections of my hometown and childhood. Although I got many bruises and scratches, I never gave up even when it was hard. And I really had a good time with my dad.

和其他重要的事件比起来，我更珍惜这份回忆。因为这是我关于家乡和童年珍贵回忆的一部分。尽管我多了很多瘀青和划伤，但即使困难我也没有放弃。而且我真的和父亲度过了一段美好的时光。

Lesson 95　你从中学到了什么?
What did you learn from it?

这一部分需要描述从这个事件中学到或得到了什么，可能包括某种技能、某个道理以及某种感情等。

01 技能

First of all, I have mastered a practical skill which will be useful during my whole life.
首先，我掌握了一项实用的技能，这将对我一生有用。

> **词汇精讲 Word Study**
>
> **master**
> 英 /ˈmɑːstə(r)/
> 美 /ˈmæstər/
>
> v. 1. 精通；掌握
> She has mastered Japanese after hard work.
> 经过努力，她已经精通日语。
> 2. 控制（情绪）
> She struggled hard to master her temper.
> 她努力控制自己不发脾气。

02 道理

Then the biggest takeaway from the experience is the fact that I learnt to persevere through difficulties.
然后，这次经历中最大的收获就是我学会了在逆境中坚持不懈。

> **实用替换 Useful Alternatives**
>
> get along with different kinds of people 和不同的人相处
> cope with stress 应对压力
> deal with difficult situations 应付困难情况
> get out of a toxic relationship 摆脱不健康的关系
> love and accept myself 爱并接纳自己

> **词汇精讲 Word Study**
>
> **takeaway**
> 英 /ˈteɪkəweɪ/
> 美 /ˈteɪkəweɪ/
>
> n. 1. 外卖
> Let's have a takeaway tonight. 咱们今晚吃一顿外卖吧。
> 2. 关键信息；收获
> What's the key takeaway from this survey?
> 这次调查的主要收获是什么？

> **persevere**
> 英 /ˌpɜːsəˈvɪə(r)/
> 美 /ˌpɜːrsəˈvɪr/
>
> v. 坚持
> She persevered with her Italian lessons.
> 她孜孜不倦地学习意大利语。
> If I had persevered, I probably would have succeeded.
> 如果我当初坚持下来的话，我可能已经成功了。

03 情感

Finally, I was able to know my father better through this experience because he hadn't shown his care and love to me before.

最后，通过这次经历，我能够更好地了解我的父亲，因为他以前没有表现出他对我的关心和爱。

> **短语精讲** Phrase Study
>
> - show sth. to sb. =show sb. sth. 给……看；出示；展示
>   Have you shown your work to anyone? 你有没有把你做的活儿给谁看过？
>   Have you shown anyone your work? 你有没有给谁看过你做的活儿？

04 总结

It turned out to be a really rewarding experience. 这真是一次收获颇丰的经历。

实用替换 Useful Alternatives

单词	英式音标	美式音标	中文
unforgettable	英 /ˌʌnfəˈgetəb(ə)l/	美 /ˌʌnfəˈgetəb(ə)l/	
=memorable	英 /ˈmemərəb(ə)l/	美 /ˈmemərəb(ə)l/	令人难忘的
meaningful	英 /ˈmiːnɪŋf(ə)l/	美 /ˈmiːnɪŋf(ə)l/	有意义的
enjoyable	英 /ɪnˈdʒɔɪəb(ə)l/	美 /ɪnˈdʒɔɪəb(ə)l/	令人愉快的
exciting	英 /ɪkˈsaɪtɪŋ/	美 /ɪkˈsaɪtɪŋ/	令人兴奋的
unusual	英 /ʌnˈjuːʒuəl/	美 /ʌnˈjuːʒuəl/	不寻常的
bad	英 /bæd/	美 /bæd/	
=terrible	英 /ˈterəb(ə)l/	美 /ˈterəb(ə)l/	
=awful	英 /ˈɔːf(ə)l/	美 /ˈɔːf(ə)l/	糟糕的
meaningless	英 /ˈmiːnɪŋləs/	美 /ˈmiːnɪŋləs/	
=pointless	英 /ˈpɔɪntləs/	美 /ˈpɔɪntləs/	毫无意义的

> **短语精讲** Phrase Study
>
> - turn out to be + a. /n. 结果是；证明是
>   The truth turned out to be stranger than we had expected. 真相比我们想象的更离奇。
>   The party turned out to be a huge disappointment. 这个派对太让我失望了。

Unit 19　描述事件 Describe an Event

> **词汇精讲**
> **Word Study**
>
> **rewarding**
> 英 /rɪˈwɔːdɪŋ/
> 美 /rɪˈwɔːrdɪŋ/
>
> a. 1. 有所收获的
> It was a rewarding experience. 这是一场收获颇丰的经历。
> 2. 报酬高的
> Her work is financially rewarding. 她工作的报酬很高。

✓ 表达示例 Example

What did you learn from it? 你从中学到了什么？

I learnt a lot from this experience. First of all, I have mastered a practical skill which will be useful during my whole life. Then the biggest takeaway from the experience is the fact that I learnt to persevere through difficulties. Finally, I was able to know my father better through this experience because he hadn't shown his care and love to me before. It turned out to be a really rewarding experience.

我从这次的经历中学到了很多。首先，我掌握了一项实用的技能，这将对我一生有用。然后，这次经历中最大的收获就是我学会了在逆境中坚持不懈。最后，通过这次经历，我能够更好地了解我的父亲，因为他以前没有表现出他对我的关心和爱。这真是一次收获颇丰的经历。

▶ 描述事件汇总

Do you have any experiences that made a lasting impression on you?
你是否有给你留下深刻印象的经历？

Of course. I have many memories of important events in my life, but the one that stands out the most is I learnt to ride a bike. I was only six at that time. I planned to cycle to school with my friends, so I started to learn it at the park near our apartment every afternoon.

It was my dad who taught me how to ride a bike. He was really patient and caring. At first, he explained to me the theory how to keep my balance on the bike. Then he held the bike by the seat post as I rode along the road. I felt secure to be with him. It will always be one of my fondest memories with my dad.

In general, my learning to ride a bike can be divided into three stages. In the beginning, I was frightened and nervous because I didn't know how to keep my balance on the bike. As I became more skilled in doing it, I found it really interesting and exciting. When I finally could cycle to school by myself, I gained a great sense of achievement.

I treasure this memory over other important events, because it's part of my precious recollections of my hometown and childhood. Although I got many bruises and scratches, I never gave up even when it was hard. And I really had a good time with my dad.

I also learnt a lot from this experience. First of all, I have mastered a practical skill which will be useful during my whole life. Then the biggest takeaway from the experience is the fact that I learnt to persevere through difficulties. Finally, I was able to know my father better through this experience because he hadn't shown his care and love to me before. It turned out to be a really rewarding experience.

当然，我记得人生中的许多重要事件，但是印象最深刻的是我学骑自行车。当时我只有六岁。我计划和朋友一起骑车去上学。所以我开始每天下午在公寓附近的一个公园里学习骑自行车。

是我爸爸教我骑自行车的。他非常有耐心且体贴。一开始，他向我解释如何在自行车上保持平衡，然后我沿路骑车时他会扶住座管。在他身边我感到很安心。这将永远是我与爸爸最美好的回忆之一。

总的来说，我学骑自行车的过程可以分为三个阶段。一开始，我感到害怕和紧张，因为我不知道如何在自行车上保持平衡。随着我变得更加熟练，我发现骑自行车真的很有趣且令人兴奋。当我终于可以独自骑车去学校时，我获得了巨大的成就感。

和其他重要的事件比起来，我更珍惜这份回忆。因为这是我关于家乡和童年珍贵回忆的一部分。尽管我多了很多瘀青和划伤，但即使困难我也没有放弃。而且我真的和父亲度过了一段美好的时光。

我也从这次的经历中学到了很多。首先，我掌握了一项实用的技能，这将对我一生有用。然后，这次经历中最大的收获就是我学会了在逆境中坚持不懈。最后，通过这次经历，我能够更好地了解我的父亲，因为他以前没有表现出他对我的关心和爱。这真是一次收获颇丰的经历。

Unit 20　描述物品　Describe an Object

Lesson 96　你收到过的最好的礼物是什么?
What is the best gift you have ever received?

本单元我们将以描述"收到过的最好的礼物"为例，用 5 小节的内容来学习如何通过 5W1H 原则来描述一件物品，即这个礼物是什么（what）、你什么时候得到的（when）、谁送给你的（who）、你为什么得到这个礼物（why）、你如何使用这个礼物（how）以及你为什么喜欢这个礼物（why）。

这一部分需要描述这个物品是什么，以及这个物品是什么样的，其中可能包括这个物品的形状、大小、重量、质地和颜色等特点。

01　物品类型

The best gift I have been given is a digital camera.
我收到过的最好的礼物是一台数码相机。

实用替换 Useful Alternatives

electronics	英 /ɪˌlekˈtrɒnɪks/	美 /ɪˌlekˈtrɑːnɪks/	电子产品
cellphone	英 /ˈselˌfəʊn/	美 /ˈselfoʊn/	手机
laptop	英 /ˈlæptɒp/	美 /ˈlæptɑːp/	笔记本电脑
television	英 /ˈtelɪvɪʒ(ə)n/	美 /ˈtelɪvɪʒ(ə)n/	电视
digital camera	英 /ˈdɪdʒɪt(ə)l ˈkæm(ə)rə/	美 /ˈdɪdʒɪt(ə)l ˈkæm(ə)rə/	数码相机
cosmetics	英 /kɒzˈmetɪks/	美 /kɑːzˈmetɪks/	化妆品
lipstick	英 /ˈlɪpstɪk/	美 /ˈlɪpstɪk/	口红
eyeliner	英 /ˈaɪlaɪnə(r)/	美 /ˈaɪlaɪnər/	眼线笔
mascara	英 /mæˈskɑːrə/	美 /mæˈskærə/	睫毛膏
perfume	英 /ˈpɜːfjuːm/	美 /pərˈfjuːm/	香水
foundation	英 /faʊnˈdeɪʃ(ə)n/	美 /faʊnˈdeɪʃ(ə)n/	粉底
eye shadow	英 /aɪ ˈʃædəʊ/	美 /aɪ ˈʃædoʊ/	眼影
stationery	英 /ˈsteɪʃənri/	美 /ˈsteɪʃəneri/	文具
pen	英 /pen/	美 /pen/	钢笔
pencil	英 /ˈpens(ə)l/	美 /ˈpens(ə)l/	铅笔
notebook	英 /ˈnəʊtbʊk/	美 /ˈnoʊtbʊk/	笔记本
book	英 /bʊk/	美 /bʊk/	书
pencil case 笔盒			
jewelry	英 /ˈdʒuːəlri/	美 /ˈdʒuːəlri/	珠宝
ring	英 /rɪŋ/	美 /rɪŋ/	戒指
necklace	英 /ˈnekləs/	美 /ˈnekləs/	项链
bracelet	英 /ˈbreɪslət/	美 /ˈbreɪslət/	手链
earrings	英 /ˈɪərɪŋz/	美 /ˈɪrɪŋz/	耳环

others 其他

watch	英 /wɒtʃ/	美 /wɑːtʃ/	手表
flower	英 /ˈflaʊə(r)/	美 /ˈflaʊər/	花
mug	英 /mʌɡ/	美 /mʌɡ/	马克杯
cup	英 /kʌp/	美 /kʌp/	杯子

soft toy 布玩偶

02 形状、大小和重量

It's very thin and light. 它很轻薄。

实用替换 Useful Alternatives

（1）形状

long	英 /lɒŋ/	美 /lɔːŋ/	长的
short	英 /ʃɔːt/	美 /ʃɔːrt/	短的
thick	英 /θɪk/	美 /θɪk/	厚的
thin	英 /θɪn/	美 /θɪn/	薄的
round	英 /raʊnd/	美 /raʊnd/	圆形的
rectangular	英 /rekˈtæŋɡjələ(r)/	美 /rekˈtæŋɡjələr/	长方形的
square	英 /skweə(r)/	美 /skwer/	正方形的
triangular	英 /traɪˈæŋɡjələ(r)/	美 /traɪˈæŋɡjələr/	三角形的
diamond-shaped	英 /ˈdaɪmənd ʃeɪpt/	美 /ˈdaɪmənd ʃeɪpt/	菱形的
oval-shaped	英 /ˈəʊv(ə)l ʃeɪpt/	美 /ˈəʊv(ə)l ʃeɪpt/	椭圆形的
star-shaped	英 /ˈstɑː(r) ʃeɪpt/	美 /ˈstɑːr ʃeɪpt/	星形的
heart-shaped	英 /ˈhɑːt ʃeɪpt/	美 /ˈhɑːrt ʃeɪpt/	心形的

（2）重量

heavy	英 /ˈhevi/	美 /ˈhevi/	重的
light	英 /laɪt/	美 /laɪt/	轻的

medium heavy 中等重量的

（3）大小

mini	英 /ˈmɪni/	美 /ˈmɪni/	迷你的
tiny	英 /ˈtaɪni/	美 /ˈtaɪni/	微型的
small	英 /smɔːl/	美 /smɔːl/	小的
medium	英 /ˈmiːdiəm/	美 /ˈmiːdiəm/	中的
large	英 /lɑːdʒ/	美 /lɑːrdʒ/	大的
huge	英 /hjuːdʒ/	美 /hjuːdʒ/	
=gigantic	英 /dʒaɪˈɡæntɪk/	美 /dʒaɪˈɡæntɪk/	巨大的

extra large 加大的

03 质地

I love the metallic texture of it. 我喜欢它的金属质感。

实用替换 Useful Alternatives

smooth	英 /smuːð/	美 /smuːð/	光滑的
rough	英 /rʌf/	美 /rʌf/	粗糙的
hard	英 /hɑːd/	美 /hɑːrd/	硬的
soft	英 /sɒft/	美 /sɔːft/	软的
coarse	英 /kɔːs/	美 /kɔːrs/	粗的；大颗粒的
fine	英 /faɪn/	美 /faɪn/	细的；小颗粒的
silky	英 /ˈsɪlki/	美 /ˈsɪlki/	如丝绸般的
polished	英 /ˈpɒlɪʃt/	美 /ˈpɑːlɪʃt/	抛光的
fluffy	英 /ˈflʌfi/	美 /ˈflʌfi/	绒毛般的
matte	英 /mæt/	美 /mæt/	哑光的
glossy	英 /ˈglɒsi/	美 /ˈglɑːsi/	有光泽的

04 颜色

The color silver is also my favorite. 它的银色也刚好是我最喜欢的颜色。

实用替换 Useful Alternatives

red	英 /red/	美 /red/	红色的
orange	英 /ˈɒrɪndʒ/	美 /ˈɔːrɪndʒ/	橘色的
yellow	英 /ˈjeləʊ/	美 /ˈjeloʊ/	黄色的
green	英 /griːn/	美 /griːn/	绿色的
blue	英 /bluː/	美 /bluː/	蓝色的
indigo	英 /ˈɪndɪgəʊ/	美 /ˈɪndɪgoʊ/	靛蓝的；青色的
purple	英 /ˈpɜːp(ə)l/	美 /ˈpɜːrp(ə)l/	紫色的
pink	英 /pɪŋk/	美 /pɪŋk/	粉色的
gold	英 /gəʊld/	美 /goʊld/	金色的
brown	英 /braʊn/	美 /braʊn/	棕色的
grey/gray	英 /greɪ/	美 /greɪ/	灰色的
black	英 /blæk/	美 /blæk/	黑色的
white	英 /waɪt/	美 /waɪt/	白色的

05 总结

I had wanted it for so long that it was extra special when I got it.

我想要一台数码相机很久了，以至于当我得到它的时候，它变得格外特别。

词汇精讲 Word Study

extra
英 /'ekstrə/
美 /'ekstrə/

a. 额外的；附加的
Breakfast is provided at no extra charge.
供应早餐，不另收费。

ad. 额外；另外；外加
I need to earn a bit extra this month.
我这个月需要挣点外快。

n. 额外的事物；另外收费的事物
The monthly fee is fixed and there are no hidden extras.
月费是固定的，没有隐藏的额外收费。

 表达示例 Example

What is the best gift you have ever received?
你收到过的最好的礼物是什么？

> The best gift I have been given is a digital camera. It's very thin and light. I love the metallic texture of it and the color silver is also my favorite. I had wanted it for so long that it was extra special when I got it.
>
> 我收到过的最好的礼物是一台数码相机。它非常轻薄。我喜欢它的金属质感，它的银色也是我的最爱。我想要一台数码相机很久了，以至于当我得到它的时候，它变得格外特别。

Lesson 97 你什么时候收到这个礼物的？谁送给你的？
When did you receive the gift and who gave it to you?

这一部分需要描述你是什么时候收到这件物品的（when）、是谁送的（who），以及你当时的心情。

01 时间

I received it several years ago. 我几年前收到的这个礼物。

实用替换 Useful Alternatives

three years/months/weeks/days ago 三年 / 个月 / 周 / 天前
recently 最近
at Christmas 在圣诞节
on the wedding anniversary 在结婚纪念日
on my 21st birthday 在我 21 岁生日时
when I was a child 当我小的时候
when I was seven years old 在我七岁的时候

At that time, I just graduated from college. 当时我刚大学毕业。

实用替换 Useful Alternatives

I was going to attend elementary school 我准备上小学
I was in middle school 我在上初中
I just graduated from high school 我刚高中毕业
I found my first/a new job 我找到了第一份 / 新工作
I was new to the place/office 我刚来这个地方 / 公司

02 人物

My aunt bought it for me. 我姑姑给我买的这个礼物。

实用替换 Useful Alternatives

my mum/dad/brother/sister 我的妈妈 / 爸爸 / 兄弟 / 姐妹
my wife/husband 我的妻子 / 丈夫
my girlfriend/boyfriend 我的女 / 男朋友
my friend 我的朋友
my colleague 我的同事
my classmate/roommate 我的同学 / 室友
my teacher/supervisor 我的老师 / 导师

03 心情

I felt so pumped up when I received it. I will never forget the moment I opened the gift box. 收到它的时候,我非常激动。我永远不会忘记打开礼品盒的那一刻。

实用替换 Useful Alternatives

thrilled	英 /θrɪld/	美 /θrɪld/	
=excited	英 /ɪk'saɪtɪd/	美 /ɪk'saɪtɪd/	兴奋的
touched	英 /tʌtʃt/	美 /tʌtʃt/	感动的
encouraged	英 /ɪn'kʌrɪdʒd/	美 /ɪn'kɜːrɪdʒd/	受到鼓舞的
surprised	英 /sə'praɪzd/	美 /sər'praɪzd/	惊讶的
bad	英 /bæd/	美 /bæd/	感到愧疚的
guilty	英 /'gɪlti/	美 /'gɪlti/	感到内疚的
disappointed	英 /ˌdɪsə'pɔɪntɪd/	美 /ˌdɪsə'pɔɪntɪd/	失望的
insulted	英 /ɪn'sʌltɪd/	美 /ɪn'sʌltɪd/	受到侮辱的

短语精讲 Phrase Study

- be pumped (up) 兴奋的,激动的
  She is very pumped up for the concert on this weekend.
  她为周末的演唱会感到兴奋不已。
  I'm feeling pumped up before the interview. 面试前我感到很兴奋。

✓ 表达示例 Example

When did you receive the gift and who gave it to you?
你什么时候收到这个礼物的?谁送给你的?

I received it several years ago. At that time, I just graduated from college. My aunt bought it for me. I felt so pumped up when I received it. I will never forget the moment I opened the gift box.
我几年前收到的这个礼物,当时我刚大学毕业。我姑姑给我买的这个礼物。收到它的时候,我非常激动。我永远都不会忘记打开礼品盒的那一刻。

Lesson 98　你为什么收到这份礼物？
Why did you receive this gift?

这一部分需要描述收到这份礼物的原因，可能包括庆祝、奖励、纪念、感情等。

01 礼物类型

It was a **graduation gift**. 这是一个毕业礼物。

实用替换 Useful Alternatives

| souvenir | 英 /ˌsuːvəˈnɪə(r)/ | 美 /ˌsuːvəˈnɪr/ | 纪念品 |

birthday gift 生日礼物　　　　　　New Year's gift 新年礼物
Christmas gift 圣诞礼物　　　　　anniversary gift 周年纪念日礼物
Valentine's Day gift 情人节礼物　　wedding gift 结婚礼物

02 庆祝 / 奖励 / 纪念

I had a tough year with lots of exams and I worked really hard.
我度过了艰难的一年，参加了很多考试，而且我非常努力。

实用替换 Useful Alternatives

具体原因：
It was my 18th birthday. 是我 18 岁生日。
I was discharged from the hospital. 我获准出院了。
I found a great job. 我找到了一份好工作。
I got a promotion. 我得到了晋升。
I made progress in my studies. 我在学习上取得了进步。
I won the game/competition. 我赢得了比赛 / 竞赛。

Therefore, my aunt thought it would be a great **comfort** to me.
因此，我姑姑认为这份礼物对我来说会是一个极大的安慰。

实用替换 Useful Alternatives

reward	英 /rɪˈwɔːd/	美 /rɪˈwɔːrd/	奖励
encouragement	英 /ɪnˈkʌrɪdʒmənt/	美 /ɪnˈkɜːrɪdʒmənt/	鼓励
compliment	英 /ˈkɒmplɪmənt/	美 /ˈkɑːmplɪmənt/	褒奖，荣誉
surprise	英 /səˈpraɪz/	美 /sərˈpraɪz/	惊喜

词汇精讲 Word Study

comfort
英 /ˈkʌmfət/
美 /ˈkʌmfərt/

n. 安慰；慰藉；宽慰

I took comfort from his words. 我从他的话中得到了安慰。
If it's any comfort to you, I'm in the same situation.
就当是一句安慰的话，我的情况也跟你一样。

03 感情好

Moreover, my aunt cared about me very much. 而且我姑姑非常关心我。

短语精讲 Phrase Study

- **care about sb.** 关心，关怀
  There is nothing I care about more than my children. 我最关心我的孩子。
  I really care about you. 我真的很在乎你。

04 自己想要

She knew that I had been longing for it but I couldn't afford it, so it was very kind of her to give me this gift.
她知道我一直都想要一台数码相机，但我负担不起，所以她送给我这个礼物真是太好了。

实用替换 Useful Alternatives

无法得到某样物品的原因：
I couldn't afford it. 我负担不起。
I didn't know how to buy it. 我不知道怎样可以买到它。
It's over my budget. 超出了我的预算。
I wanted to wait for discounts and sales. 我想等到打折促销的时候。
I was unable to make up my mind. 我还没有下定决心。
There wasn't enough space in my room to put it.
我的房间里没有足够的空间来放置它。

短语精讲 Phrase Study

- **long for sb. /sth.**（尤指对看似不会很快发生的事）渴望
  She longs for performing on stage. 她渴望上台表演。
  I've always longed for a new car. 我一直想要一辆新车。

词汇精讲 Word Study	
afford 英 /əˈfɔːd/ 美 /əˈfɔːrd/	v. 担负得起；提供 Few people can afford it. 几乎没人买得起。 I can't afford to buy a house. 我买不起房。

✓ 表达示例 Example

Why did you receive this gift? 你为什么收到这份礼物？

It was a graduation gift. I had a tough year with lots of exams and I worked really hard. Therefore, my aunt thought it would be a great comfort to me. Moreover, my aunt cared about me very much. She knew that I had been longing for it but I couldn't afford it, so it was very kind of her to give me this gift.

这是一份毕业礼物。我度过了艰难的一年，参加了很多考试，而且我真的很努力。因此，我姑姑认为这份礼物对我来说会是一个极大的安慰。而且她很关心我，她知道我一直都想要一台数码相机，但我负担不起，所以她给我这个礼物真是太好了。

Lesson 99 你是如何使用它的?
How do you use it?

这一部分需要描述如何使用这一物品，其中包括使用该物品的年限、频率和时段，使用的场合和具体用途等方面。

01 使用的年限、频率和时段

The camera has been with me for years. 这台相机已经陪伴我多年。

实用替换 Useful Alternatives

for years/months/weeks/days 数年 / 月 / 周 / 天
for（more than）five years （超过）五年
since I was a kid 从我还是小孩的时候
since I was ten years old 从我 10 岁的时候
since I was in college 从我上大学的时候

I use it once or twice a week, usually on the weekends.
我每周使用相机一到两次，通常是在周末。

实用替换 Useful Alternatives

（1）频率的表达方式
    a. 每……
    every + day/night/Saturday/weekend/month/year 每天 / 晚 / 周六 / 周末 / 月 / 年
    b. 次数 + a + 时间
    once a week 一周一次　　　　　　twice a month 一个月两次
    three times a year 一年三次　　　　four to five times a year 一年四到五次
    c. 频率副词

always	英 /ˈɔːlweɪz/	美 /ˈɔːlweɪz/	总是
usually	英 /ˈjuːʒuəli/	美 /ˈjuːʒuəli/	通常
often	英 /ˈɒf(ə)n/	美 /ˈɔːf(ə)n/	经常
sometimes	英 /ˈsʌmtaɪmz/	美 /ˈsʌmtaɪmz/	有时
seldom	英 /ˈseldəm/	美 /ˈseldəm/	很少
hardly	英 /ˈhɑːdli/	美 /ˈhɑːrdli/	几乎不
never	英 /ˈnevə(r)/	美 /ˈnevər/	从不

（2）时段的表达方式
    in the morning/afternoon/evening 在早上 / 下午 / 晚上
    on the way to school/work 在去上学 / 班的路上
    on the way home 在回家的路上　　at work 在工作的时候
    in class/during the class 在课堂上　　after school/work 放学 / 下班后
    during holidays 假期时

02 使用的场合

Whenever I go on a trip or attend special occasions, I will take the camera with me.
每当我去旅行或出席特殊场合时，我都会带上这台相机。

实用替换 Useful Alternatives

I need to work/study 我需要工作/学习
I need to meet someone important 我需要去见重要的人
I am at home/in the office 我在家/办公室
I feel bored 我感到无聊
I want to have a rest 我想休息
I want to read books 我想读书

短语精讲 Phrase Study

- go on a trip 去旅游
  They went on a trip to the mountains. 他们到山里去旅游了。
  We're going on a trip to Guilin this summer. 我们这个夏天要去桂林旅游。

词汇精讲 Word Study

occasion
英 /əˈkeɪʒn/
美 /əˈkeɪʒn/

n. 1. 场合，时刻
I've met him on several occasions.
我曾见过他几次。

2. 重大（或特殊）活动
The graduation ceremony is a memorable occasion.
毕业典礼是一场难忘的仪式。

3. 时机
I will tell him the truth if the occasion arises.
等时机成熟，我会告诉他真相的。

4. 起因
I've had no occasion to visit him recently.
我最近无缘去拜访他。

03 具体用途

I can use it to take photos of my friends and family members, or capture a moving moment or beautiful scenery.
我可以用它为我的朋友和家人照相，或者捕捉动人的瞬间和美丽的风景。

实用替换 Useful Alternatives

iPad: read books, magazines and papers
iPad：阅读书籍、杂志和论文
laptop/television: watch movies and other videos
笔记本电脑/电视：看电影和其他视频
notebook: take notes in class/meetings
笔记本：在课堂/会议上做笔记
cosmetics/clothes: make me look more beautiful
化妆品/衣服：让我看起来更美
cellphone: contact my friends or use a variety of apps
手机：联系朋友或使用各种应用程序

04 总结

The camera has become an indispensable part of my life.
这台相机已成为我生活中不可或缺的一部分。

词汇精讲 Word Study

indispensable
英 /ˌɪndɪˈspensəb(ə)l/
美 /ˌɪndɪˈspensəb(ə)l/

a. 必不可少的，必需的
Coffee is indispensable to me.
咖啡对于我来说是不可或缺的。
He is an indispensable assistant.
他是一名不可或缺的助手。

✓ 表达示例 Example

How do you use it? 你是如何使用它的？

The camera has been with me for years. I use it once or twice a week, usually on the weekends. Whenever I go on a trip or attend special occasions, I will take the camera with me. I can use it to take photos of my friends and family members, or capture a moving moment or beautiful scenery. The camera has become an indispensable part of my life.

这台相机已经陪伴我多年。我每周使用一到两次，通常是在周末。每当我去旅行或参加特殊场合时，我都会随身携带这台相机。我可以用它为我的朋友和家人拍照，或者捕捉动人的瞬间和美丽的风景。这台相机已成为我生活中不可或缺的一部分。

Lesson 100　你为什么这么喜欢这份礼物?
Why do you like this gift so much?

这一部分需要描述你为什么喜欢这件礼物，比如这个物品很实用、质量好、有意义等。

01　很实用

I like this gift. The camera is very light and convenient, so I can carry it with me everywhere.

我喜欢这份礼物。这台相机非常轻巧方便，所以我可以随身携带。

实用替换 Useful Alternatives

（1）描述实用性的形容词

单词	英	美	中文
useful	/'juːsf(ə)l/	/'juːsf(ə)l/	有用的
functional	/'fʌŋkʃən(ə)l/	/'fʌŋkʃən(ə)l/	实用的
comfortable	/'kʌmftəb(ə)l/	/'kʌmftəb(ə)l/	舒适的
suitable	/'suːtəb(ə)l/	/'suːtəb(ə)l/	合适的
essential =indispensable	/ɪ'senʃ(ə)l/ /ˌɪndɪ'spensəb(ə)l/	/ɪ'senʃ(ə)l/ /ˌɪndɪ'spensəb(ə)l/	必不可少的
portable	/'pɔːtəb(ə)l/	/'pɔːrtəb(ə)l/	便携的
economical	/ˌiːkə'nɒmɪk(ə)l/	/ˌiːkə'nɑːmɪk(ə)l/	节约的；经济的
easy to operate			容易操作的

（2）描述实用性的细节

hold it with just one hand 一只手就可以拿住它
use it anytime I want 我可以随时使用它
use it to do a variety of things 用它来做各种各样的事情

02　质量好

Another advantage of it is that it's very high-quality and durable.

这台相机的另一个优点是它质量很好且耐用。

实用替换 Useful Alternatives

单词	英	美	中文
exquisite	/ɪk'skwɪzɪt/	/ɪk'skwɪzɪt/	精致的，精美的
flawless	/'flɔːləs/	/'flɔːləs/	无瑕的
perfect	/'pɜːfɪkt/	/'pɜːrfɪkt/	完美的
first-rate	/ˌfɜːst 'reɪt/	/ˌfɜːrst 'reɪt/	一流的
fine	/faɪn/	/faɪn/	漂亮的；精湛的
solid	/'sɒlɪd/	/'sɑːlɪd/	结实的
delicate	/'delɪkət/	/'delɪkət/	精密的

词汇精讲 Word Study

high-quality
英 /ˌhaɪ ˈkwɒləti/
美 /ˌhaɪ ˈkwɑːləti/

a. The store sells a range of high-quality wines.
这家商店出售一系列高品质的葡萄酒。
All these dishes are prepared with high-quality ingredients.
所有这些菜都是用高品质的食材制作的。

durable
英 /ˈdjʊərəb(ə)l/
美 /ˈdʊrəb(ə)l/

a. 持久的，耐用的
The material is very flexible and durable.
这种材料非常有弹性且耐用。
The suitcase is made of durable materials.
这个手提箱是由耐用的材料制成的。

03 有意义

But the most important thing is that it reminds me of the challenging time and the love I've received from my family.
但是最重要的是它让我想起曾经充满挑战的日子，以及我从家人那里得到的爱。

实用替换 Useful Alternatives

the effort I made 我所做出的努力
those wonderful days 那些美好的日子
the excitement and pleasure I felt at that time 我当时激动、愉快的心情
the people who helped me 帮助过我的人

短语精讲 Phrase Study

- remind sb. of sb./sth. 使想起（类似的人、地方、事物等）
  She reminds me of my sister. 她使我想起了我的姐姐。
  It reminds me of the good old days. 它让我想起美好的旧时光。

词汇精讲 Word Study

challenging
英 /ˈtʃælɪndʒɪŋ/
美 /ˈtʃælɪndʒɪŋ/

a. 挑战性的；考验能力的
It's a challenging job.
这是一份具有挑战性的工作。
This has been a challenging time for us all.
这对我们所有人来说都是充满挑战的一段时间。

04 总结

That's why I treasure it so much. 所以我非常珍视这台相机。

- That's why... 这就是……的原因
  That's why I quit my job. 这就是我辞职的原因。
  That's why I left so early. 这就是我早早离开的原因。

✓ 表达示例 Example

Why do you like this gift so much? 你为什么这么喜欢这件礼物?

I like this gift. The camera is very light and convenient, so I can carry it with me everywhere. Another advantage of it is that it's very high-quality and durable. But the most important thing is that it reminds me of the challenging time and the love I've received from my family. That's why I treasure it so much.

我喜欢这份礼物。这台相机非常轻巧方便,所以我可以随身携带。这台相机的另一个优点是它质量很好且耐用。但是最重要的是它让我想起曾经充满挑战的日子,以及我从家人那里得到的爱。所以我非常珍视这台相机。

▶ 描述物品汇总

What's the best gift you've ever been given? 你收到过的最好的礼物是什么?

The best gift I have been given is a digital camera. It's very thin and light. I love the metallic texture of it and the color silver is also my favorite. I had wanted it for so long that it was extra special when I got it.

I received it several years ago. At that time, I just graduated from college. My aunt bought it for me. I felt so pumped up when I received it. I will never forget the moment I opened the gift box.

It was a graduation gift. I had a tough year with lots of exams and I worked really hard. Therefore, my aunt thought it would be a great comfort to me. Moreover, my aunt cared about me very much. She knew that I had been longing for it but I couldn't afford it, so it was very kind of her to give me this gift.

The camera has been with me for years. I use it once or twice a week, usually on the weekends. Whenever I go on a trip or attend special occasions, I will take the camera with me. I can use it to take photos of my friends and family members, or capture a moving moment or beautiful scenery. The camera has become an indispensable part of my life.

I like this gift. The camera is very light and convenient, so I can carry it with me everywhere. Another advantage of it is that it's very high-quality and durable. But the most important thing is that it reminds me of the challenging time and the love I've received from my family. That's why I treasure it so much.

我收到过的最好的礼物是一台数码相机。它非常轻薄。我喜欢它的金属质感，它的银色也是我的最爱。我想要一台数码相机很久了，以至于当我得到它的时候，它变得格外特别。

我几年前收到的这个礼物，当时我刚大学毕业。我姑姑给我买的这个礼物。收到它的时候，我非常激动。我永远都不会忘记打开礼品盒的那一刻。

这是一份毕业礼物。我度过了艰难的一年，参加了很多考试，而且我真的很努力。因此我姑姑认为这份礼物对我来说会是一个极大的安慰。而且她很关心我，她知道我一直都想要一台数码相机，但我负担不起，所以她给我这个礼物真是太好了。

这台相机已经陪伴我多年。我每周使用一到两次，通常是在周末。每当我去旅行或参加特殊场合时，我都会随身携带这台相机。我可以用它为我的朋友和家人拍照，或者捕捉动人的瞬间和美丽的风景。这台相机已成为我生活中不可或缺的一部分。

我喜欢这份礼物。这台相机非常轻巧方便，所以我可以随身携带。这台相机的另一个优点是它质量很好且耐用。但是最重要的是它让我想起曾经充满挑战的日子，以及我从家人那里得到的爱。所以我非常珍视这台相机。

Chapter Five

表达观点

导 语

  本章"表达观点"涵盖了社会、生活、教育、工作四大模块，共 20 个热门话题。

  我们在讨论任何一个复杂话题的时候，不应该只看到该事物好的一面或者坏的一面，而是应该学会看到事物的两面性，也就是该事物的利和弊（pros and cons）。所以，本章节中的每个话题都将围绕其利（pros）与弊（cons）展开。这意味着，在讨论如网红文化或 996 工作制等现象时，我们不会停留在表面，而是深入分析其对社会、个人生活和职业发展的积极和消极影响。

  通过本章的学习，你将能够更自信地在英语环境中分享你对各种话题的深刻见解，表达清晰有力的观点，并在讨论中展示你对事物复杂性的理解和尊重。你将学会如何平衡论证，以一种开放和建设性的态度参与到更广泛的对话中。现在，就让我们一起开始，用英语深入这个复杂多彩的世界，发现、理解并表达那些具有时代特征的关键议题吧！

Unit 21   社会话题 Social Issues

Lesson 101   垃圾分类
Garbage Classification

> **What do you think about garbage classification?**
> 你如何看待垃圾分类？

01 利与弊 Pros and Cons

☞ 利 Pros

1. It can help reduce waste. 垃圾分类有助于减少浪费。
2. It can help reduce pollution. 垃圾分类有助于减少污染。
3. It can help cultivate good habits. 垃圾分类有助于培养良好的习惯。

☞ 弊 Cons

1. It's time-consuming. 垃圾分类很耗时。
2. It's complicated. 垃圾分类很复杂。
3. You can be fined. 可能会被罚款。

02 知识要点 Key Language Points

词汇精讲 Word Study		
garbage 英 /ˈɡɑːbɪdʒ/ 美 /ˈɡɑːrbɪdʒ/	*n.*	1. 垃圾，废物 Could you take out the garbage? 你能把垃圾拿出去扔掉吗？ 2. 废话；无用（或不正确）的资料 What you just said is just a bunch of garbage. 你刚才说的就是一堆废话。
classification 英 /ˌklæsɪfɪˈkeɪʃ(ə)n/ 美 /ˌklæsɪfɪˈkeɪʃ(ə)n/	*n.*	分类，分级；分类法；类别，级别 Doing garbage classification in a right way can turn waste into wealth. 正确实施垃圾分类能够变废为宝。
waste 英 /weɪst/ 美 /weɪst/	*v.* *n.*	浪费；消耗 He wasted too much time on online games. 他浪费了太多时间在网络游戏上。 1. 浪费 They recycle used plastic bottles to reduce waste. 他们回收塑料瓶以减少浪费。 2. 白费；糟蹋 It is a waste of time to talk with you. 和你说话真是浪费时间。 3. 垃圾；废物；废料 How should we dispose of these industrial wastes? 我们应该如何处理这些工业废料？

pollution
英 /pə'luːʃ(ə)n/
美 /pə'luːʃ(ə)n/

n. 污染；玷污；弄脏
Our health is being threatened by air pollution.
空气污染正威胁着我们的健康。

cultivate
英 /'kʌltɪveɪt/
美 /'kʌltɪveɪt/

v. 1. 耕作，种植
The farmers there cultivate mainly maize.
那里的农民主要种植玉米。
2. 培养，陶冶
She cultivated a positive attitude towards life.
她树立了积极的生活态度。

fine
英 /faɪn/
美 /faɪn/

n. 罚金；罚款
The usual punishment is a fine. 通常处以罚款。

v. 处……以罚金
She was fined for speeding. 她因超速而被罚款。

beneficial
英 /ˌbenɪ'fɪʃl/
美 /ˌbenɪ'fɪʃl/

a. 有利的，有益的
Moderate exercise is beneficial to our health.
适度的运动有益于我们的健康。

短语 & 句型 Phrases and Sentence Structures

- help（sb.）with sth. 帮（某人）做某事
  Jo will help（me）with the housework. 乔会帮（我）做家务。
- help（sb.）（to）do sth. 帮（某人）做某事
  Come and help（me）（to）lift this box. 过来帮（我）抬一下这个盒子。
- help（sb.）in doing sth. 帮（某人）做某事
  Following these steps will help in improving work efficiency.
  遵循这些步骤将有助于提高工作效率。

✓ 表达示例 Example

What do you think about garbage classification? 你如何看待垃圾分类？

> Garbage classification is beneficial to our society as it can help reduce waste and pollution. However, it can be very complicated and time-consuming.
> 垃圾分类对我们的社会是有益的，因为它可以帮助减少浪费和污染。但是垃圾分类也非常复杂和耗时。

知识拓展
More to Know

- Garbage Classification/Waste Sorting 垃圾分类
  dry waste 干垃圾　　　　　　wet waste 湿垃圾
  kitchen waste 厨余垃圾　　　 other waste 其他垃圾
  hazardous waste 有害垃圾
  （hazardous　英/ˈhæzədəs/　美/ˈhæzərdəs/　有害的）
  recyclable waste 可回收垃圾
  （recyclable　英/ˌriːˈsaɪkləbl/　美/ˌriːˈsaɪkləbl/　可回收的）

- Waste Disposal 垃圾处理相关
  landfill　　　英/ˈlændfɪl/　　美/ˈlændfɪl/　　垃圾填埋场
  dustbin　　　英/ˈdʌstbɪn/　　美/ˈdʌstbɪn/　　垃圾桶（英）
  dustman　　 英/ˈdʌstmən/　　美/ˈdʌstmən/　　清除垃圾的工人（英）
  the three R's—reduce, reuse and recycle
  环保 3R——减少浪费、重复使用、回收利用
  garbage/trash can 垃圾桶（美）
  garbage man/collector 清除垃圾的工人（美）

Lesson 102 网红
Internet Celebrities

> **What do you think about Internet celebrities?**
> 你如何看待网红?

01 利与弊 Pros and Cons

👉 利 Pros

1. Anyone can be famous. 任何人都有成名的机会。
2. You can inspire millions of people. 可以激励数百万人。
3. You can earn a lot of money. 可以挣很多钱。

👉 弊 Cons

1. You can have less privacy. 隐私可能会被曝光。
2. You can create online feuds and hate. 可能会在网上制造冲突,引发矛盾。
3. People constantly judge Internet celebrities. 人们一直对网红评头论足。

02 知识要点 Key Language Points

词汇精讲 Word Study		
inspire 英 /ɪn'spaɪə(r)/ 美 /ɪn'spaɪər/	v.	1. 鼓舞,给……以灵感 Her speech has inspired many people. 她的演讲鼓舞了很多人。 2. 吸气 When you inspire, you draw air into your lungs. 你吸气时,便是将空气吸入肺部。
privacy 英 /'prɪvəsi/ 美 /'praɪvəsi/	n.	1. 隐私 The right to privacy is protected by the Constitution. 隐私权受宪法的保护。 2. 独处的(不受外界干扰的)状态 I hate sharing a bedroom. I never get any privacy. 我不喜欢共享卧室,这样我就没有任何隐私了。
feud 英 /fju:d/ 美 /fju:d/	n. v.	长期不和;争吵不休;世仇 I fear starting a neighborhood feud. 我担心会引发邻里争执。 长期争斗;争吵不休;世代结仇 The two tribes feuded with each other for generations. 这两个部族世代为敌。
constantly 英 /'kɒnstəntli/ 美 /'kɑ:nstəntli/	ad.	不断地;重复地 The car business is constantly changing. 汽车行业在不断变化。

judge

英 /dʒʌdʒ/
美 /dʒʌdʒ/

v. 1. 判断；断定；认为
   To judge from what he said, he was very disappointed.
   从他的话来看，他非常失望。
2. 评价；鉴定；指责
   You have no right to judge other people.
   你没有权利对他人评头论足。
3. （竞赛）评判；裁判
   I've been asked to judge the children's poetry competition.
   我曾被要求担任儿童诗歌大赛的评委。
4. （法庭）审理；裁决
   The man was finally judged guilty. 那个人最终被判有罪。

n. 1. 法官；审判员
   The judge sentenced him to four years in prison. 法官判他四年监禁。
2. 裁判员；评委
   He served as a judge at the dancing contest.
   他在舞蹈比赛中担任评委。

downside

英 /ˈdaʊnsaɪd/
美 /ˈdaʊnsaɪd/

n. 缺点；不利方面
   The downside of living here is that it is expensive.
   生活在这里的缺点是物价很高。

短语 & 句型 Phrases and Sentence Structures

- a lot of/lots of 大量；许多
  She received a lot of birthday gifts today. 今天她收到了很多生日礼物。
  I've got lots of work to do. 我有很多工作要做。

✓ 表达示例 Example

What do you think about Internet celebrities? 你如何看待网红？

There are a lot of online celebrities nowadays. It's great because anyone can be famous, but there are downsides too, like being judged by many people.
如今网上有很多网红。这很好，因为任何人都可以出名，但这也有不利之处，比如会被很多人评头论足。

Unit 21　社会话题 Social Issues

知识拓展
More to Know

- About Internet Celebrity 网红相关
  Internet celebrity/social media influencer 网红
  key opinion leader（KOL）意见领袖
  social media 社交媒体
  we-media/self-media 自媒体
  Internet celebrity economy 网红经济
  vlog 视频博客

- Genres 网红种类
  fashion   英 /ˈfæʃ(ə)n/   美 /ˈfæʃ(ə)n/   时尚
  beauty   英 /ˈbjuːti/   美 /ˈbjuːti/   美妆
  education   英 /ˌedʒuˈkeɪʃ(ə)n/ 美 /ˌedʒuˈkeɪʃ(ə)n/ 教育
  technology   英 /tekˈnɒlədʒi/   美 /tekˈnɑːlədʒi/   技术
  politics   英 /ˈpɒlətɪks/   美 /ˈpɑːlətɪks/   政治
  entertainment 英 /ˌentəˈteɪnmənt/ 美 /ˌentərˈteɪnmənt/ 娱乐
  sports   英 /spɔːts/   美 /spɔːrts/   体育
  gourmet   英 /ˈɡʊəmeɪ/   美 /ˈɡʊrmeɪ/   美食
  video games 电子游戏

- Social Media Sites 社交媒体网站
  Weibo 微博   YouTube 油管
  Snapchat 色拉布   TikTok 抖音国际版
  Instagram 照片墙   Facebook 脸书
  Twitter 推特   Bilibili B 站

289

Lesson 103 叫车服务
Ride-hailing Services

> **What do you think about ride-hailing services?**
> 你如何看待叫车服务?

01 利与弊 Pros and Cons

利 Pros

1. They are convenient. 叫车服务十分便利。
2. They're reliable because of the location tracking system.
   因为有定位系统,叫车服务变得很可靠。
3. They can create many jobs. 叫车服务可以创造许多就业岗位。

弊 Cons

1. They have safety risks. 叫车服务有安全隐患。
2. They may leak personal information. 叫车服务可能会泄露个人信息。
3. The wait can be long. 可能要排很久的队。

02 知识要点 Key Language Points

词汇精讲 Word Study		
hail 英 /heɪl/ 美 /heɪl/	v.	1. 赞扬(或称颂)……为……(尤用于报章等) The concert was hailed as a great success. 这场音乐会被称颂为一次巨大的成功。 2. 招手(请出租车或公共汽车停下) I hurried away to hail a taxi. 我赶紧去叫出租车。 3. 下冰雹 It's hailing! 下冰雹了!
reliable 英 /rɪˈlaɪəb(ə)l/ 美 /rɪˈlaɪəb(ə)l/	a.	1. 可信赖的 Vincent is really reliable. You can trust him. 文森特真的可靠,你可以信赖他。 2. 真实可信的 Our information comes from a reliable source. 我们的消息来源可靠。
safety 英 /ˈseɪfti/ 美 /ˈseɪfti/	n.	1. 安全,平安 They crossed the road in safety. 他们安全地穿过了马路。 2. 安全性 I'm worried about the safety of the system. 我担心该系统的安全性。 3. 安全的地方 They managed to run to safety. 他们设法跑到了安全处。

risk
英 /rɪsk/
美 /rɪsk/

n. 1. 危险，风险
That's a risk I'm not prepared to take. 我不愿意去冒这个险。
2. 引起危险的事物（或人）
Excessive drinking is a major health risk. 酗酒是健康的一大隐患。

v. 1. 使……面临危险/风险
I'm not risking my life in that old car. 我不会冒生命危险坐那辆旧车。
2. 冒……风险
She risked death to save you. 她冒着生命危险去救你。
3. 冒险做；大胆做
It was a dangerous challenge but he still decided to risk it.
这是一个危险的挑战，但他仍然决定冒险。

leak
英 /liːk/
美 /liːk/

v. 1. 漏
The roof is leaking. 屋顶在漏雨。
2. 泄露
He leaked the news to the press. 他把消息泄露给了媒体。

n. 1. 漏洞；裂缝；缝隙
There is a leak in the roof. 屋顶有个洞。
2. （秘密信息的）透露
The company had a data leak last year. 该公司去年发生了数据泄露的情况。

personal
英 /ˈpɜːsənl/
美 /ˈpɜːrsənl/

a. 1. 个人的，私人的（用于名词前）
The novel is written from personal experience.
这本小说是根据个人亲身经历写成的。
2. 人际的（用于名词前）
It's important to have good personal relationships.
拥有良好的人际关系很重要。
3. 私人的，私事的
I'd like to talk to you about something personal. 我想和你谈点私事。
4. 亲自的；本人的
I will give the matter my personal attention. 我将亲自处理此事。
5. 针对个人的；人身攻击的
It's nothing personal. 我并不是针对你。

definitely
英 /ˈdefɪnətli/
美 /ˈdefɪnətli/

ad. 肯定地，明确地
I can't tell you definitely when I will come.
我不能肯定地告诉你，我什么时候来。

incident
英 /ˈɪnsɪdənt/
美 /ˈɪnsɪdənt/

n. 1. 发生的事情（尤指不寻常的或讨厌的）
This incident colored her whole life. 这个事件影响了她的一生。
2. 严重事件，暴力事件（如犯罪、事故、袭击等）
There was a shooting incident near here last night.
昨夜这附近发生了枪击事件。

短语 & 句型 Phrases and Sentence Structures

- ride-hailing service 叫车服务，打车服务
  Uber's largest source of revenue is its ride-hailing service.
  优步最大的收入来源是它的叫车服务。
- because of 因为
  I am here because of you. 我是为了你来到这里的。
  The game has been cancelled because of the weather. 由于天气原因，比赛已被取消。

✓ 表达示例 Example

What do you think about ride-hailing services? 你如何看待叫车服务？

Ride-hailing apps like Didi have definitely made our lives much more convenient. However, certain incidents have shown that there can be safety risks.

像滴滴这样的叫车应用程序肯定使我们的生活更加方便。但是，某些事件表明，其中可能存在安全隐患。

知识拓展 More to Know

- About Ride-hailing Service 叫车服务相关

taxi	英 /ˈtæksi/	美 /ˈtæksi/	出租车
express	英 /ɪkˈspres/	美 /ɪkˈspres/	快车
premier	英 /ˈpremɪə(r)/	美 /prɪˈmɪr/	专车
ride-sharing/carpooling	英 /ˈkɑːpuːlɪŋ/	美 /ˈkɑːrpuːlɪŋ/	拼车
Didi Chuxing 滴滴出行	Uber 优步		
ride-hailing apps 打车软件			

Lesson 104 共享单车
Bike Sharing

> **What do you think about bike sharing?**
> 你如何看待共享单车？

01 利与弊 Pros and Cons

利 Pros

1. It's convenient. 共享单车很方便。
2. It's cheap. 共享单车很便宜。
3. There are some environmental benefits. 对保护环境有一些益处。

弊 Cons

1. There are way too many bikes. 自行车太多了。
2. They create bike graveyards. 共享单车制造了自行车垃圾场。
3. They may not be parked properly after someone uses it.
   共享单车在使用后可能会被停放在不恰当的地方。

02 知识要点 Key Language Points

词汇精讲 Word Study		
environmental 英 /ɪnˌvaɪrən'ment(ə)l/ 美 /ɪnˌvaɪrən'ment(ə)l/	*a.*	环境的；自然环境的 The government is facing pressure from environmental campaigners. 政府面临来自环保主义者的压力。
benefit 英 /'benɪfɪt/ 美 /'benɪfɪt/	*n.*	1. 优势；益处 The discovery of oil brought many benefits to the area. 石油的发现给该地区带来了诸多好处。 2. 福利；奖金；保险金 In addition to my salary, I got medical benefits. 除了我的工资之外，我还得到了医疗保险金。
	v.	1. 对某人有用；使受益 It will benefit the next generation. 这将使下一代受益。 2. 得利于；得益于 Who will benefit from the reform? 谁将会从这次的改革中获益？
way 英 /weɪ/　美 /weɪ/	*ad.*	大大地；远远地 This shirt is way too big. 这件衬衫太大了。
graveyard 英 /'greɪvjɑːd/ 美 /'greɪvjɑːrd/	*n.*	1. 墓地，坟场（常在教堂附近） There is a graveyard near the church. 教堂附近有一片墓地。 2. 垃圾场；废物堆积处 This had once been a port, but now it is a graveyard of rusting bikes. 这里一度是港口，但是现在成了生锈自行车的堆积处。

park
英 /pɑːk/
美 /pɑːrk/

v. 1. 坐下（或站着）
I would park myself in front of the television after work.
我下班后就会坐在电视前（看电视）。
2. 停放车辆
He found a place to park the car. 他找到了一个停车的地方。

properly
英 /ˈprɒpəli/
美 /ˈprɑːpərli/

ad. 1. 正确地；适当地
The television isn't working properly. 这台电视机运作不正常。
2. 得体地；恰当地
When will these kids learn to behave properly?
这些孩子什么时候才会学着举止得体呢？
3. 真正地；实际上
The subject is not, properly speaking, a science.
这个学科，确切地说，并不是科学。

短语 & 句型 Phrases and Sentence Structures

- way too 实在太……（表强调）
Life is way too short. 人的一生实在太短暂了。
That's way too expensive! 这实在太贵了！

✓ 表达示例 Example

What do you think about bike sharing? 你如何看待共享单车？

Bike sharing is very convenient and cheap. However, companies have produced way too many bikes and have created bike graveyards.
共享单车非常方便且便宜。但是，这些公司生产了太多自行车，造成了自行车垃圾场。

知识拓展 More to Know

- About Bike Sharing 共享单车相关
acquisition 英 /ˌækwɪˈzɪʃn/ 美 /ˌækwɪˈzɪʃn/ 收购
bike-sharing industry 共享单车行业   bike-sharing system 共享单车系统
bike-sharing app 共享单车应用程序   shared bike 共享单车
designated docking points 指定停车点   QR code（QR = Quick Response）二维码
smart lock 智能锁   start-up 创业公司

Lesson 105　移动支付
Mobile Payments

> **What do you think about mobile payments?**
> 你如何看待移动支付？

01 利与弊 Pros and Cons

利 Pros

1. They're quick and convenient. 移动支付速度快，很便利。
2. You don't have to take cash or cards. 你不需要带现金或者银行卡。
3. You can save time from looking for change. 你可以节省找零钱的时间。

弊 Cons

1. They're not that secure. 移动支付不是那么安全。
2. Your phone can be stolen or the battery can die.
   你的手机可能会被偷，或者会没电。
3. They're easier to track, which might result in some problems about privacy.
   移动支付更容易被追踪，这可能会导致一些有关隐私的问题。

02 知识要点 Key Language Points

词汇精讲 Word Study

mobile
英 /'məʊbaɪl/
美 /'moʊbl/

a. 1. 非固定的；可移动的
There is a mobile shop nearby. 这附近有一个流动商店。
Mobile payments are growing rapidly. 移动支付正在迅速发展。
2. 易于变换社会阶层（或工作、住处）的；流动性的
It is one of the least socially mobile countries in the world.
这是全世界社会流动性最低的国家之一。
3. 多变的；易变的
He used his mobile features to express sadness and disappointment.
他用自己灵活多变的五官来表达伤心和失望。

payment
英 /'peɪmənt/
美 /'peɪmənt/

n. 1. 支付
The supermarket has introduced a new method of payment.
这家超市引进了一种新的支付方式。
2. 支付的款项
Goods will be delivered after payment. 货物将在收到付款后交付。

cash
英 /kæʃ/
美 /kæʃ/

n. 1. 现金
How much cash do you have on you? 你身上带有多少现金？
2. （任何形式的）金钱；资金
I'm short of cash right now. 我眼下正缺钱。

v. 兑现支票
Where can I cash a check? 我能在哪儿兑现支票？

change
英 /tʃeɪndʒ/
美 /tʃeɪndʒ/

n. 1. 变化；变革
We're living in an era of great change. 我们正生活在大变革的时代。
2. 找给的零钱
Keep the change. 不用找了。

v. 1. 改变；变换
Let's change a topic. 我们换个话题吧。
2. 换乘；转乘
I stopped in Moscow only to change planes. 我为了转机才在莫斯科停留。

secure
英 /sɪˈkjʊə(r)/
美 /sɪˈkjʊr/

a. 1. 安全的；可靠的
He put his valuables in a secure place.
他把他的贵重物品放在一个安全的地方。
2. 牢固的；稳固的
I don't think the ladder is secure. 我认为这个梯子不牢固。
3. 无忧虑的；安心的
I felt secure about my future. 我并不担忧我的未来。

v. 1. 得到，获得
She finally secured a good job. 她终于得到了一份好工作。
2. 使安全，保卫
They tried to secure the website from attacks by hackers.
他们努力保护该网站不受到黑客的攻击。

steal
（stole, stolen）
英 /stiːl/
美 /stiːl/

v. 1. 偷；窃取
My wallet was stolen. 我的钱包被偷了。
2. 偷偷地（悄悄地）移动
She stole out of the room so as not to be noticed by him.
她蹑手蹑脚地从屋里出去了，以免被他发现。

die
英 /daɪ/
美 /daɪ/

v. 1. 死亡；凋谢
Her husband died suddenly last week. 她的丈夫上周突然去世了。
2. 消亡；灭亡
The old customs are dying. 旧的习俗正在消亡。
3. 停止运转；没电
My phone battery just died. 我的手机刚刚没电了。

Unit 21 社会话题 Social Issues

短语 & 句型 Phrases and Sentence Structures

- result in 造成；导致

  The accident has resulted in hundreds of deaths. 这起事故已造成数百人死亡。
  Sleeping deprivation might result in lower concentration.
  睡眠不足可能导致注意力不集中。

- You can (not) do sth. if... 如果……，你（不）能……

  You can have a rest if you finish the work. 如果你完成了工作，就可以休息一下。
  You can't get admitted if you don't meet the requirements.
  如果你达不到要求，就不能被录取。

✓ 表达示例 Example

What do you think about mobile payments? 你如何看待移动支付？

We all use mobile payments now because they're quick and convenient. But they're not that secure and you can't pay if your phone has been stolen.

现在我们都使用移动支付，因为它们既快捷又方便。但是它们并不是那么安全，而且如果你的手机被偷，你就无法支付了。

知识拓展 More to Know

- About Mobile Payment 移动支付相关

passcode	英 /ˈpɑːskəʊd/	美 /ˈpæskoʊd/	密码
barcode	英 /ˈbɑːkəʊd/	美 /ˈbɑːrkoʊd/	条形码
recognition	英 /ˌrekəɡˈnɪʃn/	美 /ˌrekəɡˈnɪʃ(ə)n/	认出；识别

  QR code 二维码　　　　electronic bill 电子账单
  fingerprint recognition 指纹识别
  (fingerprint　英 /ˈfɪŋɡəprɪnt/　美 /ˈfɪŋɡərprɪnt/　指纹)
  facial recognition 面部识别
  (facial　　　英 /ˈfeɪʃ(ə)l/　　美 /ˈfeɪʃ(ə)l/　　面部的)
  transaction fee 手续费
  (transaction　英 /trænˈzækʃ(ə)n/　美 /trænˈzækʃ(ə)n/　交易，业务)

- Mobile Payment Providers 常见的移动支付提供商

  WeChat Pay 微信支付　　　Alipay 支付宝
  Huawei Pay 华为支付　　　Apple Pay 苹果支付
  Google Pay 谷歌支付　　　PayPal Mobile 贝宝移动端

Unit 22 生活话题 Daily Life

Lesson 106 健身 Going to the Gym

> What do you think about people going to the gym?
> 你如何看待健身？

01 利与弊 Pros and Cons

👉 利 Pros

1. It keeps you fit and look good. 健身使你保持健康并显得气色好。
2. It reduces stress. 健身可以减轻压力。
3. It helps you deal with sleep disorders. 健身可以帮助你解决睡眠障碍。

👉 弊 Cons

1. It is tiring. 健身很累。
2. It may do harm to your body. 健身可能会对你的身体造成损伤。
3. It requires self-discipline. 健身需要自律。

02 知识要点 Key Language Points

词汇精讲 Word Study		
gym 英 /dʒɪm/ 美 /dʒɪm/	*n.* 1.	体育馆 I played basketball in the gym with my friends. 我在体育馆里和朋友打篮球。
	2.	健身房 I go to the gym every day after work. 我每天下班后都去健身房。
disorder 英 /dɪsˈɔːdə(r)/ 美 /dɪsˈɔːrdər/	*n.* 1.	混乱，杂乱，骚乱 The whole classroom is in disorder. 整个教室一片混乱。
	2.	失调；紊乱；不适；疾病 The woman is suffering from eating disorders. 这位女性患有进食障碍。 The most common sleep disorder is insomnia. 最常见的睡眠障碍是失眠。
self-discipline 英 /ˌself ˈdɪsəplɪn/ 美 /ˌself ˈdɪsəplɪn/	*n.*	自律能力；自我约束能力 It takes a lot of self-discipline to go to the gym every day. 每天去健身房是需要很强的自律能力的。

短语 & 句型 Phrases and Sentence Structures

- 和 keep 有关的句型
  1. keep + *a.*
     Keep calm, everyone. 请大家保持冷静。
  2. keep + sb. + *a.*
     Workout can keep you fit. 锻炼可以让你保持健康。
  3. keep + sb. + *ad.* /*prep.*
     Don't keep us in suspense. 别卖关子了。
  4. keep + sb. + *v*-ing
     I'm sorry to keep you waiting. 对不起,让你久等了。

- deal with
  1. 对付;应付;对待
     Her daily job is to deal with different kinds of customers.
     她的日常工作是与不同类型的客人打交道。
  2. 解决;处理;应付
     It's a difficult problem to deal with. 这个问题很难处理。
  3. 涉及;论及;关于
     The book deals with some environmental issues.
     这本书涉及了一些环境问题。

- do harm to sb. /sth. 伤害;损害
  A mistake like that will do a lot of harm to his reputation.
  这样的错误将会严重损害他的声誉。

✓ 表达示例 Example

What do you think about people going to the gym? 你如何看待健身?

> People should go to the gym more to keep fit and look good. But not everyone likes the gym because it's really tiring and may do harm to your body.
>
> 人们应该更多地去健身房,以保持健康并拥有好气色。但是,并非所有人都喜欢健身房,因为健身确实很累,并且可能会对你的身体造成伤害。

- About Gym 健身房相关
  membership card 会员卡　　　　fitness coach/instructor 健身教练
  personal trainer 私人教练　　　personal training session 私教课
  fitness equipment 健身器械　　　fitness moves 健身动作

Lesson 107 外卖
Take-out Meals

> **What do you think about take-out meals?**
> 你如何看待外卖？

01 利与弊 Pros and Cons

利 Pros

1. They are convenient. 外卖很方便。
2. There are so many varieties. 外卖有特别多的种类。
3. They taste good. 外卖很好吃。

弊 Cons

1. They can be unhealthy. 外卖可能不健康。
2. They are more expensive than cooking. 外卖比自己做饭的成本高。
3. They can make you lazy. 外卖可能会让你变懒。

02 知识要点 Key Language Points

词汇精讲 Word Study

variety
英 /vəˈraɪəti/
美 /vəˈraɪəti/

n.
1. 多种类；多样式
   There is a wide variety of patterns to choose from.
   有种类繁多的图案可供选择。
2. 多样性；多元性
   We want more variety in our diet.
   我们想要饮食更加多样化。
3. （植物、语言等的）变种，变体；异体；品种
   It is a rare variety of rose.
   这是稀有的玫瑰品种。

unhealthy
英 /ʌnˈhelθi/
美 /ʌnˈhelθi/

a.
1. 不健康的；虚弱的
   They looked very unhealthy.
   他们看起来非常不健康。
2. 损害健康的；对身体有害的
   Rock stars usually have unhealthy lifestyles.
   摇滚明星的生活方式通常是不健康的。
3. 反常的；不良的
   He had an unhealthy interest in luxuries.
   他对奢侈品有种病态的兴趣。

order

英 /ˈɔːdə(r)/
美 /ˈɔːrdər/

v. 1. 命令；指挥；要求
The policeman ordered him to put down the gun.
警察命令他放下枪。

2. 订购；订货；订服务
Shall I order a taxi for you? 要我帮你叫辆出租车吗？

3. 点（酒菜等）
I ordered a hamburger. 我点了一个汉堡。

4. 组织；安排
I need time to order my thoughts. 我需要时间梳理一下思路。

n. 1. 顺序；次序
The names are listed in alphabetical order. 名字是按字母顺序排列的。

2. 订单
We have orders coming from the whole world.
我们有来自全世界的订单。

短语 & 句型 Phrases and Sentence Structures

- 主语 + feel/look/sound/taste/smell/... + a. 用于表示主语的特征或状态
  I feel tired. 我很累。
  You look great. 你看起来很棒。
  It tastes good. 它的味道很好。
  The dish smells terrible. 这道菜闻起来很糟糕。

- 与 more than 有关的句型
  1. more + a. /ad. + than，表示比较，比……更……
     She is more intelligent than her brother. 她比她的哥哥聪明。
  2. 多于，大于，超过
     We have known each other for more than ten years. 我们认识十多年了。
  3. 不只是，不仅仅是
     She is more than a teacher to me. We are close friends.
     她对我来说不仅仅是老师。我们还是密友。
  4. 非常，十分
     He is more than smart. 他非常聪明。

- make + sb. /sth. + a. 使变成；使成为
  The news made me happy. 这消息让我开心。
  We need to make it clear what we are going to do.
  我们需要弄清楚我们要做什么。

✓ 表达示例 Example

What do you think about take-out meals? 你如何看待外卖?

> We order take-out meals because they taste good and they're convenient. Ordering too often is not good because they're usually unhealthy and they can make you lazy.
>
> 我们点外卖是因为它们味道很好，而且很方便。但是点外卖过于频繁并不好，因为它们通常不健康，并且会使你变得懒惰。

- **About Take-out Meals 外卖相关**

  delivery　　　英/dɪˈlɪvəri/　　　美/dɪˈlɪvəri/　　　派送，外送
  take-out/take-away/carry-out 外卖　　　food delivery app 外卖软件
  home delivery 送餐上门　　　delivery guy 外卖小哥，派送员
  doggy bag/to-go box 打包袋 / 盒　　　positive/negative comment 好 / 差评
  star rating 星级评价

Lesson 108 相亲
Blind Dating

> **What do you think about blind dating?**
> 你如何看待相亲？

01 利与弊 Pros and Cons

☞ 利 Pros

1. It saves time. 相亲节省时间。
2. It might eventually lead to a relationship. 相亲可能最终会发展成一段感情。
3. It can let you meet new people. 相亲可以认识新朋友。

☞ 弊 Cons

1. It could be dangerous. 相亲可能很危险。
2. You might feel disappointed. 你可能会感到失望。
3. It could be awkward. 相亲可能会尴尬。

02 知识要点 Key Language Points

词汇精讲 Word Study

save
英 /seɪv/
美 /seɪv/

v.
1. 救助，拯救
   She saved a little girl. 她救了一个小女孩。
2. 节约，节省
   We should try to save water. 我们应设法节约用水。
3. 攒钱，储蓄
   I'm saving for a new bike. 我正攒钱买辆新自行车。
4. 保存
   Please save the image as a JPG file. 请把图像保存为 JPG 文件。
5. 保留，留下
   Save some food for me. 给我留点吃的。
6. 免去；免得
   The prize money saved her from having to find a job.
   这笔奖金让她不用再去找工作了。

eventually
英 /ɪˈventʃuəli/
美 /ɪˈventʃuəli/

ad. 最后，终于
Eventually, your child will lead her own life as an independent adult.
最后，你的孩子将作为独立的成年人过她自己的生活。

dangerous
英 /ˈdeɪndʒərəs/
美 /ˈdeɪndʒərəs/

a. 有危险的；不安全的
Extreme sports can be very dangerous.
极限运动可能非常危险。

disappointed
英 /ˌdɪsəˈpɔɪntɪd/
美 /ˌdɪsəˈpɔɪntɪd/

a. 感到失望的，沮丧的
I am very disappointed with myself.
我对自己感到非常失望。

super
英 /ˈsuːpə(r)/
美 /ˈsuːpər/

a. 极好的；超级的
We had a super time this weekend. 我们这周末过得非常开心。

ad. 特别；格外
She is super considerate. 她超级体贴。

短语 & 句型 Phrases and Sentence Structures

- lead to 导致
Too much work and too little rest may lead to illness.
过多的工作加上太少的休息可能会使人生病。
His carelessness led to his failure. 他的粗心导致了失败。

✓ 表达示例 Example

What do you think about blind dating? 你如何看待相亲?

Blind dating saves time for people who are super busy. Going on blind dates might eventually lead to a relationship, but often, it could be awkward.

相亲为超级忙的人节省了时间。相亲可能最终会发展成一段感情，但通常情况下，这可能会很尴尬。

- About Blind Dating 相亲相关

知识拓展 More to Know

profile	英 /ˈprəʊfaɪl/	美 /ˈproʊfaɪl/	个人简介
matchmaker	英 /ˈmætʃmeɪkə(r)/	美 /ˈmætʃmeɪkər/	媒人
marriage	英 /ˈmærɪdʒ/	美 /ˈmærɪdʒ/	婚姻

blind dating 相亲　　　　　blind date 相亲局
online dating 线上交友　　　online dating service 线上交友服务
dating game show 约会 / 相亲节目
online dating website/app 线上交友网站 / 应用程序

Lesson 109　熬夜
Staying up Late

> **What are your opinions on staying up late?**
> 你如何看待熬夜？

01　利与弊 Pros and Cons

利 Pros

1. You can enjoy fun nightlife. 可以享受有趣的夜生活。
2. You can get more work done. 可以完成更多的工作。
3. It is a good time to have deep conversations. 熬夜是深入谈话的好时机。

弊 Cons

1. It causes sleep deprivation. 熬夜导致睡眠不足。
2. You may have difficulty waking up in the morning. 早上你可能很难醒来。
3. It can lead to insomnia. 熬夜可能会导致失眠。

02　知识要点 Key Language Points

词汇精讲 Word Study

nightlife
英 /ˈnaɪtlaɪf/
美 /ˈnaɪtlaɪf/

n. 夜生活
There isn't much nightlife in my hometown.
我的家乡没什么夜生活。
New York's energetic nightlife is second to none.
纽约充满活力的夜生活不亚于任何地方。

deprivation
英 /ˌdeprɪˈveɪʃ(ə)n/
美 /ˌdeprɪˈveɪʃ(ə)n/

n. 1. 剥夺；丧失；匮乏
If sleep deprivation continues, anxiety disorders may occur.
如果持续睡眠不足，则可能会出现焦虑症。
I suffered from sleep deprivation caused by overwhelming stress.
压力太大导致我睡眠不足。
2. 贫困
People suffer serious deprivation here. 这里的人们非常贫困。

optimal
英 /ˈɒptɪməl/
美 /ˈɑːptəməl/

a. 最优的，最佳的
I do exercise three times a week for optimal health.
为了达到最佳健康状态，我每周运动三次。

短语 & 句型 Phrases and Sentence Structures

- it is a good time to do sth. 是做某事的好时机
  It is a good time to buy a house. 是买房的好时机。
  Is it a good time to talk? 我们现在能聊聊吗?

- have（no/a lot of/considerable）difficulty（in）doing sth. 做某事（没有 / 有很多 / 有相当多的）困难
  I always have difficulty in getting along with strangers. 我和陌生人总是很难相处。
  I have no difficulty in learning English. 我在学习英语上没有困难。

- wake up 醒来
  Wake up! You are going to be late! 快醒醒！你要迟到了！
  What time do you usually wake up in the morning? 你早晨通常几点钟醒?

✓ 表达示例 Example

What are your opinions on staying up late? 你如何看待熬夜？

> For lots of young people, nighttime is the optimal time to go out and enjoy fun nightlife. It is also a good time to have deep conversations but it can lead to sleep deprivation.
>
> 对于很多年轻人来说，夜间是外出享受有趣夜生活的最佳时间，也是进行深入对话的好时机，但它可能会导致睡眠不足。

知识拓展 More to Know

- About Staying up 熬夜相关
  insomnia　　英 /ɪnˈsɒmnɪə/　　美 /ɪnˈsɑːmnɪə/　　失眠
  stay up 熬夜
  burn the midnight oil 开夜车（学习或工作）
  pull an all-nighter 通宵（学习或工作）
  night owl 夜猫子
  lack of sleep/sleep deprivation 睡眠不足
  dark circles 黑眼圈

Lesson 110　代购
Daigou

> **What do you think about buying things abroad on behalf of someone else?** 你如何看待代购？

01 利与弊 Pros and Cons

利 Pros

1. You can get the products you want without having to go abroad.
   不必自己出国就可以得到想要的商品。
2. It is cheaper than buying the same overseas product in China.
   与在中国购买同样的海外商品相比，代购更便宜。
3. It has created a new business model. 代购创造了一种新的商业模式。

弊 Cons

1. You don't have a guarantee. 没有保障。
2. You might buy the wrong size. 可能会买错尺寸。
3. Goods might not be delivered on time. 买的东西可能不会按时送达。

02 知识要点 Key Language Points

词汇精讲 Word Study		
abroad 英 /ə'brɔːd/ 美 /ə'brɔːd/	ad.	1. 到（或在）国外 I studied abroad for two years. 我在国外学习了两年。 2. 在传播，在流传 There is a rumor abroad that he is going to be the next manager. 有传闻称他要成为下一任经理。
overseas 英 /ˌəʊvə'siːz/ 美 /ˌoʊvər'siːz/	ad.	在海外 He works overseas. 他在国外工作。
	a.	在海外的 The number of overseas students has been increasing in recent years. 近几年，外国留学生的数量一直在持续增加。
business 英 /'bɪznəs/ 美 /'bɪznəs/	n.	1. 商业；买卖；生意 He went into business after graduation. 他毕业后就去经商了。 2. 商务；公事 He's away on business. 他出差去了。 3. 营业状况 Business is bad. 生意不景气。 4. 公司；企业 He started his own business. 他创办了自己的企业。

guarantee

英 /ˌgærənˈtiː/
美 /ˌgærənˈtiː/

v. 1. 保证；担保；保障
The ticket will guarantee you free entry. 这张票可保证你免费入场。

2. 使必然发生；确保
These days getting a degree doesn't guarantee you a job.
如今获得学位并不能保证你就有工作。

n. 1. 保证；担保
He gave me a guarantee that it would never happen again.
他向我保证这样的事情不会再发生了。

2. 保修单
The watch is still under guarantee. 这只手表仍在保修期内。

短语 & 句型 Phrases and Sentence Structures

- on behalf of sb. = on sb.'s behalf
  1. 代表（或代替）某人
     She wasn't able to be present, so I signed the form on her behalf.
     她无法到场，所以我代表她签署了表格。
  2. 因为某人；为了某人
     Don't worry on my behalf. 别为我担心。
  3. 为帮助某人；为某人好
     They're willing to do anything on their child's behalf.
     他们愿意做任何事来帮助他们的孩子。

- 和 time 有关的短语
  1. on time 按时
     She always arrives on time. 她总是按时到。
  2. in time 及时
     We were just in time for the bus. 我们刚好赶上那班公交车。
  3. in no time 立刻，马上
     He made a reply in no time. 他马上进行了答复。
  4. at no time 在任何时候（都不）
     At no time can we give up learning. 在任何时候，我们都不能放弃学习。
  5. at times 有时，间或
     At times I had an overwhelming desire to see him. 有时我会非常非常想见他。
  6. from time to time 时常，不时地
     His daughter visited him from time to time when he was ill.
     他生病的时候，他的女儿时常去探望他。

✓ 表达示例 Example

What do you think about buying things abroad on behalf of someone else?
你如何看待代购？

People use this service because it means you can get the products you want without having to go abroad. However, you don't have a guarantee and you might buy the wrong size.

人们使用这项服务是因为它意味着不必自己出国就可以得到想要的商品。但是，你没有任何保证，还可能会购买错误的尺码。

知识拓展 More to Know

- Ways to Express "Daigou" 表示"代购"的词组
  Daigou
  =proxy shopping
  （proxy 英 /'prɒksi/　美 /'prɑːksi/）
  =overseas surrogate shopping
  （surrogate 英 /'sʌrəgət/　美 /'sɜːrəgət/）
  =buying things abroad on behalf of someone else

- About Daigou 代购相关
discount	英 /'dɪskaʊnt/	美 /'dɪskaʊnt/	折扣
customs	英 /'kʌstəmz/	美 /'kʌstəmz/	海关
commission	英 /kə'mɪʃ(ə)n/	美 /kə'mɪʃ(ə)n/	佣金；回扣
genuine	英 /'dʒenjuɪn/	美 /'dʒenjuɪn/	真的；正版的
fake	英 /feɪk/	美 /feɪk/	冒牌的

  duty-free store 免税店

- Types of Product 代购产品类型
clothing	英 /'kləʊðɪŋ/	美 /'kloʊðɪŋ/	服装
cosmetics	英 /kɒz'metɪks/	美 /kɑːz'metɪks/	化妆品
perfume	英 /'pɜːfjuːm/	美 /pər'fjuːm/	香水
infant formula	英 /'ɪnfənt 'fɔːmjələ/	美 /'ɪnfənt 'fɔːrmjələ/	婴儿配方奶粉
wine	英 /waɪn/	美 /waɪn/	酒

  skin care products 护肤品
  health & personal care 健康和个人护理品
  luxury goods 奢侈品
  electronic products/electronics 电子产品

Unit 23 教育话题 Education

Lesson 111 出国留学 Studying Abroad

What do you think about studying abroad?
你如何看待出国留学?

01 利与弊 Pros and Cons

利 Pros

1. It provides you with an opportunity to experience new cultures and foods.
   出国留学为你提供了体验全新文化和食物的机会。
2. You can learn new languages through immersion.
   你可以沉浸式地学习新的语言。
3. You can build an international network.
   你可以建立一个国际关系网。

弊 Cons

1. You may become homesick. 你可能会想家。
2. It can be expensive. 留学可能会花费很多钱。
3. You can be isolated. 你可能会孤单。

02 知识要点 Key Language Points

词汇精讲 Word Study

experience
英 /ɪkˈspɪəriəns/
美 /ɪkˈspɪriəns/

n. 1. 经验
Do you have any previous experience of this type of work?
你之前有做这种工作的经验吗?

2. 经历;阅历
The book is based on personal experience.
这本书是根据个人经历写成的。

3. 体验
That is an unforgettable experience.
那真是一次难忘的体验。

v. 1. 经历;经受;遭受
We had never experienced this kind of holiday before.
我们以前从未有过这样的假期。

2. 感受;体会;体验
I experienced a moment of panic as I boarded the plane.
我上飞机时曾一度感到恐慌。

Unit 23　教育话题 Education

immersion
英 /ɪˈmɜːʃn/
美 /ɪˈmɜːrʒn/

n. 1. 浸没；浸
Immersion in cold water results in rapid loss of heat.
浸入冷水中会导致热量快速损失。
2. 沉浸；专心；陷入
You can learn a new language quickly through immersion.
你可以沉浸式地快速学习新语言。

network
英 /ˈnetwɜːk/
美 /ˈnetwɜːrk/

n. 1. 关系网；人际网
He tried to expand his network of friends.
他努力扩大自己的交际网。
2. 广播网，电视网
ABC is one of the major television networks in the United States.
ABC 是美国主要的电视网络之一。
3. 网络
It is a computer network with more than 200 terminals.
这是一个拥有 200 多个终端的计算机网络。

homesick
英 /ˈhəʊmsɪk/
美 /ˈhoʊmsɪk/

a. 思乡的；想家的
I became homesick recently. 我最近想家了。
"I started feeling homesick," she recalled.
"我开始了乡愁，"她回忆道。

isolate
英 /ˈaɪsəleɪt/
美 /ˈaɪsəleɪt/

v. 使隔离，使孤立
You can never isolate yourself from society.
你永远不能脱离社会。

短语 & 句型 Phrases and Sentence Structures

- provide sb. with sth. = provide sth. for sb. 为某人提供某物
  He provided us with food and water. =He provided food and water for us.
  他为我们提供了食物和水。
  Tom will provide you with the answer. =Tom will provide the answer for you.
  汤姆将会告诉你答案。

✓ 表达示例 Example

What do you think about studying abroad? 你如何看待出国留学？

Studying abroad can be tough especially if it's expensive and you're very homesick. However, a lot of students still go to experience new cultures and foods.

如果出国留学费用很昂贵而且你想家的话，这件事可能会很艰难。但是，仍有许多学生去体验新的文化和美食。

知识拓展
More to Know

- About Application 留学申请相关

application	英 /ˌæplɪˈkeɪʃ(ə)n/	美 /ˌæplɪˈkeɪʃ(ə)n/	申请
deadline	英 /ˈdedlaɪn/	美 /ˈdedlaɪn/	截止日期
admission	英 /ədˈmɪʃ(ə)n/	美 /ədˈmɪʃ(ə)n/	录取
visa	英 /ˈviːzə/	美 /ˈviːzə/	签证
scholarship	英 /ˈskɒləʃɪp/	美 /ˈskɑːlərʃɪp/	奖学金
transcript	英 /ˈtrænskrɪpt/	美 /ˈtrænskrɪpt/	成绩单

undergraduate/graduate program 本科生 / 研究生项目
online application system 网上申请系统
financial aid 助学金   application fee 申请费
required materials 申请必备材料   letter of recommendation 推荐信
personal statement 自我陈述   statement of purpose 目标陈述

Lesson 112　在线学习
Online Learning

> **What do you think about online learning?**
> 你如何看待在线学习？

01　利与弊 Pros and Cons

👉 利 Pros

1. It's flexible. 在线学习很灵活。
2. There are so many resources online. 网上有很多资源。
3. You can do it anywhere. All you need is Internet.
   你可以在任何地方进行在线学习，只要有网就行。

👉 弊 Cons

1. It's hard to focus sometimes. 在线学习有时很难集中注意力。
2. There is less tutor-student interaction. 在线学习的师生互动更少。
3. It can be tedious and boring. 在线学习可能是冗长乏味的。

02　知识要点 Key Language Points

词汇精讲 Word Study	
flexible 英 /ˈfleksəb(ə)l/ 美 /ˈfleksəb(ə)l/	a. 灵活的；可变动的 The company decided to adopt a flexible work schedule. 该公司决定采用弹性工作制。
resource 英 /rɪˈsɔːs/ 美 /ˈriːsɔːrs/	n. 1. 资源；财力 The school doesn't have the resources to renovate the library. 学校没有钱来翻修图书馆。 2. 有助于实现目标的东西；资料 Library is a valuable resource. 图书馆是一种宝贵的资源。
focus 英 /ˈfəʊkəs/ 美 /ˈfoʊkəs/	v. （使）聚焦；（使）集中 You should focus your attention on the most crucial issues. 你应该将注意力集中在最关键的问题上。 n. 焦点；中心 She is the focus of my life. 她是我生活的中心。

tutor
英 /'tju:tə(r)/
美 /'tu:tər/

n. 1. 导师
She is my literature tutor. 她是我的文学导师。
2. 家庭教师，私人教师
His parents got him a tutor to help with his English.
他父母给他找了一个家庭教师来帮助他学习英语。

v. 当……导师，当……家庭教师
He tutored me in physics. 他是我的物理家庭教师。

interaction
英 /ˌɪntər'ækʃ(ə)n/
美 /ˌɪntər'ækʃ(ə)n/

n. 交流，互动
She is really good at face-to-face interaction with customers.
她非常擅长与客户面对面的交流。

tedious
英 /'ti:diəs/
美 /'ti:diəs/

a. 冗长乏味的，沉闷的
Her presentation was tedious.
她的展示冗长而乏味。

boring
英 /'bɔ:rɪŋ/
美 /'bɔ:rɪŋ/

a. 无聊的；令人厌烦的
The movie was so boring that I fell asleep.
这个电影太无聊，以至于我都睡着了。

replace
英 /rɪ'pleɪs/
美 /rɪ'pleɪs/

v. 1. 代替，取代
Do you think robots will replace all the workers in the future?
你觉得机器人会在未来取代所有的工人吗？
2. 更换，调换
All the old computers need replacing. 所有的旧电脑都需要更换。
3. 把……放回原处
I replaced the cup on the table. 我把杯子放回了桌上。

in-person
英 /ɪn'pɜ:sn/
美 /ɪn'pɜ:rsn/

a. 亲自的，有真人参与的
The in-person interview has changed to a video interview.
线下面试已更改为视频面试了。

短语 & 句型 Phrases and Sentence Structures

- All sb. need(s) is... 某人所需要的只是……
  All you need is love.（Beatles）你所需要的只是爱。（披头士乐队）
  All you need is friends. 你所需要的只是朋友。
  All I need is you. 我只需要你。
  All we need is money. 我们所需要的只是钱。
- be popular with 受到……的欢迎
  The restaurant is popular with students. 这家餐厅受学生们欢迎。
  The product is popular with young women. 这个产品在年轻女性中很受欢迎。

表达示例 Example

What do you think about online learning? 你如何看待在线学习?

> Online learning is popular with the younger generation as it's flexible and there are so many resources online. But it cannot replace in-person teaching because there is less tutor-student interaction.
>
> 在线学习在年轻一代中很受欢迎，因为它很灵活，并且在线资源很多。但是它不能代替线下教学，因为师生之间的互动较少。

知识拓展 More to Know

- **About Online Learning 在线学习相关**

platform	英 /ˈplætfɔːm/	美 /ˈplætfɔːrm/	平台
teacher	英 /ˈtiːtʃə(r)/	美 /ˈtiːtʃər/	老师
course	英 /kɔːs/	美 /kɔːrs/	课程

distance learning 远程学习　　　　online learning 线上学习
mobile learning 移动学习　　　　teaching assistant 助教
live-streaming course 直播课　　　recorded course 录播课
audio lecture 音频课　　　　　　video lecture 视频课

Lesson 113 学习第二语言
Learning a Second Language

> **What do you think of the importance of learning a second language?** 你如何看待学习第二门语言的重要性?

01 利与弊 Pros and Cons

👉 利 Pros

1. It makes traveling and doing business around the world easier.
   学习第二语言让你到全世界旅游和做生意变得更简单。
2. It allows you to deepen your understanding of other cultures.
   学习第二语言让你加深对其他文化的理解。
3. You can communicate with more people. 可以和更多人交流。

👉 弊 Cons

1. It is not easy to learn. 第二语言并不好学。
2. It can be expensive to get lessons. 学习第二语言的课程花费可能会很贵。
3. Your native language may be neglected. 母语可能会被忽视。

02 知识要点 Key Language Points

词汇精讲 Word Study	
understanding 英 /ˌʌndəˈstændɪŋ/ 美 /ˌʌndərˈstændɪŋ/	*n.* 1. 理解;领悟;了解 She has a basic understanding of computers. 她对计算机有基本的了解。 2. 理解;谅解;体谅 We would like to thank you for your patience and understanding. 我们感谢您的耐心和理解。
communicate 英 /kəˈmjuːnɪkeɪt/ 美 /kəˈmjuːnɪkeɪt/	*v.* 1. 通讯;交际,交流 We usually communicate by e-mail. 我们一般通过邮件交流。 2. 连接,相通 Her bedroom communicates with the bathroom. 她的卧室和浴室连通。 3. 传达,传播 A bank must communicate an image that it is secure. 安全是一家银行必须要传递给公众的形象。 4. 传染 This epidemic is communicated through air. 这种流行病通过空气传播。

native
英 /ˈneɪtɪv/
美 /ˈneɪtɪv/

a. 1. 出生地的；儿时居住地的
Her native language is Korean. 她的母语是朝鲜语。
2. 本地的；当地的
He is a native American. 他是土生土长的美国人。
3. 土著的；土著人的
Indians are native peoples of the United States.
印第安人是美国的原住民。
4. 原产于某地的；土产的
The koala is native to Australia. 考拉是澳大利亚的本土物种。

neglect
英 /nɪˈglekt/
美 /nɪˈglekt/

v. 忽视，忽略，疏忽
He neglected his studies when he was a child. 他小时候忽视了学习。
n. 忽视，忽略；未被重视
He was dismissed for the neglect of his duty. 他因玩忽职守被解雇了。

短语 & 句型 Phrases and Sentence Structures

- around the world/all over the world 世界各地，全世界
I want to travel around the world. 我想环游世界。
Attitudes to masks have changed all over the world.
世界各地对口罩的态度发生了变化。

 表达示例 Example

What do you think of the importance of learning a second language?
你如何看待学习第二门语言的重要性？

Learning a second language is important because you can communicate with more people. However, it's not easy to learn and can be expensive to get lessons.
学习第二语言很重要，因为你可以与更多的人交流。但是，学习起来并不容易，而且上课的成本可能很高。

- About Second Language 第二语言相关
accent   英 /ˈæksent/   美 /ˈæksent/   口音
mother tongue/native language 母语   first language（L1）第一语言；母语
second language（L2）第二语言   second language acquisition（SLA）第二语言习得
critical period for language acquisition 语言习得的关键期
language learner 语言学习者   language input/output 语言输入/输出

Lesson 114　补习班
Cram Classes

> **What do you think about cram classes?**
> 你如何看待补习班？

01 利与弊 Pros and Cons

👉 利 Pros

1. They can help students who are falling behind to catch up.
   补习班可以帮助落后的学生赶上来。
2. They help students who want to learn more to improve their understanding of certain subjects.
   补习班帮助那些想要学习更多知识的学生提高对某些科目的理解。
3. They can make students concentrate on their study.
   补习班可以使学生集中精力在学习上。

👉 弊 Cons

1. Children no longer have time to enjoy their childhood.
   孩子们不再有时间享受童年。
2. They kill creativity and interest. 补习班扼杀创造力和兴趣。
3. They can increase the children's burden. 补习班会增加孩子们的负担。

02 知识要点 Key Language Points

词汇精讲 Word Study

cram
英 /kræm/
美 /kræm/

v. （为应考）临时死记硬背
He's been cramming for his exams all week.
他整个星期都一直在拼命准备应考。

n. （应考）突击准备，死记硬背
Her parents sent her to a cram school in order to improve her scores.
她的父母把她送到一所补习学校，以提高她的成绩。

concentrate
英 /ˈkɒnsntreɪt/
美 /ˈkɑːnsntreɪt/

v. 1. 全神贯注，全力以赴
   She is concentrating on her work. 她正在专心工作。
2. 集中，集聚
   Most of the city's population is concentrated in the downtown area.
   这个城市的大部分人口都集中在市中心。

n. 浓缩物，浓缩液
   I bought a bottle of apple juice concentrate. 我买了一瓶苹果浓缩汁。

creativity
英 /ˌkriːeɪˈtɪvəti/
美 /ˌkriːeɪˈtɪvəti/

n. 创造力，创造性
Too many rules might kill creativity.
太多规则可能会扼杀创造力。

interest
英 /ˈɪntrəst; ˈɪntrest/
美 /ˈɪntrəst; ˈɪntrest/

n. 1. 兴趣；关注
Just out of interest, why did you come here?
我只是好奇问问，你为什么来这儿？
2. 业余爱好
Her main interests are music and painting.
她的主要爱好是音乐和绘画。
3. 利息
Interest rates have declined by 2%. 利率下降了 2%。
4. 好处；利益
She was acting entirely in her own interests.
她这么做完全是为了自己的利益。

v. 使感兴趣；使关注
I have interested myself in dance. 我对舞蹈有了兴趣。

increase
v. 英 /ɪnˈkriːs/
　 美 /ɪnˈkriːs/
n. 英 /ˈɪŋkriːs/
　 美 /ˈɪŋkriːs/

v. 增长，增多；增加
The price of oil increased. 石油价格上涨了。

n. 增长，增多；增加
A good advertising campaign can lead to a significant increase in sales.
好的广告宣传能使销量大幅增加。

burden
英 /ˈbɜːdn/
美 /ˈbɜːrdn/

n. 重担；精神负担
Buying a house has become a burden on many young people.
买房已成为许多年轻人的负担。

v. 1. 烦扰
I don't want to burden him with my problems.
我不想让他为我的问题操心。
2. 负担，装载
The little girl went upstairs, burdened with a huge suitcase.
这个小女孩扛着一个大箱子上楼。

短语 & 句型 Phrases and Sentence Structures

- fall behind 落后，跟不上
  He fell behind with his schoolwork. 他学校的功课落下了。
  Catch up. Don't fall behind. 跟上，不要落后了。
- catch up
  1. 赶上，追上（某人或某物）
  I stopped and waited for her to catch up. 我停住脚步等她赶上来。

2. 赶上，达到（标准、水平等）
We'll do our best to catch up with the advanced world levels.
我们将努力赶上世界先进水平。

3. 补做，赶做
Summer vacation is the perfect time to catch up on the books you meant to read.
暑假是把想读却没读的书恶补一下的最佳时机。

4. 了解近况，叙旧
Let's have dinner and catch up. 咱们一起吃个晚饭叙叙旧吧。

- no longer/not any longer 不再……
  She no longer lives here. =She doesn't live here any longer. 她不再住在这里。
  I could stand it no longer. =I couldn't stand it any longer. 我受不了了。

- have time to do sth. 有时间去做某事
  Cheer up! You still have time to try it again. 振作起来！你还有时间再试一次。
  We don't often have time to talk. 我们经常没有时间和彼此说说话。

✓ 表达示例 Example

What do you think about cram classes? 你如何看待补习班？

Cram classes can help students who are falling behind to catch up and students who want to learn more to improve their understanding of certain subjects. However, since studying has taken up more of children's lives than anything else, a lot of children no longer have time to enjoy their childhood.

补习班可以帮助落后的学生赶上来，也可以帮助想要学习更多知识的学生提高对某些学科的理解。但是，由于学习已经占据了孩子们生活的绝大部分时间，因此许多孩子不再有时间享受他们的童年。

知识拓展 More to Know

- About Cram Class 补习班相关
  subject 英 /ˈsʌbdʒɪkt/ 美 /ˈsʌbdʒɪkt/ 学科
  cram school/crammer 英 /ˈkræmə(r)/ 美 /ˈkræmər/ 补习学校
  cram class 补习班
  　　　　　　　　　　　　　　　standardized exam 标准化考试
  entrance examination 入学考试　　language test 语言考试
  examination-oriented education 应试教育　　quality education 素质教育

Lesson 115 课外活动
Extracurricular Activities

> **What do you think about extracurricular activities?**
> 你如何看待课外活动？

01 利与弊 Pros and Cons

利 Pros

1. They can help you improve social skills and make new friends.
   课外活动有助于提高社交能力和结交新朋友。
2. They can give students the chance to explore their interests.
   课外活动可以给学生机会去探索他们的兴趣爱好。
3. Students can learn to manage their time properly.
   学生可以学会合理管理时间。

弊 Cons

1. There are too many schedules in a short time. 在短时间内有太多的日程安排。
2. They may lead to extra expenses. 课外活动可能会导致额外的开支。
3. They can be tiring. 课外活动可能会很累。

02 知识要点 Key Language Points

词汇精讲 Word Study

extracurricular
英 /ˌekstrəkəˈrɪkjələ(r)/
美 /ˌekstrəkəˈrɪkjələr/

a. 课外的；课程以外的
She has participated in many extracurricular activities.
她参加了许多课外活动。

social
英 /ˈsəʊʃl/
美 /ˈsoʊʃl/

a. 1. 社会的
She is deeply concerned about these social issues.
她对这些社会问题深感担忧。
2. 交际的，社交的
She has a busy social life. 她的社交生活很繁忙。

explore
英 /ɪkˈsplɔː(r)/
美 /ɪkˈsplɔːr/

v. 1. 探险，探索
I would like to explore a new city on foot.
我喜欢徒步探索一座新的城市。
2. 仔细查阅，探究
They decided to explore this issue more fully.
他们决定更充分地探究这个问题。

manage
英 /ˈmænɪdʒ/
美 /ˈmænɪdʒ/

v. 1. 管理，负责（机构、企业、系统等）
We need people who are good at managing.
我们需要擅长管理的人。

2. 管理（时间、金钱等）
You need to learn how to manage your time.
你需要学会如何管理好自己的时间。

3. 完成（困难的事）；勉力完成
How did you manage to persuade him?
你是怎么说服他的？

schedule
英 /ˈʃedjuːl/
美 /ˈskedʒuːl/

n. 1. 工作计划；日程安排
The conference was held on schedule.
会议如期举行。

2. 清单，明细表
Could you send me a pricing schedule?
您能给我发一份价目表吗？

v. 安排，排定
The meeting is scheduled for Monday morning.
会议安排在周一早上。

expense
英 /ɪkˈspens/
美 /ɪkˈspens/

n. 1. 花费，消费
The house was renovated at great expense.
这个房子翻修花了好大一笔钱。

2. 费用，开支
We have to cut down on our living expenses.
我们不得不减少我们的生活开支。

3. 业务费用
You can claim back your travel expenses. 你可以报销差旅费。

短语 & 句型 Phrases and Sentence Structures

- make friends（with sb.）（和某人）成为朋友
  Did you make any friends at school? 你在学校交到朋友了吗？
  I made some friends at the party. 我在聚会上交了些朋友。

✓ 表达示例 Example

What do you think about extracurricular activities? 你如何看待课外活动？

Unit 23　教育话题 Education

Extracurricular activities can be very beneficial because it gives students the chance to explore their interests and students can learn to manage their time properly. But they might lead to extra expenses and can be tiring.

课外活动非常有益，因为它让学生有机会探索自己的兴趣爱好，而且学生可以学习合理管理自己的时间。但是课外活动可能会导致额外的支出，并且可能很累人。

- Types of Extracurricular Activities 课外活动的类型
  seminar　　英/'semɪnɑː(r)/　美/'semɪnɑːr/　研讨会
  community service 社区服务　　voluntary service 志愿服务
  student organization 学生组织　　students' union 学生会
  part-time job 兼职

Unit 24 工作话题 Work

Lesson 116 创业 Starting a Business

> **What do you think about people starting their own company?** 你如何看待创业？

01 利与弊 Pros and Cons

利 Pros

1. You have greater autonomy. 你有更大的自主权。
2. You can be flexible with your time. 你可以灵活安排你的时间。
3. You are your own boss. 你是自己的老板。

弊 Cons

1. You have no security. 创业没有保障。
2. Everything is on you. 你需要负担所有的费用。
3. You have to manage everything by yourself. 你必须自己管理一切事务。

02 知识要点 Key Language Points

词汇精讲 Word Study

autonomy
英 /ɔːˈtɒnəmi/
美 /ɔːˈtɑːnəmi/

n. 1. 自治，自治权
The local government demanded greater autonomy.
当地政府要求更大的自治权。
2. 自主；自主权
Parents should give their children greater autonomy in their own lives.
家长应该在生活上给孩子们更大的自主权。

security
英 /sɪˈkjʊərəti/
美 /sɪˈkjʊrəti/

n. 1. 安全，保障
It is important to maintain our national security.
保障我们的国家安全非常重要。
2. 抵押品
His house was held as security for the loan. 他以房子为抵押得到这笔贷款。
3. 担保；保证
Job security has been a thing of the past. 稳定的工作已经是过去的事了。
4. 安全；平安
Friendship can provide me with a sense of security. 友情能给我带来安全感。

on
英 /ɒn/
美 /ɑːn/

prep. 以……支付；由……支付
It's on me. 这顿我请。

Unit 24　工作话题 Work

短语 & 句型 Phrases and Sentence Structures

- **by oneself** 独自地
  I finished the work by myself. 我独自完成了工作。
  They wanted to spend the evening by themselves. 他们想要单独度过这个夜晚。

✓ 表达示例 Example

What do you think about people starting their own company? 你如何看待创业？

Starting your own company can be very exciting as you have greater autonomy and you can be flexible with your time. The downside is that you have no security, and everything is on you.

创办自己的公司可能会令人非常兴奋，因为你拥有更大的自主权，而且可以灵活安排自己的时间。缺点是创业没有保障，而且你需要负担所有费用。

知识拓展 More to Know

- **About Starting a Business** 创业相关

	英	美	
company	/ˈkʌmpəni/	/ˈkʌmpəni/	
=firm	/fɜːm/	/fɜːrm/	公司
invest	/ɪnˈvest/	/ɪnˈvest/	(v.) 投资
investment	/ɪnˈvestmənt/	/ɪnˈvestmənt/	(n.) 投资
investor	/ɪnˈvestə(r)/	/ɪnˈvestər/	投资者
boss	/bɒs/	/bɔːs/	老板
employer	/ɪmˈplɔɪə(r)/	/ɪmˈplɔɪər/	雇主
employee	/ɪmˈplɔɪiː/	/ɪmˈplɔɪiː/	雇员
market	/ˈmɑːkɪt/	/ˈmɑːrkɪt/	市场
customer	/ˈkʌstəmə(r)/	/ˈkʌstəmər/	顾客
consumer	/kənˈsjuːmə(r)/	/kənˈsuːmər/	消费者
product	/ˈprɒdʌkt/	/ˈprɑːdʌkt/	产品
service	/ˈsɜːvɪs/	/ˈsɜːrvɪs/	服务
profit	/ˈprɒfɪt/	/ˈprɑːfɪt/	利润
cost	/kɒst/	/kɔːst/	成本

start-up 创业公司　　target/focus group 目标群体

Lesson 117 996 工作制
996 Working Hour System

> What do you think about the 996 working hour system?
> 你如何看待 996 工作制?

01 利与弊 Pros and Cons

👉 利 Pros
1. You can make more money. 你可以赚更多的钱。
2. It allows you to concentrate on your job. 996 工作制让你专注于工作。
3. It is beneficial to the company. 996 工作制对公司是有益的。

👉 弊 Cons
1. The staff may be tired out which will affect productivity at work.
   员工们可能会筋疲力尽,从而影响工作效率。
2. It will leave you with no time for yourself. 你将没有自己的时间。
3. Overwork might cause health issues. 劳累过度可能会导致健康问题。

02 知识要点 Key Language Points

词汇精讲 Word Study	
productivity 英 /ˌprɒdʌkˈtɪvəti/ 美 /ˌproʊdʌkˈtɪvəti/	*n.* 生产力;生产率 A great working environment will increase productivity. 良好的工作环境将提高生产率。
leave 英 /liːv/ 美 /liːv/	*v.* 1. 离开 I'm leaving now. 我要走了。 2. 让……处于(某种状态、某地等) Just leave the door open. 让门开着吧。 3. 使发生;造成,使留下为(某种结果) You left me no choice. 你让我别无选择。 4. 忘了带,留下 I left my phone on the taxi. 我把手机落在出租车上了。 5. 不立刻做;不马上处理 He always leaves everything until the last minute. 他总是把事情留到最后一刻才做。 6. 把……留交;交托;委托 Leave it with me—I can handle it. 把这事交给我吧——我能解决。

overwork
英 /ˌəʊvəˈwɜːk/
美 /ˌoʊvərˈwɜːrk/

n. 劳累过度；过分辛苦
He got sick through overwork. 他因劳累过度生病了。

v. （使）过度劳累，过分努力
You look tired. Have you been overworking?
你似乎很疲倦，是不是近来劳累过度了？

cause
英 /kɔːz/
美 /kɔːz/

n. 1. 原因；起因
Unemployment is a major cause of poverty.
失业是贫困的一个主要原因。

2. 理由；动机；缘故
There is no cause for concern. 没有理由担忧。

3. （支持或为之奋斗的）事业，目标，理想
They are fighting for a great cause. 他们为一项伟大的事业而奋斗。

v. 使发生；造成；引起；导致
He is always causing trouble. 他总是惹麻烦。

useful
英 /ˈjuːsf(ə)l/
美 /ˈjuːsf(ə)l/

a. 有用的；有益的；实用的；有帮助的
This information could prove useful. 这条信息也许有用。

短语 & 句型 Phrases and Sentence Structures

- **make money** 挣钱；赚钱
  Many people want to be rich without the process of making money.
  很多人想变富有，却不想经历挣钱的过程。
  She made some money by selling second-hand clothes online.
  她通过在网上卖二手衣服赚了一些钱。

- **tired out** 筋疲力尽的；疲惫不堪的
  I am tried out now after the long journey. 经过漫长的旅程，我现在很累。
  Bill was tired out so he took the day off. 比尔太累了，所以请了一天假。

✓ 表达示例 Example

What do you think about the 996 working hour system? 你如何看待 996 工作制？

The 996 working hour system is useful if you want to make more money. However, working long hours per week can make you tired out and leave you with no time for yourself.

如果你想赚更多的钱，那么 996 工作制非常有用。但是，每周长时间工作会使你筋疲力尽，而且你将没有自己的时间。

- About 996 Working Hour System 996 工作制相关

salary	英 /ˈsæləri/	美 /ˈsæləri/	工资
overtime	英 /ˈəʊvətaɪm/	美 /ˈoʊvərtaɪm/	加班
laborer	英 /ˈleɪbərə(r)/	美 /ˈleɪbərər/	劳动者

996 working hour system 996工作制
work schedule 工作时间表
Internet industry 互联网行业
IT（Information Technology）company 信息技术公司
labor/employment law 劳动法

Lesson 118　居家办公
Working from Home

> **What do you think of working from home?**
> 你如何看待居家办公？

01 利与弊 Pros and Cons

利 Pros

1. It can cut out the daily commute. 居家办公可以省去每天通勤的时间。
2. You can have a more flexible schedule. 你的时间会更灵活。
3. You can achieve a better work-life balance. 你可以更好地平衡工作和生活。

弊 Cons

1. You may have more distractions at home, like kids, pets and family trifles.
   在家可能有更多让你分心的事情，比如说孩子、宠物和家庭琐事。
2. You may have insufficient communication with co-workers.
   可能无法和同事进行充分的沟通。
3. You might have to be on call 24 hours. 可能得全天随叫随到。

02 知识要点 Key Language Points

词汇精讲 Word Study

commute
英 /kəˈmjuːt/
美 /kəˈmjuːt/

v. 1. （乘公共汽车、火车、汽车等）上下班往返，通勤
   She commutes from Beijing and Langfang every day.
   她每天往返于北京与廊坊之间。
2. 减刑
   His death sentence was commuted to life imprisonment.
   他的死刑被减为无期徒刑。

n. 上下班交通
   I have a long commute to work. 我的通勤路程很远。

balance
英 /ˈbæləns/
美 /ˈbæləns/

v. 1. 保持平衡
   She balanced the cup on her knee. 她把杯子在膝盖上放稳。
2. 相抵；抵消
   His lack of experience was balanced by a willingness to learn.
   他的好学弥补了他经验的不足。
3. 同等重视（相对的两个事物或方面）
   He tries to balance home life and career. 他试图兼顾家庭生活和事业。
4. 比较（两个相对的事物）；权衡重要性
   You have to balance the advantages of living in a big city against the disadvantages. 你必须权衡在大城市生活的利与弊。

5. 结算（账目）；（使）收支相等
Be very careful when you balance the books! 结算账目时要格外细心！

n. 1. 均衡；平衡；均势
Try to keep a balance between work and relaxation.
尽量保持工作与休闲的平衡。

2. 平衡能力
She lost her balance and fell off. 她失去平衡摔了下来。

3. 余额，余数，结存
I'd like to check the balance in my account, please.
我想查一下我的账户余额。

4. 尾款
The balance of $500 must be paid within 90 days.
500美元的尾款必须于90天之内付清。

distraction
英 /dɪˈstrækʃ(ə)n/
美 /dɪˈstrækʃ(ə)n/

n. 1. 分心的事
I find there are too many distractions when I begin to study at home.
开始在家学习时，我发现让人分心的事情太多了。

2. 心烦意乱；精神错乱
The noise outside the classroom is driving me to distraction.
教室外面的噪音让我感到心烦意乱。

3. 娱乐，消遣
Hiking is one of the distractions of country life.
徒步旅行是乡村生活的娱乐之一。

trifle
英 /ˈtraɪf(ə)l/
美 /ˈtraɪf(ə)l/

n. 琐事，小事；不值钱的东西
I don't want to bother him over such trifles. 我不想因为这些小事麻烦他。

v. 怠慢，轻视
He is not a person to be trifled with. 他这个人怠慢不得。

insufficient
英 /ˌɪnsəˈfɪʃ(ə)nt/
美 /ˌɪnsəˈfɪʃ(ə)nt/

a. 不充分的；不足的；不够重要的
The case was thrown out because of insufficient evidence.
由于证据不足，该案被驳回了。

communication
英 /kəˌmjuːnɪˈkeɪʃ(ə)n/
美 /kəˌmjuːnɪˈkeɪʃ(ə)n/

n. 1. 交流，交际
I want to improve my communication skills. 我想提高我的沟通能力。

2. 通信（或交通）工具；交通联系
Communication technology has developed rapidly in recent years.
通信技术在近几年发展得很快。

短语 & 句型 Phrases and Sentence Structures

- on call 随叫随到
  Doctor Liu is on call at all times. 不论什么时候刘医生都随叫随到。
  In theory, I'm on call day and night. 理论上我是全天随时待命的。

表达示例 Example

What do you think of working from home? 你如何看待居家办公？

> Many people love to work from home, which can allow them to cut out the daily commute and enjoy a more flexible schedule, but they may have insufficient communication with co-workers.
>
> 许多人喜欢居家办公，这可以让他们省去日常通勤的时间并享受更灵活的日程安排，但他们与同事的沟通可能不足。

知识拓展 More to Know

- About Working from Home 居家办公相关

microphone	英 /ˈmaɪkrəfəʊn/	美 /ˈmaɪkrəfoʊn/	麦克风
mute	英 /mjuːt/	美 /mjuːt/	静音
volume	英 /ˈvɒljuːm/	美 /ˈvɑːljəm/	音量
camera	英 /ˈkæm(ə)rə/	美 /ˈkæm(ə)rə/	摄像头

remote working 远程办公　　remote team 远程合作团队
screen sharing 屏幕共享　　video conference 视频会议

Lesson 119 跳槽
Changing Jobs

> **What do you think about changing jobs?**
> 你如何看待跳槽？

01 利与弊 Pros and Cons

利 Pros

1. You can compare jobs and see what you really want to do.
   你可以比较不同的工作，看看什么是你真正想做的。
2. You can accumulate experience in many different areas.
   你可以积累在许多不同领域的工作经验。
3. You can move up in salary more quickly.
   你的薪水会涨得更快。

弊 Cons

1. Many companies are reluctant to hire job hoppers.
   许多公司不愿意雇用频繁跳槽的人。
2. You need time to adapt to the new environment.
   你需要时间来适应新环境。
3. It might have a bad influence on your long-term career goals.
   跳槽可能会对你的长期职业规划有不好的影响。

02 知识要点 Key Language Points

词汇精讲 Word Study

compare
英 /kəmˈpeə(r)/
美 /kəmˈper/

v. 1. 比较，对照
Living standards improved enormously compared to 40 years ago.
与40年前相比，生活水平得到了极大提高。

2. 把……做比较
People compared him to Mark Twain.
人们将他与马克·吐温相提并论。

accumulate
英 /əˈkjuːmjəleɪt/
美 /əˈkjuːmjəleɪt/

v. 积累，堆积
He has gradually accumulated a large fortune.
他逐渐积累了一大笔财富。

hop
英 /hɒp/
美 /hɑːp/

v. 1. （动物或鸟）齐足跳行
The rabbit hopped across the grass.
这只兔子在草丛中跳跃。

2. 单脚跳
I hopped down three steps. 我单脚跳下三级台阶。

3. 突然快速去某处
She hopped out of bed when the alarm clock went off.
闹钟一响，她就猛地起床了。

4. 换来换去；不断更换
I like to hop from channel to channel when I watch TV.
我看电视时喜欢不断地转换频道。

influence
英 /ˈɪnfluəns/
美 /ˈɪnfluəns/

n. 1. 影响，作用
His speech had a profound influence on me.
他的演讲对我产生了深远的影响。

2. 影响力，势力
She exerted her influence to make him give up the opportunity.
她施加她的影响力，好让他放弃这个机会。

3. 产生影响力的人
He is a bad influence on his son. 他对儿子有不好的影响。

v. 影响
She attempted to influence his decision. 她试图影响他的决定。

long-term
英 /ˌlɒŋ ˈtɜːm/
美 /ˌlɔːŋ ˈtɜːrm/

a. 长期的
You need to set some long-term goals.
你需要制定一些长期的目标。

短语 & 句型 Phrases and Sentence Structures

- be reluctant to do sth. 不情愿做某事；勉强做某事
  I am reluctant to ask for help. 我不愿意请求帮助。
  He is reluctant to talk with others. 他不愿意和别人说话。

- adapt (yourself) to sth. 适应（新环境、新情况等）
  He has adapted to the new environment. 他已经适应了新环境。
  It took me a while to adapt to the new position. 我花了一段时间适应新的职位。

- job hopper 频繁变换工作的人
  People may question regular job hoppers' loyalty.
  人们可能会质疑经常跳槽者的忠诚度。

✓ 表达示例 Example

What do you think about changing jobs? 你如何看待跳槽？

> Changing jobs can let you accumulate experience in many different areas and move up in salary more quickly. However, you may need time to adapt to the new environment.
>
> 换工作可以让你在许多不同的领域积累经验，并更快地提高薪水。但是，你可能需要时间来适应新环境。

知识拓展 More to Know

- About Changing Jobs 跳槽相关

resignation	英 /ˌrezɪgˈneɪʃ(ə)n/	美 /ˌrezɪgˈneɪʃ(ə)n/	辞职
experience	英 /ɪkˈspɪəriəns/	美 /ɪkˈspɪriəns/	经验
skill	英 /skɪl/	美 /skɪl/	技能
project	英 /ˈprɒdʒekt/	美 /ˈprɑːdʒekt/	项目
network	英 /ˈnetwɜːk/	美 /ˈnetwɜːrk/	关系网，人际网
promotion	英 /prəˈməʊʃ(ə)n/	美 /prəˈmoʊʃ(ə)n/	升职
title	英 /ˈtaɪt(ə)l/	美 /ˈtaɪt(ə)l/	职称
salary	英 /ˈsæləri/	美 /ˈsæləri/	薪资
benefit	英 /ˈbenɪfɪt/	美 /ˈbenɪfɪt/	福利

Lesson 120 斜杠青年
Slash Career

> What do you think about taking a slash career?
> 你如何看待斜杠青年？

01 利与弊 Pros and Cons

利 Pros

1. You can enjoy multiple income sources. 你可以享受多种收入来源。
2. You can experience different work positions in different fields.
   你可以体验不同领域的不同职位。
3. You can develop several skills. 你可以练就很多技能。

弊 Cons

1. It can be very tiring and stressful.
   做斜杠青年可能会很累且压力很大。
2. You might have no time to enjoy your life or stay with your friends and family.
   你可能没有时间享受生活或与朋友和家人在一起。
3. You might end up being adept at nothing.
   你可能到头来什么都做不精。

02 知识要点 Key Language Points

词汇精讲 Word Study	
slash 英 /slæʃ/ 美 /slæʃ/	*n.* 斜杠；斜线号 You often write a slash between alternatives, for example, "and/or". 你通常可以在可替代项之间使用斜杠（/），比如，"and/or"。 The room functions as a guest bedroom slash study. 这个房间既可以做客房也可以做书房。
multiple 英 /ˈmʌltɪpl/ 美 /ˈmʌltɪpl/	*a.* 复合的，多重的，多样的 Your answer to the multiple choice question was wrong. 这道多选题你选错了。 *n.* 倍数 6 and 12 are multiples of 3. 6 和 12 都是 3 的倍数。
source 英 /sɔːs/ 美 /sɔːrs/	*n.* 1.（河的）源头，根源 The source of the Yangtze River is the Tibetan Plateau. 长江的发源地是青藏高原。 2. 来源，出处 My main source of income is teaching English. 我的主要收入来源是教英语。

短语 & 句型 Phrases and Sentence Structures

- slash career 斜杠事业，身兼多职
  A slash career is one in which a person makes multiple income sources simultaneously from different careers.
  斜杠事业是指一个人同时从不同的职业中获得多种收入来源的一种职业道路。

- end up 到头来，结果
  I ended up doing all the work by myself. 结果所有的活儿都是我一个人干了。
  Every time they had dinner together, they ended up in a bad mood.
  每次他们一起吃晚饭，结果都是不欢而散。

- be adept at/in (doing) sth. 擅长／精于做某事
  She's very adept at dealing with the media. 她很擅长应对媒体。
  He is adept at fixing computers. 他擅长修电脑。

✓ 表达示例 Example

What do you think about taking a slash career? 你如何看待斜杠青年？

Taking a slash career can make you enjoy multiple income sources and you can develop several skills. But it can be very tiring and stressful and you might have no time to enjoy your life or stay with your friends and family.

成为斜杠青年可以让你享受多种收入来源，还可以练就多种技能。但这可能会非常累人且压力很大，你可能没有时间享受生活或与朋友和家人在一起。

知识拓展 More to Know

- About Slash Career 斜杠青年相关
  slashie　　英/slæʃi/　　美/slæʃi/　　斜杠青年
  day job 正职　　　　　　side job 副业
  freelance work/job 自由职业，特约工作
  freelancer/self-employed person 自由职业者